Education and Cultural Citizenship

Nick Stevenson

Los Angeles | London | New Delhi
Singapore | Washington DC

Theory, Culture & Society

Theory, Culture & Society caters for the resurgence of interest in culture within contemporary social science and the humanities. Building on the heritage of classical social theory, the book series examines ways in which this tradition has been reshaped by a new generation of theorists. It also publishes theoretically informed analyses of everyday life, popular culture and new intellectual movements.

EDITOR: Mike Featherstone, *Nottingham Trent University*

THE TCS CENTRE
The Theory, Culture & Society book series, the journals *Theory, Culture & Society* and *Body & Society*, and related conference, seminar and postgraduate programmes operate from the TCS Centre at Nottingham Trent University. For further details of the TCS Centre's activities please contact:

The TCS Centre
School of Arts and Humanities
Nottingham Trent University
Clifton Lane, Nottingham NG11 8NS, UK
email: tcs@ntu.ac.uk
web: http://sagepub.net/tcs/

Recent volumes include:

Inhuman Nature
Nigel Clark

The Domestic Economy of the Soul
John O'Neill

Race, Sport and Politics
Ben Carrington

Intensive Culture
Scott Lash

Peer to Peer and the Music Industry
Matthew David

'Nick Stevenson skilfully draws upon a welter of leading thinkers from the liberal, socialist, critical-theory and multiculturalist canons in developing his argument that leading ideas about education are umbilically tied to notions of the good society. The pluralistic and un-dogmatic manner in which he sifts these accounts, and his insistence upon the centrality of democratic citizenship, make this a timely and important contribution to current debates about the nature and purpose of schools.'
Michael Kenny, Professor, Department of Politics, University of Sheffield

'In *Education and Cultural Citizenship* Nick Stevenson presents a powerful argument concerning how education can and should promote democracy, accompanied by critiques of how all-too-often education fails to do so. Full of strong ideas, arguments, engagement with key thinkers, Stevenson's book should be of great interest to all concerned with the nexus of democracy and education.'
Douglas Kellner, UCLA, author of *Guys and Guns Amok* and *Media Spectacle and the Crisis of Democracy*

First published 2011

SAGE Publications Ltd
1 Oliver's Yard
55 City Road
London EC1Y 1SP

SAGE Publications Inc.
2455 Teller Road
Thousand Oaks, California 91320

SAGE Publications India Pvt Ltd
B 1/I 1 Mohan Cooperative Industrial Area
Mathura Road, Post Bag 7
New Delhi 110 044

SAGE Publications Asia-Pacific Pte Ltd
33 Pekin Street #02-01
Far East Square
Singapore 048763

Library of Congress Control Number: 2010939199

British Library Cataloguing in Publication data

A catalogue record for this book is available from the British Library

ISBN 978-1-84860-646-3
ISBN 978-1-84860-647-0 (pbk)

Typeset by C&M Digitals (P) Ltd, Chennai, India
Printed by CPI Antony Rowe, Chippenham, Wiltshire
Printed on paper from sustainable resources

For Alastair Stevenson, Ida James, Eve James,
Joseph Hurd and Charlotte Hurd

Contents

About the Author

Nick Stevenson is a Reader in Cultural Sociology, University of Nottingham. His most recent books include *David Bowie* (2006, Polity Press), *Cultural Citizenship* (2003, OUP), *Culture and Citizenship* (2001, Sage), *Understanding Media Cultures* (2001, Sage) *Making Sense of Men's Lifestyle Magazines* (written with Peter Jackson and Kate Brooks) (Polity, 2000) and *The Transformation of the Media* (1999, Longman). He is currently writing a short book on freedom for Routledge.

Acknowledgements

I would like to thank many of the people who have helped with the production of this book – in particular my partner Lucy James, whose faith, love and encouragement have been crucial when my sense of purpose has started to flag.

I would also like to thank Nottingham University for having such a good education library. This was always a pleasant place to work, and I spent many a happy afternoon there. Further, my publishers SAGE (especially Chris Rojek and Jai Seaman) have been excellent as usual.

Most books have a connection to the personal life of the author and this one is no different. Without the ties to my own and my sister Jane's children I doubt I would ever have written on this topic. I have followed their first steps into the world with great interest and it has become clear just how significant an influence education is on the shaping of our identities. This has also led me to rethink my own education and I would like to thank all of them for sharing with me many of their experiences. This book is dedicated to them.

During the writing of this book both of my parents Dermis and June and Lucy's father Maurice died. I would like to thank all of the people who helped me during this period. Your parents are of course your first and most important educators and I would like to remember them here. Not a day goes by when they are not missed or their considerable influence is not noted.

I would also like to thank my education policy advisors Mark Bevan, Toby Greaney, Matt Varley and Stewart Philpott for keeping me up to speed with current developments in education and their personal and professional lives. I can only hope they are not too horrified by the arguments contained within this book. Thanks too to Diane Beechcroft, David Rose and Colin Lago who offered a different kind of education.

In a more academic and professional context I have learned a great deal from the conversations of Anthony Elliott, Angharad Beckett, Stella Hart, Jagdish Patel, John Downey, Jim McGuigan, David Moore, David Hesmondhaugh, Paul Ransome, Nick Couldry, Robert Unwin, Maurice Roche and numerous colleagues in the school of Sociology and Social Policy. Here I especially want to thank the anonymous reader and Professor Mike Kenny for their critical and incisive comments.

Finally I would like to thank my thoughtful teachers Mr Dome, Mr Sawford, Miss Stevens, Paul Bellaby, John Bowen, Steven Webb and Anthony Giddens for their wise guidance in years gone by.

Permissions

I would also like to thank the following journals for permission to republish parts of the following:

Nick Stevenson (2010) 'Cultural citizenship, education and democracy: redefining the good society', *Citizenship Studies* 14(3): 275–292.
Nick Stevenson (2009) 'Critical pedagogy, democracy and capitalism: education without enemies or borders', *Review of Education, Pedagogy and Cultural Studies* 32(1): 86–92.
Nick Stevenson (2009) 'European democratic socialism, multiculturalism and the third way', *Cultural Studies* 23(1): 48–69.

They all appear here in a modified form.

1

Introduction

What kind of education is suitable for citizens of modern democratic and culturally diverse modern societies? This is the question that has troubled me most while writing this book. Notably, as we shall see, it has also puzzled a number of the leading writers on education. There is, however, no one simple answer to this question. How we respond to this issue inevitably depends upon the point in time and space within which we seek to address questions of cultural development and democracy. Indeed, one of the arguments I shall be making here is how we might locate ourselves in terms of some of these debates, but at the same time reconstruct these arguments in new times. There is no 'neutral' answer to this question despite the agnostic view offered by some liberals. That we seek to positively identify the values of democracy will inevitably mean that we prefer certain ways of organising, living and practising education to others. For the most part this book adopts an approach that is often referred to within critical theory as 'immanent critique'. The aim of critical theory is not only to produce self-reflection and criticism, but also to argue that if education is to become meaningful then we would need to revise our current practices and seek to struggle for a more democratic society. However, in this process we have to start from where we currently stand and recognise that the realisation of a democratic education could only take place in a reconstructed society. Such a society is unlikely to arrive in any pristine form but will depend upon citizens and social movements seeking to combat social and cultural forms that aim to close down the possibility of the emergence of a culturally pluralistic, dialogic and learning education system and society. Here we will need to understand 'education' not only as a diverse set of practices that takes place within formal settings of learning like schools, colleges and universities, but also more broadly involves the media of mass communication, popular culture, literature and social movements. Here I would follow Antonio Gramsci (1971: 40) who argues that for education to be described as democratic it 'must mean that every "citizen" can "govern" and that society places him, even if only abstractly, in a general condition to achieve this'. This would mean that our democratic 'education' as citizens does not end at the school gates but includes relationships inside families, in front of the television, on the computer, inside the workplace and within civil society more generally. In this respect questions of education face in a number of directions all at once.

In making these claims I am inevitably drawing upon my own experiences and intellectual preferences as a British academic working in an institution of higher education. My own intellectual journey from the working class to the educated middle class undoubtedly colours many of the arguments discussed within this volume. This does not mean of course that many people who have made a similar transition will necessarily understand this experience in the same way that I have done. Further, I have tried as hard as possible to argue from the point of view of a critic who is keen to preserve and extend the practice of democracy in increasingly difficult times. It is just that I am aware that had I encountered education differently I might have written a different kind of book.

My argumentative strategy is to defend both a democratic form of education and one that seeks to include a wide variety of cultural experiences that are compatible with these values. There is no vision of education or understanding of its practice that is not based upon a view of the good society. Much of the debate that goes on within education it seems to me deliberately obscures this argument by reducing the role of education to overly instrumental and technical criteria. Often it seems there is no vision of the good society to defend but simply a view of education as raising 'aspirations' or of people gaining access to more and better employment. What this book seeks to achieve is to clarify the principles that are at stake in these arguments, and suggest the different ways in which the practice of democracy might become enhanced through education. In this book I want to look more closely at the meaningful practice of education and how it might serve a democratic as opposed to an authoritarian or consumerist ethos.

This book does not seek to argue from the position of scientifically conceived neutrality. This is because I doubt that such a position exists, and I think that education and the practice of democracy are more closely linked than many currently think. Indeed, part of the task I have taken on here is to rethink a number of complex and often overlapping traditions of thinking that can help us understand how education is linked to democratic forms of practice. However, before proceeding any further I had better explain what I mean by democracy and why I think it is important.

If I might at this point be allowed a personal story. My own initial education was fairly unremarkable. The infant and junior schools I attended were authoritarian places where a minor breach of the rules could often lead to harsh punishments. The schools were well ordered and disciplined but offered little by the way of creativity or imagination. With football and comic reading being my only escape these were not on the whole (with some notable exceptions) places of enjoyable learning. If anything they were mostly disciplinary institutions that passed on basic skills, but expected very little of their students. At my secondary school most of my male peers were encouraged to specialise in certain subjects (mainly wood work, metal work and technical drawing) so that they could gain employment in the wider economy. Many of the other boys were targeted by the armed services and most of the girls were taught cookery and needlework as preparation for a life of domesticity. Despite these features most of my education disallowed any critical discussion of the wider world that myself and my classmates would soon be moving into. Other than an occasional discussion within say Geography, History or English there was little sense that I was a democratic citizen in the making. This meant no discussion of labour history, feminism, racism, multiculturalism, the peace movement or any of the intellectual questions raised by these particular concerns. There was indeed very little discussion of questions that might be called ethical or moral or that asked us what kinds of people we wished to become. Education as it was practised was about passing exams to gain access to either craft apprenticeships in industry or office work. It did not seem to be about the development of curiosity, asking difficult questions or the wider development of our interests.

However, soon after leaving school I was to encounter a number of sub-cultural (namely punk, soul, Mod and the New Romantics), political (labour movement, feminism and peace) and literary (mainly Camus, Kafka, Orwell and Sartre) concerns that seemed to be asking what was it ethical to become and how I might live a meaningful, passionate and democratic life. In other words this discordant collection of cultures (not all pulling in the same direction) asked questions in a way that I had never encountered in school. Indeed, while at work I was sent on a day-release course and despite my initial sense of excitement was soon to realise that this was less about learning than training. However, this proved to be an important time for me as I was to meet other similarly alienated young people who introduced me to a world of books, music and ideas that I had not previously encountered. Much later, after eventually entering university, I discovered that education could be a place of critical inquiry and questioning in a way that did not seem to be the case in school. By this time I had formulated a number of questions that I wished to pursue and was lucky enough to find a university that offered the literary, philosophical, sociological and historical courses that might enable me to find some answers. Later, when thinking back over my life, I was struck by the difference between my early formal stages of learning and the sense of cultural vibrancy I had encountered within at least some aspects of politics, popular culture, literature and later higher education.

Since this period I have now become a parent. My children's education is of course quite different from my own, mainly due to the new class position I now occupy. Theirs is a world of books, new technology, school league tables, multi-channel television and numerous after-school clubs that is quite alien to the world in which I grew up. There is no sense that they are being prepared for life on a factory floor and the school seems genuinely interested in them as people. Yet if my early education was to prepare me for the labour market I am not sure that my children's education is any different. There is a deep concern amongst educationalists that the current focus upon passing exams, teaching to test and increasingly instrumental modes of learning is failing to develop the educational capacities of citizens in the making. In other words, if I 'learned to labour' I sometimes think that my children are being trained for the knowledge economy. If the modern economy no longer requires unskilled and skilled labour in the same ways that it did in the past the new requirements of the knowledge economy are for workers who have mastered basic literacy and keyboard skills, who are positive, hard-working, and whose idea of the good society is successful upward mobility. Here I would like to ask if these are the kinds of educated citizens required by a modern democracy? Are there indeed dangers in the context of the 'knowledge society' of education losing its value, as the economy mostly requires useful knowledge? If children are increasingly being taught to test (as seems to be the case) what happens to the ability to be able to think more independently and develop your own passions? If the needs of the economy continue to be the defining feature within education what space is there for what might be called a citizen's education? Educational institutions are undoubtedly places of learning, but which identities are made available to us there, and how important are they in making us into the kinds of people we later go on to become? To what extent is it legitimate to use education as a means of training for the labour market, and what should be the limits of this imperative? To what extent should education simply be about itself, and what are its responsibilities to the wider community? These are just some of the questions I aim to investigate within this book.

Obviously these are important questions for any society that calls itself democratic. If by democracy we mean a society that simply allows for competition between different points of view then this probably only makes minimal claims on the organisation of education. However, if what we mean by democracy includes the possibility of participation, listening, the capacity to change your mind or at least form an opinion, cultural inclusion and a society where we can deliberate on roughly equal terms then this would suggest certain forms of education rather than others. Further, if these ideas are to be meaningful then this would mean the development of an approach to education where young people were not simply 'objects' to be weighed and measured, but where they were subjects in their own right with their own ideas and passions. Here my argument is not that education should have no link to the economy (this does not seem to be possible) but that the primary driving force of education should be one that gives a priority to learning and not training, freedom and not prescription, and initiative and not conformity. Democracy in this argument is a practice as much for the classroom as it is for more public encounters. These are not new ideas. As we shall see, that democracy relies upon the critical and thoughtful nature of its citizens to govern both themselves as well as the societies in which they live lies at the heart of a long tradition of educated thinking.

However, please note that I have used the term cultural citizenship rather than democracy. This is because the idea of democracy is often associated with different systems of representation and voting procedures. By adopting the term cultural citizenship I was more concerned to group together a number of different questions that were not simply focused on questions of procedure but also on the development of cultural competencies, sensibilities and capacities within future and current citizens. In particular, the word 'culture' is important here as a way of signifying the different ways in which we might be said to participate meaningfully and critically within the broader society. It is not by virtue of our humanness or our individuality that we understand our place in the world but this can only be done through a diversity of cultural perspectives that make the world meaningful for us. Here I follow a hermeneutical tradition of argument that suggests there is no human life without the capacity to make meaning. This does not limit the inquiry to a particular view of human nature, and yet it is hard to write on education unless we believe at some level that human beings are capable of learning and of interpreting both their own and others' actions in different ways. As cultural beings then we are always caught in multiple webs of linguistic meaning. Following Clifford Geertz (1973) culture might be thought of as a web of significance spun by human action and interpretation. The task of interpreting meaning does not require us to get inside people's heads, but to understand instead the intersubjective nature of linguistic practices. We have no choice but to try and make sense of our lives in the context of the cultures in which we live. We are all, following Paul Ricoeur (1991), compelled to create a sense of our selves through particular cultural stories or narratives. How we construct and remake these narratives depends upon the meeting point between our agency, cultural context and of course wider social structures. For Ricoeur in order to construct ourselves we need access to different traditions of thinking so that they might be remade or indeed re-interpreted in the context of our own lives. How we create our lives and fashion our narratives has both a poetic and a moral component. Refusing the separation between morality and aesthetics, Ricoeur argues we are responsible for the choices we make in fashioning our personal narratives and how these then become connected to the wider community (Wall 2005).

These arguments provide one of the ways we can link questions of 'culture' to those of 'citizenship'. By 'citizenship' I mean our connection to particular social and cultural locations, the possibility of a participatory involvement in shaping our society and our understanding of our rights and responsibilities. Much has been made of the idea of citizenship in recent times, and here I would seek to defend an active, republican concept that is not neutral about the role of the citizen in democratically participating in the common life of our society. The idea of cultural citizenship therefore seeks to look at the diversity of competencies and capacities that need to be available within a democratic context to enable acts of public criticism, compassion or concern. My sense in this respect is that the cultural realm remains absolutely central to the ways in which the vast majority of people understand their role within the wider community. Returning to Ricoeur, how we choose to live our lives in relation to global injustices or oppressive systems of domination inevitably invites us to be creative agents. We can seek to reshape larger and more collective narratives as well as those connected to our personal lives. This might involve us defending the difference of the Other, arguing for justice, seeking to democratise powerful social structures, making a stand for what we believe to be 'right' or indeed living lives of service in respect of the wider community. The creativity of our shared moral lives requires not only a capacity to challenge the collective wisdom on particular issues, but also a broader understanding of the different human possibilities and a diversity of ways of living our individual as well as collective lives. Education as we shall see remains a vital resource in connecting questions of culture to those of citizenship.

We live in a time of transition. The relatively recent arrival of a consumer, technologically literate, diverse and largely politically disengaged society is changing the ways in which citizenship is experienced by the vast majority of the population. However, we also live in a world that is becoming more multicultural, unequal, global and environmentally uncertain. This means that the way we think about education needs to change, but that it also needs to do so by re-engaging with different cultural traditions and not by simply starting again. More specifically I would seek to return to the traditions of liberal socialism. This is for two main reasons. First, liberal socialist arguments recognise there is no 'Big Bang' theory of emancipation and remain as sceptical of authoritarianism on the political Right as the political Left. If liberal socialism historically sought to combine the values of liberty and equality it did so without believing in utopian solutions to social and cultural problems. Instead there is a concern that much of the Marxist Left are as authoritarian as the capitalist society they justifiably seek to criticise. Rather than arguing for a revolutionary transformation of society liberal socialism has sought to promote the idea of a common civic culture that is both relatively egalitarian and liberal. Historically this has meant support for an interventionist state that sought to contain the market, address inequality and protect civil rights. And yet the political Right sought to remake mass education in the interests of employers while preserving an elite education for the privileged. R.H. Tawney (1961) argued that capitalist society in this respect seeks to emphasise rights as opposed to responsibilities. This ultimately lead to a destructive form of individualism that simply ends with the right to secure for yourself a privileged education and high levels of personal consumption. Tawney, by reconnecting rights and responsibilities, sought to emphasise a sense of obligation to the wider community. Such a move, as we shall see, opens up the possibility of citizens not only being offered relatively equal opportunities, but also an educated culture that could enable them to develop themselves as cultural beings and not simply as raw material for 'use' in the workplace. The demand that ordinary working-class people have the right to an intellectual life and that the education system should prepare its citizens for a life within a shared community has had a long history within liberal socialist thinking. The historian Jonathan Rose (2001) has demonstrated how within the working class during the twentieth century before the rise of the mass media there existed a culture of mutual improvement based less upon reading radical texts, and more upon understanding complex works of literature. This history often found expression within the labour movement. Here many trade-union leaders spoke of their sense of exclusion from opportunities to engage in a culture of learning. What I continue to find valuable about the liberal socialist tradition is the idea that education should not be reduced to the needs of the economy and its suspicion of authoritarianism of all kinds. As Tawney (1964) was to argue, the liberal socialist critique of capitalism was just as concerned with questions of inequality and poverty as it was with the possibility of developing a new politics of citizenship. This new politics was concerned about the effects of atomised individualism and sought to connect rights, community and responsibility. Tawney recognised that economic power could undermine democracy and the quality of civic life by converting education into a means of training for the economy. Tawney (1964: 168) argued that the struggle for a democratic society promoted the argument that if 'to lead a life worthy of human beings is confined to a minority, what is commonly called freedom would more properly be described as privilege'. For Tawney a community that made life worth living would need to be built upon a sense of mutual responsibility and the freedom to develop the self. Here the question that begins to emerge is what a democratic as well as a genuinely inclusive education might be like. However, as I have indicated, there is no simple return to these ideas; instead, as we shall see, the idea of a critical and inclusive education produces a number of different problems and questions.

Liberty, equality and culture

While my own personal educational story began in the 1960s I want to return for a short while to the 1860s. Here I shall investigate a dispute between two English liberal thinkers of the nineteenth century. The 1860s no less than the 1960s were a key decade in respect of the argument of this book. Mathew Arnold and John Stuart Mill shared a good deal (amongst other things a love of the work of Marcus Aurelius) in that they both argued for the progressive potential of a democratic as opposed to an aristocratically dominated society. Further they sought to identify the appropriate culture for a democratic society. Both were formed by an Enlightenment-based culture that valued freedom of thought rather than the imposition of authority, as well as the idea of equal rights and democratic rule (Todorov 2009). And both were seeking to argue how these principles might best be established through education and political culture more generally. Democracy they each agreed would need to be different from an aristocratic society where the ability to rule was a matter of status and rank rather than discussion and persuasion. Arnold and Mill continue to remain important not only for the ways in which they chose to answer these questions but also because of the huge influence that they had in terms of defining the terms of the debate. They both asked what kind of shared culture was appropriate for democracy, and what role might the education system have in helping to shape our shared understandings? Their writing during this period seeks to answer the question of what it means to be a moral self and how we might live as democratic citizens. There are of course numerous other places to begin here, and yet it seems to me that Mill and Arnold connected questions of culture and democracy in ways that continue to have relevance for the ways we understand these debates. Further, both predated and directly influenced the work of Richard Hoggart, R.H. Tawney, John Dewey, Raymond Williams and others. Indeed I would also take George Orwell to be a direct inheritor of much of the dialogue that takes place between Mill and Arnold. Orwell (1999), who is perhaps best remembered for his nightmare vision of the Big Brother society of state control, remained a liberal socialist. For him the state was charged with the responsibility to introduce the public to an intellectual culture based upon free debate and discussion. Freedom was not simply preserved by maintaining abstract rights but had to be placed within everyone's grasp by introducing people to new ideas and concepts. For Orwell (2001) this could only conceivably be delivered by a liberal state that did not seek to press the mass working-class population into a vocational education, but instead introduced them to ideas of debate, argument and disagreement. This could, only be ensured as we shall see, by encouraging those within education to participate within democratically inspired conversations.

Central to both Mill and Arnold's concerns was how education could be related to ideas of freedom. What is crucial within a democratic context is that individuals are 'free' to become themselves, make up their own minds, and follow their own interests and passions. Freedom in the context of a democratic society means something other than what it has come to mean in a market driven and progressively state regulated society. It clearly does not mean rote learning, always offering back what the teacher wishes to hear, training, or indeed selling courses to the public in order to enhance their future earning potential. A life that is worth living instead depends upon citizens who are driven to make up their own minds, who will jealously cling to liberal freedoms and be willing to explore ideas and perspectives that they might initially find strange or threatening. Yet as both Arnold and Mill in their different ways understood how we do this needs to be a matter of careful debate and discussion. And what remains central to this discussion in our own time is a recognition of the centrality of questions of liberty. In this respect, education in a democratic context is primarily concerned with questions of freedom rather than, say, happiness, class mobility or indeed any other value that I would care to mention. Of course what we mean by 'freedom' has to be more precisely described and culturally located. What Arnold and Mill took to be 'freedom' has undoubtedly changed over time. In our society the word 'freedom' is often connected to neoliberal versions of capitalism where it has come to mean the cutting of state welfare, economic individualism, an attack on trade unionism and progressive consumerism (Harvey 2005). However, there continue to exist other definitions of freedom that are concerned with the possible extension of liberty of thought and more autonomous ways of living for everyone. This has over the course of the twentieth century become a staple of democratic socialist and liberal modes of thinking. George Orwell (2001) argued that it was only when socialism and liberalism were combined that we could talk of freedom in any meaningful sense. That is, 'freedom' would not be meaningful if we feared unemployment, if work was insecure, if citizens were treated unequally and had inadequate resources to live a meaningful life. The problem was that working-class people often desired economic security while it was intellectuals who wanted individual liberty. It was the project of liberal socialism to bring these two aspects together. The coming together of a social state, an equal society and liberal freedoms would convert the idea of freedom into a value that was lived rather than simply remaining an abstract idea. While neither Mill nor Arnold took these arguments as far as Orwell they would both have resisted the idea that freedom was simply market freedom.

Like Orwell, Mathew Arnold recognised that the state had a crucial role to play in the formation of democratic citizens. Arnold's trip to post-revolutionary France had convinced him of the desirability of state-run schools to lift the level of civilisation for the majority. Arnold (1861/1970) had noted how the French state-run schools had successfully raised the cultural standards of both the middle and lower classes. In the liberal culture of the time these views were not popular as the state was seen as acting as a device that restricted personal forms of liberty. This was per-haps most evident in the view of John Stuart Mill (1859/1974: 59), who perceived the central struggle of the age as between 'liberty and author-ity'. The key principle at stake in his work was to establish the culture of liberty as the culture that could best serve the wider democratic society. For Mill, state-run schools could not be trusted not to impose uniformity upon private individuals (Collini 1998). It was the despotic power of the state that most liberals of this period feared would undermine a shared culture of liberty. Without a shared culture of active citizens who were capable of forming their own views and unafraid of being out of step with mass opinion there could be no democracy worthy of the name (Ginsborg 2008: 45). Hence, while Mill focused upon the repressive power of the state, he was also concerned about how the forming of mass opinion could become a kind of external coercion (Ryan 1970). Such was Mill's concern to defend personal liberty he defended the 'right' of parents to choose an education that was best suited to their children and upheld the view that 'attempts by the state to bias the conclusions of its citizens on disputed subjects are evil' (Mill 1859/1974: 178). This meant that he opposed state education and thought it should for the most part remain in privately run institutions, although these were in need of considerable reform.

Mill's (1873/1924: 25) account of his own education makes for interest-ing reading in this context as he describes how his father impressed upon him an educated culture of logic, Greek and Latin, 'making his opinion the ultimate standard'. Mill identified his own education as being that which we might deem appropriate for the upright and public-orientated figure that he was to become. Mill, however, also talked engagingly about his own self-education after a period of formal instruction. He describes a moment of self-revelation when he read Jeremy Bentham's work on utilitarianism and later shows how his ability to read and reflect helped him find his way out of a depressive state. Mill realised that despite his work as a liberal reformer and public moralist his own education had provided him with certain analytical qualities and because of this he had little personal sense of sympathy and connection with others. Mill (1873/1924) admits that this left him with 'no delight in virtue, or the general good'. He went on to conclude, as he eventually found his way out of his depression, that he had previously underestimated 'the internal culture of the individual' (1873/1924: 121). Eventually he was to find in Romantic poetry (especially Wordsworth) the capacity to both connect with his own inner feelings and to experience an acute sympathy with others as well as nature. Notable here is the role that educated culture plays not only within public morality, but also in helping us make sense of our own inner world. Despite Mill's depressive state what becomes obvious in reading his work is the importance he places on personal forms of liberty. There is no sense that Romantic poetry is for everyone, but more that in the context of his own journey and struggle that this moment held particular significance. Indeed what is notable is that Mill was able to engage in the practice of self-education that values the constant search for ideas and different perspectives that would enable him to make sense of his own time. In this Mill's own story suggests that once he was able to free himself from his father's dominance he could authentically pose himself complex problems and questions that did not necessarily have any easy answers. Mill's stand for the liberty of the individual can work at both a personal as well as a social and cultural level where we are free to ask our own questions and discover our own solutions.

Raymond Williams (1958: 81) commenting on Mill's personal crisis objects that human feelings are too quickly relegated to the private sphere by Mill's account. Mill's impersonal insistence on a culture of individualised liberty leaves too much out of the public content of education. Here Williams makes the point that a public education requires more than simply instruction in the use of impersonal reason but also the cultivation of human feelings and compassion that should not be too quickly relegated to the private realm. Williams is here suggesting that public education is as much a matter of cognitive ability as it is of the development of different emotional capacities. This perhaps brings us to the work of Mathew Arnold who sought the public cultivation of the self through artistic, poetic and philosophical forms of expression.

Indeed when Matthew Arnold read Mill's great work on liberty he was duly impressed and found a great deal to agree upon. However, Arnold's notion of 'liberty' differed from that held by Mill. Arnold (1869/1970) was critical of the prevailing liberal thought of his time as it propagated a culture of simply doing as one pleased. For Arnold this potentially led not only to poor behaviour that would often end in violence, but also to an indifference on matters of culture. As a classicist and a school inspector he argued that the English obsession with liberty as the primary value was preventing the development of a more democratic model of education that was concerned with the development of the self. This could only be achieved through the state sector given the inadequacy of the private institutions that currently governed the provision of education for the middle classes. As Arnold argued (1869/1970: 203), 'I am a Liberal, yet I am a Liberal tempered by experience, reflexion, and renouncement, and I am, above all, a believer in culture'. Culture for Arnold aimed at human perfection, the development of the self and the transformation of our identities. This was being undermined by the faith that many liberals placed in the free market, factory machinery and material progress. Industrial capitalism was no lover of culture, preferring to focus instead upon wealth and material success. A culture that valued liberty above everything else was readily translated into the individual right to remain ignorant. Culture, for Arnold (1869/1970: 219), should be valued above everything else and confront us with the fact that 'the truth of beauty and sweetness are essential characters of a complete human perfection'. Culture suggests citizens move beyond a celebration of liberty for its own sake in order to fashion themselves as more complex and sympathetic beings. Indeed it is a means of bridging the divide between social classes and of producing a society of cultivated selves. These cultured selves require access to education so we can engage in the development of 'our best self' that can only emerge once we recognise not liberty but the value of 'service' in producing 'perfected humanity' (Arnold 1869/1970: 291). Here we perhaps need to note that by using terms such as 'perfection' or more often 'sweetness and light' Arnold seeks to make a stand for the role of culture in the exploration of the self. Culture produces an educative self that offers the possibility of developing both aesthetic and moral selves.

However, as Williams (1958: 133) points out, Arnold in his enthusiasm to bring educated culture to the vast majority of the people ended up endorsing an authoritarian model of education. Here the state was granted the power to define what was meant by perfection and to offer a form of civilisation that would educate the masses. This was, as Williams implies, less a democratic model of education than the imposition of state control. Raymond Williams is an important figure within this argument as he admires Mill's emphasis upon the idea of the liberty of the individual (if not the split between an instrumental public ethic and a private realm of feeling) and Arnold's emphasis upon the critical potential of culture (if not his authoritarianism). Indeed both could be said to be defending the idea of the cultivated liberal individual against what might be called a fear of the masses. Behind Mill's insistent defence of liberal individuality as opposed to the conformity of mass opinion and Arnold's desire to bring the culture of civilisation to ordinary people lies 'the unfitness of the masses – they will riot, they will strike they will not take an interest – such is the nature of that brute' (Williams 1958: 303). The fear here was that the coming culture of democracy would end in Mill's case in crushing individuality and in Arnold's in becoming indifferent to questions of cultural value. Instead Williams more optimistically sees within the culture of democracy the possibility of fashioning new identities and selves, and above all of reorganising the dominant relations of cultural transmission in such a way that did not simply reaffirm the atomised individualism of Mill or the authoritarianism of Arnold. This is not to argue that Mill and Arnold's fears were unreasonable, but that within a democracy new forms of authority and different kinds of educative relationship are required. A genuinely democratic education, Williams reasons, would need to steer clear of the idea that it was the state's role simply to impose civilisation upon its citizens and would need to respect the different levels of engagement offered by citizens. For Williams (1958: 304) education was involved in reciprocal human relationships and had the status of an 'offering' that was 'not an attempt to dominate, but to communicate, to achieve reception and response'.

Democratic education and liberal socialism

A democratic culture, argues Williams (1958: 305), should seek to reaffirm what he calls an 'equality of being'. Such a culture is one that seeks to build mutually respectful relations between teachers and the taught. This only becomes possible if intellectuals give up notions of simply imposing culture upon 'the masses' and admit that learning is not simply the realisation of the sovereign individual but more often than not involves the formation of complex human relationships. Education should be (as Mill's own experience bears out) less an instruction, and more what Williams (1958: 304) refers to as a 'living response'. This means that a democratic version of education needs to be open to the process of interpretation and complex engagements that is brought by teachers and the taught within learning relationships. Rather than seeing citizens as abstract individuals (as is characteristic of much of Mill's thought), Williams argues we need to be able to appreciate the diversity of ways whereby citizens can become themselves and form attachments to different communities. Here Williams (1958: 318) argues that educative culture should indeed seek to foster a sense of service or duty towards the community in a way that does not find a place within the dominant culture of individualism. Such a view would be outlawed by Mill given that it offers a particular way of life as being superior to another. However, we might question here whether education can actually be as neutral as Mill suggests. As Amy Gutman (1987) argues the view that the state has no right to bias in terms of suggesting how citizens should live has been used by liberals to defend the notion of 'neutrality' within education. In this not only schools but also parents must be warned against passing on their particular prejudices. However, such a view is quite impractical and probably impossible. Democratic states cannot really afford to be neutral about how citizens choose to live. Such states need to foster a sense of connection to 'our' histories, cultures and of course democratic ways of life that are shared in common with others. This is not done because of a sense of innate superiority but simply because citizens are unlikely to feel a basic sense of duty otherwise. This of course does not mean that the state should be allowed to 'impose' particular understandings of historically significant public events as these should be open to a number of competing interpretations. This would suggest that not only do citizens need equal access to a high-quality education, but that citizens also need to form an understanding of history, politics and the culture of the nation and its relationship with the wider world. Here a liberal socialist argument would need to maintain that all members of the community need to make sense of the national story. A shared culture of democratic citizenship requires access to a number of competing narratives in respect of who 'we' are now and who 'we' used to be in the past.

Further, a liberal socialist view of education (as I indicated earlier) does not simply emphasise individual rights but also stresses the responsibilities citizens owe to the wider community. As Williams (1958: 317) points out ideas of service towards the community (without which education as a public service is hard to imagine) have been explicitly fostered historically by labour and socialist movements. In these the idea of service offers an alternative to the metaphor of 'the ladder' focusing upon individual escape roots. Instead of a culture of upward mobility, Williams (1958: 318) prefers the idea of 'common betterment' as it seeks to develop a commitment towards the education and development of others. Without a sense of duty to the community we are simply left with liberal indi-vidualism that under a dominance to the market can easily become trans-lated into a form of indifference towards the suffering and unmet needs of others. Liberty is the primary value for democratic forms of education but it is not the only value. Thus we can note it seems perfectly legitimate for democratic states to foster a sense of connection to their own institu-tions and histories, but not in such a way that suggests that they can't be revised or interpreted differently.

While Arnold's writing still has much to offer it can seem anachronis-tic in the twenty-first century. While I would not wish to defend notions such as the perfection of the self or indeed the central importance of a classical education what I still find germane in Arnold's writing is his cosmopolitan attachment to European culture, the idea that the state through the development of public schools could be charged with the civilisation of the community and the notion that we can seek to transform ourselves through education. Further, I also think that Arnold correctly identifies some of the major flaws within mainstream liberal thinking. Namely that the liberal championing of the culture of individual liberty is connected to the dominance of the economic system over the cultural sphere. Arnold correctly identifies that by instilling the culture of liberty as our ultimate value there is nothing to prevent citizens becoming indif-ferent, disengaged and of course under-educated. As educators we need to remember that students are indeed at liberty to reject our arguments, disagree with our conclusions and pour scorn over our judgements. Any education that refuses this challenge simply ceases to be worthy of the name.

If we judge the way that Arnold carries this out as not really appropriate for contemporary democratic societies this is hardly surprising. More recently Martin Ryle and Kate Soper (2002) sought to defend an Arnoldian definition of literary culture's role in realising the self as opposed to the one-dimensional culture of economic rationality and productivity insisted upon by capitalism. Arnold's work remains critical in the extent to which it cautions about a dominant culture that impresses itself through the fostering of competition, concern for wealth and instant transformation. However, as I have indicated, we need to be careful that it is not only a literary or (in Arnold's case) a classical culture that is capable of producing democratic forms of self-reflection and transformation. Much popular culture is also capable of taking on this role as well. Here I would suggest that we abandon the argument that a particular class of cultural objects better serves the process of producing critical forms of reflection than others. In this much recent work in cultural studies has wisely cautioned against making judgements about aspects of culture without carefully considering contexts of production, meaning and reception (Stevenson 2006). This discussion need not end in relativism. It's just that as democratic educators we are sometimes best placed when discussing reality television or the culture of celebrity rather than more 'worthy' cultural matters.

Charles Taylor (1979) hints at how this might be achieved when he argues that if mainstream liberalism offers a culture of individualism then because we are moral beings we require access to cultures of self-realisation. In other words, not only do we need space to make up our own minds, we also need to hear counter-arguments and viewpoints that at first may seem to be unreasonable. At this point I would add that we must grasp a sense of our own overlapping histories and traditions as well as a sense of how our own lives are linked to citizens of the past and future. Ultimately this is a liberal culture where we should all be granted adequate opportunity to become ourselves without the community seeking to manufacture us into being certain kinds of subjects. However, we will not able to realise ourselves without the wider community making available to us a sense of our own 'living traditions' (MacIntyre 1981: 223). A genuinely liberal, democratic and moral education would need to hold in check vocationalism, the buying of educational privilege and attempts to impose ethical, political or religious doctrines. This is not a defence of liberal agnosticism, but offering instead an education that is suitable for democratic citizens. Further, such an education would need to offer students the possibility of being the producers of knowledge and a complex understanding of themselves and their role in the world as citizens of the future. As we shall see, the provision of a critical and public education that allows citizens to become the kind of beings they wish to become is currently under threat. If education is thereby being reduced to a means to gain access to the labour market then the traditional liberal model that (in theory at least) allowed students the possibility of self and democratic exploration is in crisis. As Raymond Williams (1965: 168) argues:

> Instead of the sorting and grading process natural to a class society, we should regard human learning in a genuinely open way, as the most valuable resource we have and therefore as something which we should have to produce a special argument to limit rather than a special argument to extend.

Williams' own radicalness lay in his insistence that a liberal culture of learning was for everyone and not just the middle classes. This argument necessarily pushes liberalism in a more social direction. A mass democracy, as Arnold was ahead of Mill in realising, requires democratic institutions that are capable of addressing questions of human welfare, learning and development. An educated and participatory democracy requires an education system that is both high quality and able to offer everyone the possibility of critical forms of reflection. League tables, standardised curriculums, teaching to test and the conversion of education into exam-passing factories do not best serve this purpose. Mathew Arnold himself was critical in his own time of proposals to pay schools according to their results and thereby risk narrowing the curriculum. Here a form of education that imposes on children a cultural of aspiration or narrow ideas of what it means to lead a successful life does not best serve a democratic society. Instead a genuinely liberal education would need to link education to knowledge about our diverse traditions, an understanding of the increasing complex global world in which we live, our ecological vulnerability, issues of cultural difference, questions of justice and complex moral problems. This could not of course discount the progress of people who simply want to live overtly consumerist lifestyles, but it might be able to offer other possibilities as well. Education, as I have insisted thus far, is intimately connected with questions of freedom and will continue to be so in the future regardless of how our dominant institutions are designed and developed. As we shall see over the course of this book, these ideals need to be radically reinterpreted in order to meet the complex challenges of the present.

2

Cultural Citizenship, Education and Democracy: Redefining the Good Society

If there is no understanding of the meanings and practices of education outside of debates about the good society then how are we to proceed? Here I want to look at a conflict that has taken place within modern liberal thinking about the 'right' and the 'good'. On one side of the argument is the view that modern citizens should not be socialised into what are called 'comprehensive doctrines'. John Rawls (1996) argues that it is basically illiberal to expect citizens to uphold similar views on a plurality of perspectives. A liberal and tolerant society could expect to contain a number of different religions, ethnicities, political convictions and so on. The problem, however, is how in an individualist society we can find coherence if it is not through common values and beliefs. Here Rawls's answer is that all citizens irrespective of their orientation would need to accept liberal principles that protected basic rights and liberties that provided the framework within which different cultural beliefs and perspectives could flourish. It is, then, for Rawls 'unreasonable' for the state to force particular comprehensive doctrines upon citizens and it should instead aim to help foster pluralism. The state through education should not seek to impose a particular version of the good on the community, but should instead seek to honour distinctive ways of life that are compatible with ideas of equal rights and democracy. This of course does not mean that individual citizens do not have their own ideas of the good, but that these need to fit with a society based upon liberal principles. The priority of the right over the good entails that the rights of citizens not only place limits on freedom, but also offer the possibility of liberty to all of its citizens. Education in this setting would be required to offer a diversity of perspectives and arguments to its youngest citizens without preferring any over another as long as they were compatible with basic liberal freedoms and justice for all. Education would need to be agnostic as to how citizens chose to live, respecting their choices as long as they could be shown not to have interfered with the liberties of others.

The argument against these views suggests that far from being 'neutral' liberal societies are actually substantive doctrines themselves that offer a version of the good society which is individualistic to the core. In other words, there is no such thing as the neutral society or a social order that does not seek to regulate the behaviour and actions of its citizens in some ways rather than others. Education systems and institutions are compelled to make choices as to how they shape the horizons, identities and self-understandings of the young. Here we might turn to the work of Antonio Gramsci (1971) who argued that education should be understood in the context of the operation of power and control. There is no 'neutral' education system as the kind of education, culture and learning instituted in society is the outcome of the relationship between the dominant class and more subordinate classes. In this respect, the dominant class cannot simply impose a vision of education, but would need to negotiate within the horizons of more subordinate groups. Gramsci noted how in 1920s' Italian society the education that was offered to the young was divided between classical and vocational education. The dominant social groups could expect to have access to elite forms of education, with the working class being offered a narrow curriculum and technical forms of training. The deep divisions within education existed for a society that explicitly taught its citizens how to rule or how to labour. In other words, it was only through the development of common schools that had dispensed with the social divisions between classes that society could be said to offer a democratic schooling for everyone. What is so helpful in respect of Gramsci's (1971) analysis is the argument that education and schooling more generally cannot be conceived apart from the dominant social structures that govern society. As Henry Giroux (2000a: 128) argues, Gramsci remains critical to the way we think about education because of the way he links questions of authority and power. Giroux also goes on to to argue that a democratic education for Gramsci was less about neutrality and more about the development of democratic capacities, and that such an education would need to be struggled for by social movements from below. Here Gramsci identifies both the state and capitalism as the main agents shaping the content and context of education that would need to be confronted by alternative social and political projects. In this respect, educators and intellectuals could not afford to be indifferent or 'neutral' in the struggle for more democratic forms of culture and education.

While Gramsci cannot be simply returned to for the answers to our own dilemmas about education his comments remain enormously suggestive. Here I would argue that the idea of a liberal and democratic society is an enormous political advance offering the prospect of a critical education for the many rather than either elite schools for a minority and vocational training for the majority. A liberal or democratic education is not valued because it is neutral but because of the opportunities that it offers to develop certain sensibilities, capacities and complex cultural literacies. Such arguments are dependent upon wider frameworks of power and authority that are willing to implement and enforce a democratic education. There is no democratic education without a wider alliance of social movements, concerned citizens, trade unions and state officials who are willing to argue for its importance. A democratic education depends upon a vision that would need to become a particular political project that was connected to a contemporary vision as to how we could and indeed should organise education. What Gramsci offers the analysis in a way that is missing in Rawls is an understanding that education is linked to broader questions of cultural power and authority.

So how might such an idea become attached to ideas of cultural citizenship? Such features arguably take the debate on the practice of citizenship in contemporary societies beyond Kantian approaches that have been concerned with ideas of social contract (Rawls 1972) or procedural norms (Habermas 1996). These approaches have little connection with the social and cultural organisation of the practice of citizenship within contemporary society, and, further, also neglect to analyse the continued importance of local and national political traditions and histories of organising political sentiment and connection. Here I am also concerned that they offer an overly minimal understanding of how historical understandings of the 'good society' might become reformulated over time. Alternatively, debates by Turner (2006b) and others have sought to emphasise the ways in which citizenship is being transformed by questions of human rights. Such a view tends to suggest that a closer relationship between human rights and citizenship will enable humanity to build a future that is both cosmopolitan and socially inclusive. While I have some sympathy with this view, I think that it radically underestimates the continuing importance of the locality in organising the central features of citizenship as well as the thinning out of citizenship by neoliberalism. In this respect, despite the cosmopolitan visions offered by others such as Held (2004) and Beck (2006), they fail to address what a good society could mean in the early twenty-first century. Ultimately their descriptions depend upon a view of citizenship that is more concerned with global institutional reform than it is with the ways in which the practices of citizenship have been reformulated by social and historical change. In other words, the process of democratically arguing and struggling for a democratic education inevitably means that we will prefer certain visions of the good society over others. To return to Gramsci for a moment, it is a call for intellectuals and counter-hegemonic formations to offer a different view of what education might be from the dominant form that is currently practised and instituted (Giroux 2000a: 135). The idea of cultural citizenship needs to look carefully at the ways in which education is currently constituted by certain institutional designs and pedagogic patterns rather than others and to also look at the possibility of these becoming a site for struggle, contradiction and agency. The 'cultural' aspect of citizenship suggests that our understandings of rights and responsibilities are subject to social and historical change and dependent upon particular locations. Part of the project of cultural citizenship not only seeks to locate the struggle for certain institutional orders and visions of the good society, but also suggests, following Gramsci (1988: 348), that 'every relationship of "hegemony" is necessarily an educational relationship and occurs not only within a nation, between the various forces of which the nation is composed, but in the international and world-wide field, between complexes of national and continental civilisations'. Part of the project of cultural citizenship is to study the ways in which dominant social formations will mobilise particular ideological understandings but also to seek to map the ways in which they can be resisted and transformed. However, as should be clear by this point, the version of cultural citizenship I would hope to defend has an overtly normative stance and is suggestive of certain versions of the good society rather than others.

The idea of cultural citizenship has thus far been concerned with issues more related to respect than democracy. Cultural understandings of citizenship are not only concerned with 'formal' processes, such as who is entitled to vote and the maintenance of an active civil society, but also crucially with whose cultural practices are disrespected, marginalised, stereotyped and rendered invisible. As Renato Rosaldo (1999: 260) argues cultural citizenship is concerned with 'who needs to be visible, to be heard, and to belong'. Similarly I have sought to argue that cultural citizenship is mostly about the ability in a shared cosmopolitan context to participate in the polity while being respected and not reduced to an Other (Stevenson 2001, 2003). Cultural citizenship becomes the struggle for a communicative society that is fearful of the threat of normalisation, exclusion and silence. These features all seek to investigate the ways in which cultural diversity, technology and globalisation foster a sense of an overlapping and contested cultural domain. However, while these remain important debates, I have more recently been interested in the extent to which they currently fail to map the declining fortunes of the nation-state, widespread public cynicism, the drop in election turn-outs, the rise of privatised living patterns and more general forms of disengagement from the political sphere (Castells 1997; Putnam 2000). In addition, we might add that the growing environmental crisis, consumerism, neoliberal policies of privatisation, and the widening of the gap between rich and poor pose substantial problems for democratic societies. Yet the broader point remains that a large-scale cultural shift to a global and technological society is reconfiguring the practices and meanings of citizenship. This does not mean that the concerns of previous historical periods that feared totalitarianism or sought to construct a social state are now redundant, but it does mean the project of creating an educated and participatory society needs to be reimagined.

On this I would follow Castoriadis (1997a) in arguing that democracy is itself a social and historical creation that allows individuals to both formulate laws and place these rules under critical scrutiny. It is the struggle for the democratic and autonomous society as opposed to a society ruled by neoliberalism or an authoritarian state that should be central to the concerns of cultural citizenship. In considering questions of 'freedom' the prevailing culture of a particular society becomes all important. If freedom is to be more than an abstract norm it will mean we need to look closely at the ownership and control of the media, how schools are run, the various civic campaigns and the development of alternative and democratic spaces. As Henry Giroux (2006a) argues questions of pedagogy concern not only schools but also the ways in which people think of themselves, their sense of identity and the possibility of imagining a different world. Cultural citizenship needs to engage with more worldly contexts while connecting with the need to foster respectful, democratic, engaged and learning societies. In this setting therefore education needs to be concerned with issues such as rights as well as responsibilities. While citizens of the future require the right to participate in civic spaces they also need to consider questions of responsibility in an increasingly global and ecologically fragile world.

The good society and political theory

Recent writing on questions related to contemporary citizenship have tended to ignore the idea of the good society. More often there is a consideration of the competing traditions of liberalism, republicanism and communitarianism before this moves into a discussion about global transformations (Delanty 2000; Faulks 2000). While these debates inevitably deal with questions that are related to notions of political community, participation and individual liberty they often fail to deal with more specific cultural contexts and political traditions of thinking. In particular most of these accounts neglect to analyse ideas related to host political traditions and a number of contextual features such as the ways in which the public sphere becomes constructed in the context of everyday life. Ideas of the 'good society' are sometimes utilised by American communitarian thinkers, but these debates are mainly authoritarian in character and conceive of the cultural in an overly unified way (Etzioni 2000).

The contemporary dominance of neoliberal ideas and practices that aim to reproduce a view of the social as a place of atomised competition and free markets actively excludes any notion of the good society. However, there is a tradition of thinking on the nature of the good society that can be traced back to Aristotle and also connected to liberal socialist traditions of thought. An Aristotelian approach is mainly concerned with how citizens might be said to live well and be relatively virtuous while flourishing in the context of shared communities. Aristotle (2004) argues that the ultimate aim of life is happiness and that this is sought through practices that are ends in themselves. Ethics is a matter of practical activities where the teacher seeks to become better at teaching and the journalist better at communication. In other words, in order to be happy human beings will seek self-realisation and fulfilment. In this way of thinking, citizens become virtuous by both living and acting well. For Aristotle education was mostly concerned with the aim to make us moral people by transmitting the necessary virtues for a happy life. The most important virtue in this respect is the ability to be able to think and contemplate. We need to learn not only to be critical but also how to be virtuous and to live well. There is no happy or good life without also living virtuously. These virtues are mainly cultivated through doing virtuous acts and realising the self as a person of character. Education, then, has an explicitly moral character where ultimately we need to consider how best to become a good person and lead a happy life (Frankena 1965).

As Alasdair MacIntyre (1998) points out such views are in stark contrast to accounts that seek to formulate universal laws in order to regulate the duties of the citizen. Usually inspired by Kant such approaches attempt to tell the citizen what they should not do. A point not considered by MacIntyre is that perhaps it is not surprising in the context of European history (including two world wars, colonialism and slavery, and the Holocaust) that this kind of thinking has become prevalent. In the European context much philosophical reflection that emphasises the 'right' over the 'good' has taken place in the context of human catastrophe. However, the regime instituted by contemporary liberal society is far from 'neutral' and has been progressively colonised by a capitalist imaginary that is hostile to more democratic sentiments and understandings. Terry Eagleton (2003) has remarked that Kantian-inspired arguments are largely built upon the necessity of self-sacrifice in troubling circumstances. In this regard, there is surely no vision of the good society without a willingness to behave responsibly. It is just that to be moral can be equally about the dis-covery of a society based upon human happiness and fulfilment.

Charles Taylor (1989a) has observed that the idea of the good society switches our emphasis from what is the right course of action to what is good for all. There is no vision of the good society without also an idea of what it means to be a good person. This is a shared language of discrimina-tion that allows us to distinguish and evaluate between different acts. There is no fully inclusive culture as any description of the good society will of necessity seek to foster certain ways of life rather than others. These fea-tures inevitably require a change in language that can produce a discussion of human potential and the possibility of cultural development and learning (Taylor 1989b). Such a view arguably shifts our shared discussion into questions related to critical humanism, but also suggests that any radical movement for change needs to be concerned with issues related to educa-tion in the broadest sense. How we might build a good society on our shared capacities for dialogue and engage in processes of critical reflection while valuing the ways in which we become interconnected with one another and nature is part of what I shall explore below. In particular, notions of the good society would ask us to jettison concerns about liberal neutrality for a project that aims to produce a robust civic culture. It seems to me, however, that this is not just a matter of localising democracy but also, as John Dewey (1977) understood, of accepting that we are born rela-tional beings but not democratic beings, and unless the ability to deliberate upon matters of common concern is an ordinary feature of everyday life then such features are unlikely to take root in the wider community. It is only through democratic dialogue that society is able to put itself into question and distance itself from previously held beliefs and perspectives. Such a view necessitates the operation of a democratically contested public sphere. Charles Taylor (1995: 259) has argued that we can talk coherently about public space and the extent to which it allows for common spaces of deliberation on matters of shared interest. The issue of what is the common good needs to become a matter of ongoing controversy. It is less one of returning to Aristotle's definition of the good society, and more of recognising that what we take for the common good requires ongoing social and historical creation.

The common good has to be the outcome of a diversity of perspectives and intellectual challenge rather than simply being imposed by powerful interests and media organisations. However, if Aristotle's account of the virtues reflects the context of his time, what is equally evident is the idea that there is no living well without an account of these virtues (Urmson 1988). And while there are democratic virtues, there are also others. Many feminist writers have sought to argue that education should indeed aim to make us better people by emphasising our capacity to give care to vulnerable others. The ethic of care argument recognises that as vulnerable creatures humans (and animals) are dependent upon others. Virginia Held (2005) suggests that a morality which focuses upon our ability to be able to reason autonomously often neglects ideas of human dependence and the moral values that become associated with these lived realities. An ethic of care is less a universal ethical system and more the recognition that humans are relational beings and value the ties we have with others. An ethics of care does not necessarily replace concerns with democracy or social justice but offers an understanding as to how ethics remains related to our ability to form specific attachments with others. An ethics of care is not only concerned with our moral identities, but also seeks to create a caring society. As Nel Noddings (2002) has argued, an ethics of care suggests that just as women have learned to play a role in public then men can also learn to be carers. This cannot be brought about by imposing a particular set of virtues upon citizens, it ultimately requires a careful discussion of who we are, what we take to be important, and who we wish to become. An ethics of care in the context of education is about the ability of different stories and narratives to help cultivate moral sentiments. Noddings holds that this is especially important in contexts of violence, broken families and shattered communities. Similarly, Alasdair MacIntyre (1999) argues it is because we are bodily vulnerable creatures that we require an account of the virtues. That is, in order to flourish humans require the possibility of deliberation and social relationships that take account of our bodily needs. This does not mean that we are only mouths to feed, but that we need to deliberate on what it is good to be and become. MacIntyre highlights here the importance of self-reflection as we seek to ponder how we might best live, and what is best for those within 'our' families, communities and shared globe. Within this process MacIntyre suggests that we need to be able to find a balance between an ability to reason, argue and debate with others about the idea of the good, and equally with how we might offer care to those who are vulnerable. These features would suggest that a moral community is distinct from that of an overtly market-driven society. If a market society is mainly concerned with competitive advantage then a moral community requires virtues that would include the ability to be able to sympathetic and hospitable towards others.

Both McIntryre and the ethics of care arguments suggest that education in this respect cannot only be about our ability to reason, but must also consider our identities as potentially compassionate beings. Following Richard Rorty (1998a) these disputes do not really get us any closer to what can be seen as authentically human, rather they show us how we might imaginatively reconceive ourselves after we have given up foundational thinking. Rorty (1998a: 176) calls the possibility of reinventing how we see ourselves a 'sentimental education'. This is an education that seeks to develop a sense of sympathy with others in our shared and vulnerable world where fellow beings are suffering different kinds of abuse and indignity. Again what is important here is less that we obey a moral law, and more that through narratives and stories we recognise a shared sense of obligation. We become moved by these and other stories less out of a sense of rationality and more because we are sympathetic to the sufferings of others. The version of democratic life and education I would seek to defend is built upon the idea that we seek to explore the diverse ways in which we can offer solidarity to others, but also collectively and individually consider how we might best live. However, while recognising these different human capacities we also need to recognise that there is no sense in which these might be imposed, but that different versions of the good society need to be offered within democratic contexts. At this juncture I want to trace some of these features through the work of Hannah Arendt and Raymond Williams who can both make significant contributions to our thinking in this regard.

Hannah Arendt and the politics of thinking

If we begin our concerns about citizenship from the position of how we can be responsible and prevent the re-emergence of mass genocide, then this will be different from our attempt to build a society where the vast majority of human beings can be said to flourish. Hannah Arendt (1958), whose work was explicitly focused upon the need to defend a pluralistic public sphere against the threat of totalitarianism, could not be said to have articulated a vision of the good society beyond the need to foster a sense of personal responsibility amongst citizens and a republic built upon equal rights. However, the part of Arendt's thought I would seek to recover is based upon the importance of building a political culture based on 'thinking'.

Arendt wrote in the context of a totalitarian Europe and what she perceived as the rise of blatant criminality. The morality of the Holocaust and the gulags is made possible through an undermining of the rule of law and citizens lacking a sense of responsibility for the public realm. Arendt's (1977) reflections on the links between morality and politics find their most concrete form of expression in her discussion of the trial of Adolf

Eichmann. Here Arendt famously described the war criminal as a fairly average sort of person who was motivated to do his duty. In this respect, common sense had seemingly offered a weak barrier against political evil, given Eichmann's participation in crimes against humanity. He sought to defend himself by claiming that he was simply doing his job. This defence revealed not only someone who was willing to submit to externally defined bureaucratic rules and procedures, but also someone who had established a career in the Nazi order. Elsewhere Arendt (2000) suggested that the fact that many ordinary Germans were willing to consider themselves as cogs and functionaries detracts from the idea that each of us is individually responsible for our actions, and, further, that the SS and the Gestapo were not so much fanatics as relatively normal 'jobholders and family men' (2000: 152). In other words, it was the background of mass unemployment and a lack of regard for civic virtues that converted the ordinary 'bourgeois' into the mass man who was capable of playing his part in administered murder. Corey Robin (2007) argues that for Arendt the politics of genocide was as much about faceless bureaucracy as it was about careerism. It was, then, careerism as much as the pervasiveness of ideologies of hatred that paved the way for genocide and mass murder. Notably such an argument poses difficult questions for those who would seek to support the connection between liberal ideas of freedom and capitalism. This means that inhumanity is as much a problem for the ideologue as it is for those who seek to be pragmatic and reject all forms of critical thinking and public forms of engagement.

Elsewhere Arendt (1958) defended a pluralistic public realm where citizens were able to act creatively together and institute new projects while appreciating a diversity of perspectives and viewpoints. Hence whereas totalitarianism represents the attempt to eradicate human plurality, Arendt sought by returning to the philosophy of Ancient Greece to remind us of the republican potential of more contemporary societies. Politics is a matter for public reflection and shared plural public spaces that allow individuals to propose and try out new thoughts and a dialogue with others as well as engage in common forms of action.

Given these conclusions it is perhaps not surprising that Arendt emphasised the importance of thinking. Ultimately it was Eichmann's reliance upon clichés, stereotypes and the absence of a capacity to think for himself that attracted Arendt's attention. Notably it was also the idea of thinking as an activity that was emphasised rather than either access to knowledge or educational qualifications. In this respect, 'thinking' emphasised less the ability to produce a list of moral commandments and more an engaged practice which could be constantly involved in processes of revision and argument. Arendt (2003: 45) argued that: 'The dividing line between those who want to think and therefore have to judge by themselves, and those who do not, strikes across all social and cultural or educational differences'. For Arendt the evidence from totalitarian societies indicated that many people will simply adapt themselves to fit into the status quo. The Nazi order was able to exert its dominance over the mass of the population not because they were criminals but because they were 'respectable' people who refused or failed to think. It is the ability to doubt and be sceptical that best ensures resistance. Evil is most likely to be perpetuated by people who pragmatically adapt themselves to society without engaging in processes of self-examination. Here Arendt was not only referring back to the Socratic maxim that 'the unexamined life is not worth living', but was also nodding in the direction of Kant. According to Arendt, moral behaviour was less connected to self-love or obligations towards a shared community, and more motivated through ideas of self-regard and self-respect. In other words, it is the desire not to let the self down and the ability to recognise that we will have to live with ourselves afterwards that motivates moral behaviour. In this regard, those who refused to participate in the crimes of the Nazi regime were more often people to whom it was fairly self-evident after a short bout of thinking that such actions were wrong. As Arendt (2003: 95) commented: 'The greatest evildoers are those who don't remember because they have never given thought to the matter, and without remembrance, nothing can hold them back'. Despite these considerations, Arendt did not take the view that it was possible to create a society of thinkers. The best defence against the reoccurrence of totalitarianism was a rights-based society where citizens were encouraged to be public spirited (Canovan 1992: 163). Here Arendt underestimated the extent to which public forms of reflection presuppose communities to which citizens have a shared sense of connection. Without a bond between a number of overlapping and complex communities it is not clear why we should wish to listen to others or indeed care about their future (Taylor 1995: 276–277). Given the importance that Arendt placed upon 'thinking' and the dangers inherent in its absence surely it might be important to consider how modern societies could enhance the capacity of their citizens to both learn and think while maintaining a sense of obligation. Again, given the times that Arendt lived through, it is perhaps not surprising that she did not consider such features to be possible. Arendt's conservatism on questions of 'culture' and descriptions of a mass society seemingly foreclosed the possibility of ordinary people becoming engaged in extended forms of reflection. For Arendt (1958) art and culture were being radically undermined by a consumer society that was more concerned with the instantaneous than the durable. Art becomes undermined in a world where the vast majority of production is governed by functionality rather than the creation of relatively durable objects. In this respect, mass society is less interested in culture and more involved in the production of entertainment. While I would not wish to dismiss these reflections out of hand, it is notable that little consideration is given as to how 'culture' could become democratised so as to produce a society of collective reflection and engagement.

However, Arendt was deeply concerned with questions of education and learning. More specifically she (1993) warned that most revolutionaries of the past had simply sought to indoctrinate children. Within education, adults have to assume a responsibility for the well-being and development of the child. There is no education without responsible forms of authority. This authority does not simply rest at the level of the teacher's qualifications, but rather 'authority rests on his assumption of responsibility for that world' (Arendt 1977: 189). It is through education that we learn to balance freedom, authority and responsibility. It is the place where we renew a public world by communicating our traditions and an understanding of the past while leaving these projects open enough to become revisable by citizens of the future. In this respect, responsibility does not lie in neglecting our children or leaving their education to consumerism and the ideologies of markets or to processes of indoctrination. These citizens of the future require an education that not only reconnects them to the rich literatures and understandings of the past, but also helps provide them with critical knowledge as we seek to negotiate the future.

For Arendt as well as the early Greek philosophers we become human through our capacity to engage in autonomous thinking. This is indeed a human capacity I would seek to defend. The ability to be able to engage in autonomous forms of thinking has to be education's primary aim. However, as we have seen, human beings are also emotional beings who have a need for community and a connection with others. Norbert Elias (1998) wrote about the social relatedness of human beings and their dependence upon one another. This is most markedly the case with children who in order to become adults need to be able to relate to their parents and older members of the community. There is no model of human flourishing that can be built outside of a recognition of the ways in which human beings are capable of reshaping themselves in terms of their interdependence upon one another. These considerations are, as we shall see later, a necessary feature of any idea of the good society. Here my argument is that it is Arendt's Kantianism coupled with her conservatism on matters of culture that prevent her from considering a prospective future society where a fulfilled and reflective life is potentially within everyone's reach. Indeed, given Arendt's (1990) concern about revolutions that had been motivated by the 'social question', she would undoubtedly have been sceptical about any such aim. Ultimately what is missing from the accounts of those who seek to articulate a vision of a human society built upon a minimal set of public rules or autonomous thinking is any idea as to how citizens might be said to flourish in the context of complex relationships, communities and attachments. Despite Arendt's critical insights, her limitations in this regard bring us to the critical thought of Raymond Williams.

The long revolution and public culture

Raymond Williams was formed by a different intellectual and political climate to that of Hannah Arendt. More easily placed in a tradition of post-war democratic or liberal socialism, he explicitly sought to create the conditions of an 'educated democracy and a common culture' for everyone (Williams 1965: 176). Like many democratic socialists of his time Williams saw the development of the 'social state' as a means of promoting a more 'civilised' and democratic human society (Crossland 1956). However, Williams made his distinctive contribution in that he did not merely seek to utilise state power to promote a good society, but sought to democratise the state while promoting the conditions for common forms of cultural engagement. For Williams, ideas of culture were not simply to be contrasted with a debased mass society as Arendt had a tendency to do. Questions of culture mattered because they helped to define the very process of learning and self-transformation within contemporary society. Rather than simply defending certain works of 'civilisation' Williams emphasised the public role that mass communication, art, education and popular culture might play within modern society. In doing this, Williams (1958) also emphasised a Romantic tradition in writers from Mathew Arnold to William Morris who had sought to find within art a place of social and cultural reflection. This tradition not only tried to question the increasing dominance of market-place forms of rationality, but also potentially helped us link issues of culture to the public sphere. In this respect, Raymond Williams (1965) described the struggle for a learning and communicative society as the 'long revolution'. For him the development of cultural institutions such as broadcasting, the education system and the press were essential features within a mass democracy.

These ideas, as many others have recognised, possess a marked family resemblance with those of Jürgen Habermas (1989) on the public sphere. Like Arendt, Habermas does not so much describe a 'good society' but more explicitly seeks to outline what we might minimally expect from a society that attempts to call itself democratic. Yet unlike either Arendt or Habermas, Williams was seeking to discover a society where all might flourish while participating in an energetic civil society built upon autonomous and above all creative forms of cultural production. Indeed Habermas's writing is more closely connected to liberal ideals that seek to prioritise the right over the good. In other words, a liberal society should not seek to defend substantive doctrines but try to institute a liberal public sphere enabling them to have access to diverse opinions and perspectives. Here there is considerable confusion as to what counts as a 'substantive doctrine' and I remain unconvinced there could ever be such a thing as a neutral society, public sphere or education system (Stevenson 1999: 41–42). This is not simply to jettison the concerns of liberal political theory as I would argue that a more pressing question than 'neutrality' is how modern society might institute democratic forms of debate and reflection within a common realm.

For Williams (1965: 10) the democratic revolution could be said to be 'at a very early stage'. Despite the development of mass literacy, the prospect of participating in democratic elections and new communications technology as well as labour organisations that represented the subaltern class society remained dominated by the needs of capitalism. Only the gradual emergence of a complex socialist society could give full expression to every individual's capacity to be creative and live more realised lives. In these respects, Williams resisted the mental and manual divide instituted by a class society. Art and cultural forms of communication could be described as similarly creative activities that were concerned with: 'the sharing of common meanings, and thence common activities and purposes; the offering, reception and comparisons of new meanings, leading to the tensions and achievements of growth and change' (Williams 1965: 55). In this respect, he (1965: 56) was arguing against those who like Arendt sought to abstract art as a 'special experience', but aimed to see how they were both part of 'ordinary' processes of communication while being located in specific historical periods. Williams (1962) noted that cultural conservatives during his own time continued to argue that the state should preserve high culture against democratic tendencies and the market. He proposed that such features had a great deal in common with the commercial culture that this had been meant to oppose. The strict separation between an elite high culture and the more populist concerns of the market divided 'our culture into separate areas with no bridges between them' (Williams 1962: 108). During the 1960s Williams became interested in a new generation of people (Ken Loach, Tony Garnett, John McGrath) whose work in film, television and on the stage sought to question prevailing attitudes and assumptions particularly in respect of class politics. These individuals helped to make a public contribution by raising critical questions about the so-called classless society that many had assumed had emerged in the 1960s.

For Williams (1989) a culture in common had several aspects, but overall it was an instituted culture of dialogue rather than agreement. To be able to talk of a culture in common meant rejecting the choice between atomised privatisation or cultural communalism. However, it did mean the development of democratic public spaces of engagement built upon a shared education system that had broken with the class-bound logic of the past. The *common* element of Williams' argument concerned the ability of ordinary people – not just paid professionals – to contribute, criticise and re-interpret aspects of their culture. Within this process the meanings of 'high' or indeed 'popular' culture were not fixed in stone but required open criticism by members of the community. Notably, Williams provided a defence of the ability of literature and drama to ask critical questions of both historical and more contemporary societies. In this respect, complex works of art and criticism did not belong to the dominant class, but could be potentially commented on by everyone.

A culture in common requires the provision of institutions that transmit the knowledge, skills and resources that allow for full participation. This was no longer the Arnoldian project of simply transmitting the best works of civilisation, but one of enabling citizens to realise their critical potential. Inevitably such a project required an education system that was willing to break with 'the sorting and grading process natural to class society' (Williams 1965: 168). For Williams educational institutions not only needed to familiarise working-class students with 'high' forms of culture, but also had to allow them to develop their own arguments and perspectives that might well stop short of traditional forms of reverence. Such a project could not rely upon an image of a unified public sphere, but instead had to look to interlocking and competing public spheres from education to the media and from the arts to more overtly popular forms of expression.

Raymond Williams' working-class background meant that his initial experience of 'culture' was one of inequality. Culture was primarily experienced through a sense of being excluded from high culture (Williams 1968). He most acutely explored these features through his first two novels, *Border Country* (1960) and *Second Generation* (1964). In these, rather than simply resting on the argument that education needed to develop critical forms of understanding, Williams explored the tensions within subjective experiences involved in moving across cultural borders and boundaries. More specifically these novels give expression to some of the pain and uncertainty that was encountered by people from working-class backgrounds who moved across the borders of class. As Wendy Kohli (1993) notes, despite Williams' emphasis upon feeling most of his theoretical work is concerned with developing the democratic practice of critical reflection while remaining connected to broader communities of interest such as the labour movement. It is, however, mainly through Williams' novels that feelings of alienation, detachment and disconnection become apparent.

For Williams democratic socialism remained connected to the capability of citizens to learn through the education system and democratised public spheres. Later he would describe socialism as 'not only the general "recovery" of specifically alienated human capacities, but also, and much more decisively, the necessary institution of new and very complex communicative capacities and relationships' (Williams 1980: 62). This noted, he (1980: 249) was perceptive enough to recognise that since the early 1970s a much harsher version of capitalism had become apparent, leading to what he called 'the actual defeat of major sections of the working-class'.

The idea of 'the long revolution' offers an answer to the question of what a good society and a good life might be. The response that Williams gave was a place where ordinary people could become creative, be actively involved in the key decisions that were made in their society and develop themselves through education (Rustin 2007a). The long revolution as the learning society had to be permanently open to the challenge of new voices and perspectives, and in this respect would in more contemporary times have had to adopt a more self-consciously multicultural vocabulary. The guiding aspect of a democratic culture in common is its ability to be able to promote dialogue across a number of cultural divides and enclaves while all the time developing a common capacity to become a cultural producer and critic. Similarly Bhikhu Parekh (2000a) argues that a multicultural society needs a shared common culture fashioned out of diversity. In a multicultural society diverse cultures constantly encounter one another and change due to the presence of the other. Unless we are content to live in a society of cultural apartheid and fragmentation institutional conditions must be created to foster intercultural dialogue. While a 'common culture' cannot be engineered the opportunities for a common dialogue need to be politically created. Just as Williams argued that literature and creative practices had to be extended and criticised by working-class voices so Parekh argues that similar privileges need to be extended to 'minorities'. Within this process both Williams and Parekh highlight the centrality of cultural and educational institutions. They are both critical of monocultural institutions that aim to impose a collective conformist culture. Since Williams' time a multitude of groups have sought to interrupt the dominant culture and carve out a realm of relatively authentic forms of public expression and concern. These features can perhaps be seen as a means by which the long revolution has continued since Williams' death in the late 1980s.

However, arguments related to multiculturalism have necessarily moved the analysis on from the culturally 'bounded' national society and cultural nationalism that were assumed by much of Williams' writing. The main problem with the preceding argument is the nationalist assumption that notions of the public are constituted by exclusively national public spaces. It presents an image of publics emerging inside of exclusively national borders. Such a view is of course not without a certain resonance; however, it is blind to the ways in which cultures and publics can be said to cross over those borders. If Williams significantly underestimated these features in his work he was undoubtedly correct to warn against the idea that an unrestrained capitalism could ever deliver the common conditions for a cultural democracy. Further, we need to remind ourselves that he wrote at a time when the democratic transformation of the state, media and education seemed like a realistic prospect. In the next section, I shall argue how questions of culture and the good society might be rethought in our more cosmopolitan, networked and global times.

Recovering hope and cultural politics

As Williams foresaw, the rise of neoliberalism defeated the democratic socialist project that sought to create an educated and egalitarian public culture. The end of the Cold War did not offer new forms of hope for democratic socialism but witnessed the gradual winding up of the so-called parliamentary road to socialism. The decline of the social democratic Left has seen socialist parties across Europe adapt themselves to the harsh realities of neoliberalism. Pierre Bourdieu (2003: 29) has described neoliberalism as instituting 'a mode of domination based on the *institution of insecurity*, domination through precariousness: a deregulated financial market fosters a deregulated labour market and thereby casualisation of labor that cows workers into submission'. The concrete effect of this new hegemony is an economy that increasingly creates divisions between low-paid and low-status employment and the overworked and stressed middle classes. This division also maps onto an equally worrying cultural divide between the dominant cosmopolitan orientations of elites and more locally orientated publics who sometimes take refuge in vicious nationalism. The increasing dominance of multinational corporations, the development of a commercial culture built upon the rich lifestyles of celebrities, the erosion of public-service broadcasting, the corporatisation of the education system and of course the withering of working-class institutions like trade unions have increased the dominance of capitalism over society more generally. However, as Raymond Williams would have been among the first to point out, while being aware of dominant hegemonic processes we also need to point towards the dialectical possibilities of transformation.

Cultural processes of globalisation offer us the possibility (sometimes if only for a moment) of moving beyond the borders of nation. In this respect, our shared media space is more than the effect of the commodification strategies of media conglomerates, and better understood as a disorderly and plural space (Silverstone 2007). This at least offers us the *possibility* along with the development of the Internet of stretching our civic imaginations beyond nation. Hence the coming together of neoliberalism and globalisation speaks of a simultaneous impoverishment of our common culture while it has been substantially reinvented in a world that continually poses questions concerning cultural as well as geographical borders.

In part, then, modern societies have increasingly through the impact of diverse popular cultures, social movements and multiculturalism within education sought to progressively reconsider their relationship with issues related to cultural difference. This is inevitably an ongoing process, indeed one without end. Alberto Melucci (1996: 42) argues that what 'matters today is no longer mere learning, but rather learning *how* to learn'. By this he means that new technology permanently multiplies the range of our relationships with distant others. This has the effect in an age where the markers of class and party have been weakened of introducing new possibilities as to who we might become. This may then convert into a renewed search for 'anchors' for the self in a seemingly shifting world, but equally may open up the possibility of forging a new relationship with questions of difference and Otherness. Such features obviously point towards the possibilities of living in a global culture that is full of multicultural and technological possibility even if these features are not always realised. Further, one of the central features of living within an information-driven society has been the enhancement of the capacity for reflexivity in an age that fears normalisation. There are new opportunities in our society for learning through the media, education and other forms of cultural interaction in a society that welcomes the Other. David Chaney (2002) argues that in terms of cultural citizenship one of the key transformations has been the decline in the ability of the nation-state to sanction the culture of its citizens through the policy arena. It is now more accurate to describe the state as a 'facilitator of diversity and a mediator between its citizens and global trends and markets' (Chaney 2002: 132). The cultural institutions that the long revolution sought to reform in order to press forward an agenda of democratic learning have declined in authority. However, if consumer-led populism has indeed contributed to a more relaxed attitude towards cultural diversity it has also led to an enhanced capacity on the part of markets to define everyday life.

If the long revolution in Williams' formulation was driven by the progressive desire and leadership of the labour movement then it would seem that capitalism for now has won this particular struggle. Does this then mean that there is indeed no alternative to the continual development of the commodified and privatised self? In Geoff Eley's majestic (2002) history of the Left in Europe he argues that the struggle for socialism held together ideas of collective organisation, notions of improvement and public service. As the old working class has gone into decline since the 1970s then so have the notions that public culture, or indeed the idea that education offers anything 'better' beyond what individuals may decide to choose for themselves. Since Williams' time our shared cultural worlds have simultaneously become more commodified and multidimensional. At this point I shall argue that we need to rethink the connection between democratic forms of life and the good society. This can only be achieved by seeking to imagine what democratic public spaces might mean in the context of complex information-driven global societies.

Local cosmopolitans and the good society

The idea of the cosmopolitan has been the focus for a considerable amount of recent critical discussion (Held 2004; Beck 2006). There has also been much debate on how cosmopolitanism can be connected to questions of education (Nussbaum 1996; Gunesch 2004). The notion of the cosmopolitan usually trades upon our mutual ideas of the world or global citizens and as a form of citizenship that is able to welcome the Other. There is of course no need to choose between these two different visions and indeed many authors have sought to emphasise both strands within contemporary debates (Beck 2006). In our terms, Hannah Arendt offered a view of cosmopolitan citizenship where international law and human rights conventions increasingly emphasise individual responsibility for our actions irrespective of the official role of the state. A society built upon human rights would need to instruct its citizens that crimes committed against different religions, ethnic groups and others were an affront to our shared humanity (Fine 2000). These features necessitate the view that citizenship education would need to emphasise the critical importance of the role of human rights, democracy and pluralism.

However, within the discussion of Raymond Williams' ideas of the long revolution I expressed the concern that this vision did not describe a good society in which we all might flourish. Williams' egalitarian emphasis upon education, plurality and creativity as human goods pointed to a society where learning was not something which should be either instrumentalised or restricted to an elite. He potentially offered a more rooted version of cosmopolitanism that sympathetically welcomed the voice of the Other, but did so through a recognition of the host culture's internal complexity and mutual capacity to be creative. Similar to Appiah's (1998) version of cosmopolitanism we can take pleasure in our own cultural particularities while maintaining a dialogic interest in human differences. Such a view means that we can be loyal to host traditions, while also seeking to re-read them through a diversity of experiences and perspectives. Indeed Appiah's (2005) arguments are that educational attempts to facilitate cosmopolitan citizenship should be less concerned with promoting a detached global citizenship and more open to the realisation that in being a local citizen you can also be a good global citizen. Along with Martha Nussbaum (1997) I would seek to defend the critical importance of a liberal education for everyone. In a world of overlapping and complex loyalties we should be careful that local attachments are not dismissed as the bad Other of universal thinking. Here Nussbaum stresses the importance of Socratic dialogue and deliberative argument that aim 'to confront the passivity of the pupil' into thinking for themselves (Nussbaum 1997: 33). Education should aim to critically interrogate local traditions, to investigate how we are mixed in with globalised others and seek to develop the imaginative capacity to understand our shared world from different points of view. Such an outlook can respect local attachments while at the same time subjecting them to deliberative arguments in respect of the common good. Cosmopolitanism should not simply seek to transcend local attachments and traditions, but should also promote a critical dialogue between, for example, human rights documents, the need for critical thinking and the citizen's sense of attachment to place. This is indeed what was advocated by Paulo Freire (1993) who argued that our sense of being global citizens came less through abstract norms and was more likely to emerge through a sense of connection to particular places, and then proposed how these locations could link us less into a separatist identity than into a more interconnected identity with globally situated others.

Of course there are dangers in a return to the local such as local retrenchment and an increasing fear of outsiders. Here we might need to learn to balance the cosmopolitan and the local at the same time. This suggests a form of cosmopolitan localism that criticises the placelessness evident in certain versions of global citizenship while seeking to promote fluid and complex understandings of place (Tomlinson 1999). This perhaps only becomes possible through movements and educational settings that mutually seek to explore more democratic arrangements and a mutual sense of interconnectedness both with other people and with the natural world. Cultural citizenship needs to be redefined as a form of critical theory that seeks to develop democratic public spaces while simultaneously promoting a sense of lived connection with a number of complex and overlapping communities in time and space. It would also need to balance the demand for autonomous reflection with the recognition that citizens live within overlapping communities with which they are likely to experience different levels of connection. If Raymond Williams was able to imagine the long revolution being carried through by the labour movement this is perhaps no longer adequate for our shared global, neoliberal and post-industrial times. The retreat of the democratic state, the progressive commodification of culture and the self, the increasing power of global capital and the erosion of national democracy all mean that cultural citizenship has to be re-imagined in terms of a new set of co-ordinates that can continue to connect citizens with the practices of democratic community. If there is no vision of the good society without an attempt to reimagine the ways in which citizens may learn and find community with one another in the network age radical possibilities of transformation need to be rethought (Castells 1997).

Cultural citizenship therefore is the struggle for a democratic society that enables a diversity of citizens to lead relatively meaningful lives, that respects the formation of complex hybrid identities, offers them the protection of the social state and grants them access to a critical education which seeks to explore the possibility of living in a future that is free from domination and oppression. To be a cultural citizen means to engage in deliberative argument about what it is ethical to become, and to consider how we might lead virtuous and just lives in specific cultural locations and contexts. In our complex global society we require an education and a media culture that are able to make sense of contemporary transformations and offer us the space to share and critically interrogate our diverse experiences and practices, enabling us to consider how we might best ensure the flourishing of each and every individual. It would also mean that we are able to recognise ourselves as local, national and of course globally interconnected citizens. Such a feat would require, as I have sought to emphasise, not only our cognitive capacities to reason, but also a renewed sense of ourselves as sympathetic and compassionate beings.

3

Democratic Socialism, Multiculturalism and the Third Way: Questions of Education

The argument of the past two chapters has been that the way we understand education remains tied to our shared ideas of the good society. Further, how we imagine a good society is in turn dependent upon a number of cultural, sociological and normative features. Here I want to point to how a particular critical understanding of the possibilities of education has become undermined by the extension of neoliberalism. While the project for an educated and participatory society has a long historical lineage I have argued that it remains closely connected to notions of democracy or liberal socialism. We have already seen how the critical intervention of Raymond Williams in these debates sought to rethink questions of democracy and its relationship to politics and public forms of pedagogy. I now want to look more closely at the writing of Richard Hoggart who has also sought to defend an 'educated' version of democratic socialism. Hoggart has a certain similarity to Williams in that he is often thought of as a founder of British cultural studies and came to prominence during the late 1950s. Indeed like Williams, Hoggart has been keen to link together a critical analysis of the wider capitalist society, a complex understanding of culture and a defence of public forms of education. However, this approach is now quite marginal to debates within cultural studies as well as those seeking to reimagine democratic socialism in new times.

I shall argue that despite the criticism received from later generations of cultural and political theorists, the tradition of 'educated' democratic socialism should be rediscovered and reinvented in our own troubled days. In a later section, I shall also explore the contributions of Hoggart and Williams in relation to more contemporary ideas in respect of the 'third way' proposed by Anthony Giddens. While welcoming the call to reinvent the connection between democracy, social justice and education in a global age I shall argue that the third way should be subject to criticism. My argument will be that the recovery of democratic socialism and the prospects for a more educated society should seek to defend while also rethinking the idea of 'comprehensive' public schooling. However, this can only be achieved by a deeper engagement with the ideas of multiculturalism than has been evident thus far by those who seek to defend egalitarian forms of education. If the traditions of liberal socialism needed to be rethought in the previous chapter due to global changes here I shall seek to explore their relevance in more culturally pluralist societies.

Democratic socialism, cultural studies and education: the case of Richard Hoggart

As we saw earlier, the traditions of liberal socialist thinking remain central in respect of debates that seek to connect social justice, education and democracy. This tradition of thinking sought to steer clear of market-driven approaches that favoured vocationalism and state socialism that pressed ideological forms of indoctrination. A key argument here was that public space needed to be protected against both the market and the state, and further that the most disadvantaged members of society had the most to gain from such a political and cultural settlement given that they had not previously had the opportunity to develop themselves culturally. Many educational and cultural workers of Williams and Hoggart's generation saw that education had a value in itself and that this should not be restricted to the middle classes. For Hoggart this has meant a career spent defending the value of a genuinely public education.

Richard Hoggart (1995) provides a forceful defence of the public value of education in an age that is increasingly dominated by market values and relativism. Since the 1980s, along with the growth of a genuinely mass society and new communications technologies, the collective values of the old industrial working class and notions of public service have been increasingly assaulted by the ideologies and practices of free market capitalism. While some of these changes have allowed ordinary working-class people to shake off the yoke of deference in respect of the hierarchies of social class, Hoggart (1995: 6) describes the emergence of a society that is both 'more horizontal and diffused'. The undermining of cultural hierarchies has not introduced a more genuinely democratic public sphere, but has witnessed instead the growing dominance of the market over other social and cultural spheres. If the market has diminished the social standing of the educated middle classes it has simultaneously provided new opportunities for the cultural products of large corporations. In this respect, Hoggart accuses many on the cultural Left of adopting a form of market-friendly relativism for fear of being seen to disrespect the cultural practices of ordinary people. If there is simply a plurality of lifestyle and tastes whose 'superiority' is a matter of easily punctured snobbery, then nothing seemingly stands in the way of the commodifying logic of the dominant consumer society. The dominant hegemony of an age which refuses to admit a hierarchy of cultural tastes and preferences becomes 'stay as sweet as you are' (Hoggart 1995: 9). In this the ethos of the public is gradually replaced by progressive privatisation, atomism and a decline in the idea that citizens have a civic duty to the community. Cultural worth is no longer measured using questions of quality and value, but is more likely determined by the ability to either make a profit or in the new technocratic logic of public services to satisfy 'performance indicators' and produce 'measurable outcomes'. The increasing dominance of neoliberal capitalism has produced a dominant hegemony of the 'puritan and prim' and the 'intensely money-conscious', replacing more social democratic concerns for the common good and the urban poor (Hoggart 1995: 13). The displacement of the ethic of community where I am 'my brother's keeper' has seen the public sector caught in a vicious pincer movement where it both adopts the language and management styles of the private sector while being forced into a constant battle over scarce resources.

These social and cultural changes have particular implications for the value of education. In the mid-1990s Hoggart reported that the collapse in the public value of education and the persistence of entrenched hierarchies of social class meant vocationalism gained a new respectability in debates concerning education. This not only reflected the dominance of the market in the governance of education but was also an expression of a class-based society that increasingly aimed to teach young working-class people practical skills. The divisiveness of the education system helped create what Hoggart (2004) was later to call the 'under-educated society'. If the lives of the under-class are marked by illiteracy and narrow horizons those at the top of the social hierarchy are still able to buy educational success through access to elite private schools. The divisions of class prepare some children for a life of success and achievement and others either for exclusion or for a world of mostly dead-end employment. For Hoggart the 'right' to choose a private education is actually the 'right' to choose a competitive advantage over others. Education here is not viewed as a public good, but as a passport to success in the labour market. The concept of market choice when applied to education ends up reinforcing class divisions, however unintentionally. Hoggart's argument is that the increasing penetration of the market into education further reinforces existing class relations that in turn enhance elitist assumptions that working-class children are incapable of handling difficult works of literature and abstract concepts. These arguments, we might summarise, are not only a matter of class prejudice but also act as a form of political control.

The history of democratic or liberal socialism is marked by the idea that working people should be enabled to expand their intellectual capacities beyond those required for the functioning of the labour market. This is a history and legacy that refuses the argument that working-class people simply demanded better forms of training for the job market. Part of the history of 'educated' democratic socialism was the insistence that working-class people had intellectual tastes and the imaginative capacity to engage in a wider literature and forms of reflection (Rose 2001). For Hoggart the capitalist-based society is hostile to this tradition in two ways. First, by seeking to offer only poor levels of education and the failure to develop more critical forms of literacy this enables the political and economic system to argue that working-class people are best served through vocational forms of training. Second, a consumerist society seeks to articulate the view of a liberal right to pleasure. This is where we are the best deciders as to how we spend our leisure time. Similar to Mathew Arnold, Hoggart argues that this view misses how the dominant system seeks to manipulate our desires in some ways rather than others. Indeed it is the working class who are most likely to be manipulated by the claims of advertisers as they lack the cultural capital to see through their demands.

Hoggart's argument is that the dominance of the market over educational values and perspectives requires relativism. If capitalist-driven democracies need a compliant population who are willing to fit unquestioningly into the requirements of flexible capitalism then it is not surprising that knowledge is no longer valued in terms of its capacity to enlighten and open up repressed questions. A democratic rather than a capitalist-driven education system and society is dependent upon 'the belief in the worthwhileness of the pursuit of knowledge for its own sake, and the respect due to those who seek it' (Hoggart 1995: 302). The capacity of modern societies to offer young people equal forms of educational provision and critical forms of inquiry beyond the narrow confines of 'vocationalism' is a necessary requirement for democracy. Such arguments seek to break with the elitist traditions of education (private schools for the elite and vocationalism for the masses) and attempt to foster the genuinely critical forms of inquiry demanded in a society that is able to hold in check the colonising logic of capitalism.

Hoggart's writing needs to be seen in a democratic socialist tradition that was committed to the values of self-development, community and solidarity with the poor and dispossessed. Such views could be understood historically in terms of the split in the Second International between Communism and a reformist social democracy. For most of the twentieth century European social democracy adopted a genuinely parliamentary road to socialism while seeking to maintain a fair distribution of wealth, a mixed economy, the building of a welfare state and the empowerment of trade unions. European social democratic parties sought to establish alternative public spheres that would act as a counterweight to the dominant capitalist ethos of market competition. We might remember that despite their variety European social democratic parties were more than election-winning machines and were directly involved in the ideological and cultural organisation of the working class (Moschonas 2002). For the most part the culture of social democracy was built upon an alliance between the educated middle class and the organised working class. Both these groups historically found a common cause in seeking to mediate the more destructive tendencies of capitalism.

Richard Hoggart's classic (1957) work *The Uses of Literacy* captures some of the essential features that democratic socialism had to grapple with during this period. As Hoggart so memorably argues there are deep dangers to democracy when social progress and cultural development begin to be defined in terms of the accumulation of material possessions. Here Hoggart does not seek to deny the importance of the material improvements in the lives of the vast majority of the working class. However, what had arrived along with 'progress' was a permissive tolerance which was afraid of making critical judgements. The mood of 'democratic egalitarianism' ushered in by a market culture simply ended in an uncritical populism. This meant that anyone wishing to develop a more critical appreciation of culture was dismissed as a snob who was seeking to look down on the tastes of ordinary people. In Hoggart's judgement working-class people valued being modern and contemporary, but in such a way that this made them easy prey for an exploitative and capitalist-driven culture.

Hoggart has however been rightly criticised for his overly moralistic reaction to the arrival of commercial culture and its corrupting effect upon the working class. On this he stands accused of the view that culture can be unproblematically assigned into categories of 'good' and 'bad' (Hebdige 1979). The struggle for an emancipated society becomes entangled in a binary logic that opposes educated socialism to the market in a way that has the consequence of producing a form of condescension in respect of the cultures of the working class. Further, the feminist historian Carolyn Steedman (1986) has proposed that Hoggart's study fails to recover more subsumed stories that do not conform to working-class Labour values. Yet what it is that later work offering more contested accounts of culture than Hoggart's own displaces is his social democratic concern with the educated development of the working class. The problem Hoggart identified was the erosion of a class-based culture by 'mass opinion, the mass recreational product, and the generalized emotional response' (Hoggart 1957: 343). There was also a deeper concern that the promise of mass culture would fail to develop the critical potential evident within the scholarship boy who is 'earnest for self-improvement' (Hoggart 1957: 303). In other words, what was missing from some of the later cultural studies literature was an engagement with Richard Hoggart's central narrative that concerned the educated development of those whom industrial civilisation had relegated to the status of labouring people.

Hoggart (1982) in particular argued that a genuinely critical education could be best fostered through the development of a searching dialogue between students and teachers. In this regard, he was critical of the working-class deprivation thesis that presumes that students are simply 'blank slates' waiting to be written over with the complexities of high culture. However, he has been equally critical of educational debates that deny any language of 'improvement' or 'development', arguing that a culturally relativist approach which merely seeks to reaffirm working-class identities may be well meaning, but unintentionally reinforces the rule of the market and corporate capitalism given its dominance in shaping the aspirations of the young. For Hoggart education does not have a neutral value, but instead needs to be protected from the market so that it can become a place of critical engagement, diversity and transformation. In this respect, he (2001a) would ask that education should not be confined to basic literacy, but also encompass questions of critical literacy. Hoggart (2001a: 194) defines critical literacy as:

> blowing the gaffe on all the small and large corporations, on the humbugging, smart-alec persuaders; it means learning how to read the small print in insurance policies and guarantees on major purchasers; it means telling the doorstep cowboys of all kinds to clear off and throwing junk mail into the wastepaper

basket, unopened; it means mocking television advertisements (all too easy) – especially which go for our soft underbellies.

If critical literacy is about being able to decode the relations of dominance that are part of the everyday world of consumer capitalism it is also about the ability to be able to understand complex ideas and associations. Similarly Martha Nussbaum (1997) argues that an education driven by utilitarian sentiment reduces the complexities and meaningfulness of our lives to simple forms of calculation. In this respect, Richard Hoggart (1970a) persists with the argument that the study of literature is central to any democratic vision of education. A complex appreciation of literary culture is important because of its ability to offer new ways of seeing, new experiences and complex moral and cultural vocabularies. Both Nussbaum and Hoggart are rejecting an education that deals merely with that which is 'objective' or can be scientifically verified by focusing upon the need to develop the poetic and the imaginative potential of citizens. Much writing in cultural studies has been suspicious of this move, supposing that it automatically leads to a denigration of popular culture. Yet Hoggart (1970a: 38) also argues that while popular culture is worthy of detailed study it is unlikely to attain the level of complexity of good literature. This assumption, which has been endlessly deconstructed by postmodernism, is no longer helpful, but the defence of cultural complexity against more utilitarian calculations is still well worth making.

In this and other respects Hoggart's work is related to what his contemporary Raymond Williams (1965) called 'the long revolution' which sought to link economic, social and political issues to cultural questions. The idea at heart, as we have seen, was that in the context of the labour movement there existed the potential for an alliance between radical educationalists, politically committed artists and organised labour. All had an interest in curtailing the power of the market and the establishment of a genuinely democratic and inclusive public sphere. For Williams the long revolution maintained the historical possibility of realising the creative and learning potential of ordinary people. Notably Hoggart and Williams refused either to romanticise or to denigrate their shared if regionally distinct working-class backgrounds. Such views have a marked similarity with those of Henry Giroux (1988, 1989) given that he has consistently made the case for a critical politics of education which argues that schools and educational institutions are not merely sites of cultural reproduction but should become places of critique. For Giroux (1993a: 369), 'literacy as an emancipatory practice requires people to read, speak, and listen in the language of difference, a language in which meaning becomes multiaccentual and dispersed, and resists permanent closure'. However, there are marked differences between this position and that occupied by Hoggart and Williams. As we shall see, Hoggart and Williams remain more specifically connected to the critical potential of high culture (in particular literature) whereas Giroux's arguments contain a more multicultural emphasis. And also while Hoggart and Williams remain insufficiently located in debates outside questions of class, I would agree with Nick Couldry (2004: 10) here that 'what is urgent now is not defending the full range of cultural production and consumption from elitist judgement, but defending the possibility of any shared site (whether or not overlapping with specialized spheres of cultural production) for an emergent democratic politics'.

For Williams and Hoggart democratic socialism is caught up with the capacity of citizens to learn through the education system and democratised public spheres. Of course their views are not interchangeable. As Paul Jones (1994) argues the more cautious ideas of public service evident within Hoggart can be contrasted with Williams' more radical insistence on the need to press for a greater radical transformation of capitalism. However, before we begin to oppose Williams the Marxist with Hoggart the social democratic it should be remembered that much of Williams' (1980: 250) political writing refuses any easy separation between these different traditions. Indeed with hindsight it is perhaps more useful to assimulate both into overlapping traditions of liberal socialism.

However, the end of the Cold War did not offer new forms of hope for democratic socialism but the rise of the New Right and neoliberalism. If the plebian public spheres of the past had sought within the context of social democratic parties to articulate a vision of the future that coupled the self and communal development together with the taming of capitalism, these have sometimes been displaced by nationalistic and anti-immigrant sensibilities. For Bourdieu et al. (1999) neoliberalism is not the outcome of an opposition between the market and the state as so many would argue but a matter of state policy. Since the 1980s domains like education, housing and the public sector more generally have been reconstituted through the retreat of the state. What Hoggart describes as the loss of the ethic of public service is the result of the hegemonic operation of neoliberalism to downgrade democratic socialism as totalitarianism and couple the idea of freedom with market freedom. Any attempt to articulate a more educated and public form of engagement would need to address both the partial collapse of the culture of social democracy and the new economic and cultural divisions instituted by neoliberalism.

At this stage I want to argue that the tradition of educated democratic socialism holds considerable riches for us to draw upon while needing to be reformulated in terms of the challenges of the present. In this respect, I would agree with Andre Gorz (1994) that modern socialism should not be described as a system that competes with capitalism, but that it is concerned with the tendency of economic rationality to come to dominate other spheres and activities. In this respect, democratic socialism is concerned with 'the abolition of that domination, not the abolition of capital and the market' (Gorz 1994: 25). This inevitably means that any attempt to breathe new life into the tradition of democratic socialism would need to resist the return of ideas associated with a revolutionary avant-garde, but would also need to think about how democratic socialism might be reinvented in an era dominated by neoliberalism.

As we now know, the so-called 'golden age' of European social democracy is in the past. The installation of Keynesian economic management and the defeat of fascism paved the way for European social democracy. Until the early 1970s social democratic parties presided over a situation that was roughly marked by relatively full-employment, rising incomes and 'improving' systems of welfare. As Perry Anderson (1992a) argues, this was mostly a Northern European narrative given the later arrival of industrialisation in Southern Europe. Indeed if Northern Europe encountered its first wave of neoliberalism during the early 1980s at this point Southern Europe could be seen to be experimenting in socialism. It is in this context that the fate of the French Mitterand government was to become emblematic of the difficulties faced by European social democracy in an age of international capital.

Since this period there has emerged a new kind of social democracy (usually referred to as the 'third way') which has increasingly sought to adapt itself to the demands of the global market. If old-style social democracy depended upon an unequal balancing of the forces between capital and labour, it at least recognised working-class institutions. Educational institutions played a key role in this process, providing the universal forms of education necessary for the maintenance of full employment. In the next section I want to look more closely at the idea of the third way and how it relates to debates within education and neoliberalism.

The third way, neoliberalism and education

Despite Tony Blair's (1994) claim that education was central to the New Labour project this was surprisingly marginal in much third way thinking. Anthony Giddens (1998, 2003) argued over a number of high-profile publications for the need for social democracy to reinvent itself in order to create the possibility of the twenty-first century becoming the progressive century. As a leading sociologist it was not surprising that Giddens located the need for a rethink of social democracy within the context of radical social changes. These were of course: (1) the impact of globalisation affecting the operation of markets as well as the construction of cultural identities; (2) the development of individualism and lifestyle diversity; (3) the weakening of the divide between Right and Left in a post-socialist world; (4) the development of new political agencies outside of the conventional theatre of party politics; and (5) the rise of an ecological politics of risk that questions the Left/Right polarity. This much could be agreed upon by a number of social critics who were taking a different political stance from that of Anthony Giddens, and yet what made the third way distinctive was the argument that 'politics should take a positive attitude towards globalisation' (Giddens 1998: 64). While recognising that neoliberal forms of globalisation can indeed have a destructive impact we should be careful of retreating into a politics of protectionism and warring economic blocs. Third way politics not only seeks to break with old-style statist social democracy and neoliberalism, but also offers a new politics of citizenship that presses 'no rights without responsibilities' (Giddens 1998: 65). By this Giddens is concerned that old-style social democracy often stressed the unlimited expansion of rights in such a way that these were not sustainable in a competitive and increasingly individualised world. The key question in the context of the decline of tradition and the rise of lifestyle politics then becomes what are our duties in a fast-moving and increasingly global world? Giddens has argued that in the modern world the central questions are no longer about social justice, but about how we should live in the context of the decline of tradition. These features, as many will be aware, refer back to Giddens's earlier (1994) work on the relative decline of emancipatory politics and the rise of a reflexive politics of lifestyle.

Despite the development of new political initiatives, risks and opportunities the state remains central to the third way. However, Giddens proposes that we need to radically rethink the relationship between the state and civil society in order to help foster a deeper involvement in the political process by community and local initatives. Whereas neoliberals would wish to shrink the state, the third way is all about a reconstructed national state. Here the state should engage in processes that seek what Giddens (1998: 72) has called the 'democratizing of democracy'. This involves constitutional reform, the expansion of the public sphere, the devolution of power, citizens' juries and more flexible decision structures. These features would increase civil society's capacity to take a more active role in self-government's breaking away from old-style statist social democracy whereby the potential of civil society was rendered largely passive. The new role adopted by the state should build upon democratising pressures in order to help develop a society of 'responsible risk takers' (Giddens 1998: 100). Such action is needed to redraw debates in respect of equality where a renewed emphasis is placed not upon equality of opportunity but on the 'redistribution of possibilities' (Giddens 1998: 101).

Such a politics would need to combat the growth of two kinds of exclusion to be found in a situation where both elites as well as an underclass begin to live their lives cut off from mainstream society. In this respect, exclusion at the top and bottom of society becomes a major problem in advanced industrial societies that are witnessing rapid growth in income inequality. The way these groups are encouraged to maintain a shared commitment to the community is by the maintenance of social solidarity through institutions which can promote a good-quality public education, sustain health resources and provide genuine public amenities that aim to provide an inclusive compact amongst diverse social groups. As Giddens (1998: 108) argues 'only a welfare system that benefits most of the population will generate a common morality of citizenship'.

The third way seeks to couple the practice of responding 'positively' to technological change and global markets with a renewed emphasis on obligations in an attempt to remodel an inclusive society. The reform of the public sector is essential to prevent the relatively well off from contracting out of goods and services (they need to be offered expanded forms of choice) and thereby increasingly cutting themselves off from the poor. These features have particular implications for a politics of education, the case for high-quality forms of education being a necessity for everyone in the context of increased global competition. What's required is an expansion of educational opportunity and a reversal of the fact that between 1975 and 1995 expenditure on education as a proportion of GDP fell 'from 6.7 per cent to 5.2 per cent' (Giddens 1998: 113). According to Castells (1996: 90) if a society wishes to develop then they have little choice but to enhance their collective competitiveness. Indeed it has been the United State's inability to adopt more long-term technological and educational policies coupled with its massive indebtness that has seen the downgrading of living standards. These features might seem to gloss over the neoliberal assault on education, but they do at least point out the consequences of a failure to invest in education. To counteract this tendency 'new'-style social democracy relies upon a contract whereby the state provides citizens with the resources to make their own lives in return for which citizens recognise their responsibilities towards the wider community. In this relationship the enabling state plays the role of a 'facilitating agency' (Giddens 2003: 13). At this point Giddens gives the example that at age 11 over 25 per cent of the population lack the capacity to read and write adequately. He then argues the state cannot directly remedy the situation but it can help promote partnerships between young people, parents and the community. In this respect, the expansion of choice becomes central in order to expand the range of options for the worst off. Rather than an educational or public sector that aims to produce 'bureaucratic uniformity' the expansion of choice would hold together the contract between the middle classes and the poor. Further, the expansion of quality education for all should also be coupled with renewed attention being paid to the construction of a universal structure of day care for pre-school children. The aim here seems to be one of providing parents (particularly working-class women) with employment possibilities and of seeking to enhance the cultural capital of working-class children.

Third way or neoliberalism?

I now want to briefly consider the argument that the third way is neoliberalism in disguise. I think we can dispense with this claim fairly easily. We have already seen how social democracy has survived by being historically reconstructed. Anthony Giddens' argument cannot be dismissed as a betrayal of the socialist tradition as some of his Marxist critics have claimed (Callinicos 2001). Such claims fail to recognise the complex histories of social democracy and the genuinely new challenge offered by the partial disintegration of the labour movement and neoliberalism. Yet in taking a 'positive' attitude towards globalisation the third way fails to develop a more critical disposition towards the market's dominance over the cultural sphere. Stuart Hall (2003) has demonstrated how third way political parties like New Labour have consistently combined economic neoliberalism with more social democratic concerns. New Labour is best thought of as a hybrid regime that combines a dominant neoliberal strand with a more subordinate social democratic strand. Viewing the third way in these terms allows us to understand how New Labour has been able to balance modest forms of redistribution while progressively marketising and privatising the public sector. The role of the welfare state is no longer to support the least fortunate but to help individuals provide for themselves (where they can) and to target means-tested aid for the rest.

Neoliberalism is not simply about the 'external' operation of markets: it is also explicitly concerned with instilling certain behavioural norms. Under neoliberalism it becomes the civic duty of citizens not to become overly reliant upon the state and to become self-reliant instead. In these terms Jürgen Habermas (1999: 6) emphasised that the third way seeks to foster a society of individualised risk takers who will embark upon 'a kind of fitness training' that tries to foster 'positive' lifestyles and attitudes attuned to the demands of the global market-place. In this respect, we could argue more critically that the third way cancels the historic project of democratic socialism in order to confront the generation of those systematic inequalities and exclusions which are the outcome of the increasing dominance of global capitalism (Mouffe 2005). Whereas Giddens' version of social democracy is rightly concerned with a politics of exclusion, the question as to what is to determine the dominant ethos of education seems to be left to a world of league tables, competition and training for upward mobility. It is this aspect of the third way, and not the need to rethink social democracy, with which I would take issue. What is missing from the third way in the context of the arguments I outlined earlier is how questions of social justice and an ethic of cultural development can be pursued in a world that preserves genuinely public values in an age of global capitalism. Before I seek to answer this question, however, I want to look at how the ideas and practices of neoliberalism can be said to be progressively reconstructing education.

Neoliberalism, New Labour and education

Here I shall seek to outline some of the broad ways in which neoliberalism is seeking to convert the education system into a competitive market. Implicit in new Labour and third way strategies in respect of education has been having the appropriate attitude. Poor educational performances can no longer rely upon the 'excuse' of wider patterns of social and cultural inequality, but such features are to be overcome by the upgrading of expectations (Power and Whitty 1999). The disciplinary mechanisms by which New Labour has sought to implement this change in behaviour operate through the development of targets and league tables that enable the performance of individual schools to be judged. Ideas of market choice have lead to the rejection of 'one size fits all' comprehensive schools in favour of the increased development of 'specialist schools' or academies. Whereas comprehensives are viewed negatively as being rigidly egalitarian the development of 'specialist schools' is valued because their ability to provide 'choice'. The context of market- and consumer-driven choice has meant that schools are increasingly seeking to attract parents with children who are judged to be both 'able' and 'motivated'. Schools are able to enhance their position in the context of local competition by 'improving' the 'quality' of their intake. According to Michael Apple (2001: 413) these features institute a crucial change in focus 'from student needs to student performance and from what the school does for the student to what the student does for the school'. The argument here is that the enhanced forms of competition between educational establishments end with an increased emphasis on marketing and public relations and the exclusion of students who are either working class, from ethnic minorities or perceived to have 'special needs'. Indeed the expansion of choice, as has been widely recognised in many public debates on these questions, is most likely to favour those parents who have the cultural capital and flexible lifestyles to locate the 'better' schools. Such a situation could be said to reward both entrepreneurial attitudes on the part of parents while encouraging enhanced forms of competition amongst children. The marketisation of education not only privileges higher-status families who are best able to exercise 'choice', thereby encouraging a third way-style entrepreneurial-ism, but also enables the privileged to 'exit' those comprehensive schools that are seen to be failing.

Despite the distinctiveness of the third way it has been unable to resist the New Right's attack on the idea of comprehensive education. The idea of a well-resourced, locally-based and publicly-funded school that is able to edu-cate children across a number of social, ethnic and religious backgrounds has progressively fallen into disrepute. While the roots of this ideal remain central to the traditions of democratic socialism it is not easily understood as the province of 'old Labour'. It was the Attlee Labour government who introduced the distinction between academic, technical and practical forms of education which resulted in 80 per cent of children being placed in secondary modern schools. However, all the main political parties during the 1960s recognised the economic necessity of raising the educational level of young people. The vehicle best placed to do this was comprehensive schooling which by the early 1990s educated over 88 per cent of young people (Tomlinson 2003). It is this ideal despite being an ambivalent success story that is currently under attack. There is considerable evidence that, as I highlighted above, despite the inclu-sive ideals of comprehensive education we are now entering into a post-comprehensive era within education. This was evident in recent educational reforms suggested by the last Labour government, promoting consumer choice, the end of the 'bog standard' comprehensive, more specialist schools, the weakening of local education authorities and enhanced forms of selection. The most likely casualties of such changes, as many commentators have pointed out, are those deemed unfit to compete (Benn and Millar 2006; Tomlinson 2006).

Despite these arguments it remains the case that the third way stressed the importance of the equality of opportunity. The attempt to upgrade the performance of schools was undertaken in the context of a post-industrial economy that required high levels of educational attainment. Here we might argue that while league tables and performance-driven targets are inevitably fairly blunt mechanisms of social control we could also at least argue that the aim of the third way was to promote economic and social mobility. However, what is missing from this equation is the argument that the biggest influence on school performance remains the family back-ground of every child. To have radically improved upon class mobility third way arguments would have needed to have paid greater attention to the need to create a more equal society (Wilkinson and Pickett 2009). If the poor and excluded are not to be converted into a new 'Other' then we need to return quickly to the democratic socialist ethics of solidarity with the least advantaged while recovering the educational ideal of self-development for all social classes. It is notable for example in recent class-based talk about so-called 'chavs' (basically middle-class forms of revulsion in respect of working-class 'bad taste') and the fear evident in the recent New Labour 'Respect' agenda that the need to provide a counter-hegemonic alternative to neoliberalism is more pressing than ever. Beverley Skeggs (2004) similarly argues that dominant representations of working-class people within popular culture are of the 'Other', of middle-class values of good sense and respectability. In this context, working-class people are seen as 'beyond' the reach of educational institutions and progressive initiatives. However, in order to achieve this I shall argue that we need to rethink the legacy of democratic socialism and simultaneously pro-mote more multicultural forms of education. In other words, if 'third way' agendas on education offer a retreat from the ideas of a public edu-cation this should not be taken as an argument to seek to return to the more homogeneous communities of the past.

Education, multiculturalism and citizenship

The argument so far has suggested the need to reconnect the value of educa-tion, egalitarianism and a comprehensive education. The democratic socialist response to the neoliberal attack on the value and practice of education is to shield its practice from the operation of the market and help build inclusive institutions that are careful to integrate students from a diversity of back-grounds. However, what is missing from this argument is a recognition of more multicultural agendas. If the liberal socialism of Hoggart and Williams was built on the value of a certain kind of education this can be questioned from a number of sources. If ordinary working-class people wished to 'better' themselves through the education system this was undoubtedly both to improve their employment prospects and thereby enhance their cultural capital. However, the value of the kind of literary education proposed by Hoggart and Williams has increasingly been subject to critiques from a number of perspectives. The argument that literary culture can be easily opposed to a debased popular culture has been lost. And yet, the corporatisation of culture and the marginalisation of civic discourses and places continue to be matters of urgent concern. It is this aspect of the democratic socialist tradition I should like to retain in relation to Richard Hoggart. Later generations of cultural studies have indeed been concerned that in making these arguments Hoggart has been blind to some of the ways in which high culture can reaffirm patterns of domination and that popular culture is more internally complex than he has sometimes assumed. However, as Jonathan Rutherford (2005: 13) argues, anti-humanist approaches to cultural studies have 'lacked the ethical resources to generate new, more egalitarian social relations and identities to replace those it has undermined'. In other words, the strength of traditions of liberal socialism is that these contain (no matter how problematic) an idea of humanness and the possibility of development. While the period of the so-called culture wars between educated and popular culture continues to preoccupy many, arguably the challenge issued by the demand for more multicultural forms of education is just as profound. Whereas Hoggart and Williams sought to combat an exploitative capitalist culture by emphasising the importance of public institutions such questions do not adequately address issues related to the negotiation of cultural difference. Indeed more currently the neglect of such questions is especially striking in attempts by the political Left to defend the public values of a comprehensive system against a third way agenda driven by market choice (Benn and Millar 2006).

It is clearly necessary not only to restate the value of comprehensive education, but also to rethink it through more multicultural frames and perspectives. Notably third way arguments take a more sceptical stance in respect of multiculturalism, preferring instead to emphasise the need to create overtly national forms of solidarity (Giddens 1998: 130–132). My argument here is that a genuinely inclusive education is not simply a matter of enhancing the social and cultural capital of the excluded. We also need to struggle for an education system that welcomes the difference of the Other. By this I mean a set of cultural policies and practices that do not so much tolerate but actively include the Other.

Bhikhu Parekh (2000a, 2000b) has identified the need for a multicultural educational strategy. What makes Parekh's contribution distinctive is his argument that multicultural societies should aim to create a common culture out of difference. Such a culture, he reasons, could grow out of cross-cultural conversations and inter-cultural dialogue. The key resource in seeking to develop such sensibilities amongst its citizens is the progressive development of a genuinely multicultural education. In terms of European liberal societies this would involve the enhanced questioning of Eurocentrism and monoculturalism more generally, and the development of an 'educated' curiosity in respect of other cultures. In this simply to learn about the 'great and glorious' past of a particular ethnic or national societies not only breeds racism, but also stultifies the imagination. As Yasmin Alibhai-Brown (2001: 53) has argued, this would mean a more concerted attempt to intermix different cultural traditions by fostering knowledge about a diversity of contributions (by this she means the incorporation of Shakespeare and Salman Rushdie) and the development of more critical forms of knowledge in respect of the history of slavery and empire. While these well-intentioned attempts at rethinking a common curriculum are to be welcomed they evidently do not go far enough. The danger is that they will end up adopting a 'correct' multicultural education as opposed to the bad old nationalist history of the past. Indeed, as Modood and May (2001: 306) argue, much mainstream multiculturalism is relatively superficial (they call this a 'multiculturalism of the three "S's:" saris, samosas, and steelbands') while some of the well-intentioned anti-racist education of the past tended to reinforce essentialist categories in respect of the identities of white British students. Hence the attempt to reintegrate a multicultural agenda into comprehensive schools needs to develop more sophisticated arguments than simply pointing towards curriculum change.

Alain Touraine (2000) has attempted to argue for a form of education that seeks to realise the ideal of inter-cultural education. Such an education system would emphasise the needs of the individual over those of society or the economy. A multicultural education is not solely dependent upon having the 'right' curriculum, it should also include the subject's capacity to be communicative with themselves and others. Here public forms of education would be redrawn not only by formally mixing children from different backgrounds, but also by seeking to foster inter-cultural forms of dialogue. For this to become a possibility education would need to regain its autonomy from the market to become a laboratory that could conduct experiments in difference. Such a view of education comes close to Pierre Bourdieu's (1998) view that the state should provide students with the conditions for 'serious play'. However, I would argue that such dialogues are unlikely to end in new forms of multicultural consensus but would, like all engaged education, require what Renato Rosaldo (1994: 407) calls 'tolerable discomfort'. This is where the classroom is made aware of the fact that students are allowed to speak from different positions without the need to impose closure. As Stuart Hall (2000a, 2000b) has argued, the multicultural project actually requires the identification of rival versions of the good which are allowed expression in a genuinely heterogeneous space. In this respect, educated forms of multiculturalism are not a new form of dogmatism but seek to work through the development of critical forms of public space.

Multicultural comprehensive schools would need to reject a Romantic view of education based upon literary studies as well as liberal forms of neutrality. The idea of a form of 'soft' multiculturalism that revalues minority cultures at the margins would also need to be rejected as schools sought to be places of inter-cultural dialogue. This would not mean the descent into a form of relativism where one culture is seen to be as good as another. A genuine dialogue with some of the dominant narratives of modernity in respect of our understanding of ideas such as 'progress', 'Western civilisation' and 'development' would be more likely to produce a number of interpretations that sought to question dominant master narratives (Kalantzis and Cope 1999). The aim of inter-cultural dialogue is not 'correctness' or new forms of apartheid, but the development of educated spaces that welcome difference (Hall, 2000b). Here education is defended as a public space that not only necessarily requires enhanced forms of protection from the market, but is also able to offer a number of competing and contradictory narratives in terms of a politics of identity. These alternative narratives are produced not in the hope that they will foster believing subjects but that new forms of critical knowledge will be produced through their interrogation. Education in this reading is not only a site for the transmission of cultural capital, but also seeks to foster what Chantal Mouffe (2000) calls agonistic (struggle between adversaries) rather than antagonistic (struggle between enemies) forms of public space. By fostering educated forms of inter-cultural dialogue the aim of a multicultural education is not to reinforce enclaves as its many detractors seem to suggest or promote polarised argument through guilt tripping, but the simultaneous development of more inclusive and contested forms of public space.

Public education

The argument being presented here is that democratic socialist virtues are urgently required to promote genuinely inclusive forms of education. I have considered the threats currently being posed to such a project by neoliberalism and the third way, both of which (to different degrees) tend to subjugate the ethos and the provision of education to the market. In this respect the earlier work of previous generations of cultural studies, with the contributions of Richard Hoggart (and Raymond Williams), remains a valuable resource in seeking to promote a democratic socialist vision of education. The need for education to develop an alternative hegemony to that which is currently supplied by the dominant culture of market choice is undeniable. Comprehensive schools remain uniquely placed not only to articulate more inclusive forms of education, but to do so in such a way that provides zones of genuinely inter-cultural communication. If democratic socialism has been historically connected with ideals of working-class self-development these virtues now need to be expanded to include a range of diverse and competing educated narratives that may try to dismantle overt nationalism and ethnic exclusivity. If the struggle for an 'educated' culture and society could reconnect egalitarian ideals and claims to difference then perhaps more progressive forces might be able to challenge the intellectual dominance of both neoliberalism and the third way in respect of education.

Class societies regularly promote feelings of disrespect and hierarchy. Richard Wilkinson (2006) argues that the levels of inequality promoted by neoliberal social policies undermine the common life of the community promoting increasingly individualistic forms of competition. Growing competition for status, employment, houses and consumer goods promotes a stressful society where many people feel vulnerable to being considered inferior. If social integration is good for citizens' sense of well-being then competitive individualistic market cultures promote a sense of being a disrespected second-class citizen. A sense of a lack of status leads not only to poor personal health but also to a general lack of self-worth and confidence more generally. Further, class-divided societies promote feelings of superiority and self-satisfied privilege amongst the better off as well. This language has no room for Hoggart's (1970b: 77) social democratic acceptance that middle-class children will of course begin their educational careers with a number of class-specific advantages. This would include not only an ability to pay for education equipment and space within the home but also a closer association with the dominant culture of learning and education. It is only a democratic education that can give all children an equal chance to develop themselves. However, we should note that the cultures of disrespect in terms of the working classes would be difficult to root out even by the most progressive and democratic of educators. As bell hooks (2000a: 46) reminds us conspicuous consumption rather than education is often the most available means the poor have of escaping a sense of class shame. A society that has sought to banish the divisions of class would of course also seek to emphasise the importance of sharing resources, of sharing respectful dialogue, and of sharing solidarity with the poor.

Capitalistic cultures of greed and excess can only be encountered by developing common cultures of democracy where what is important is not what you own but your ability to ask questions, live ethically and develop a sense of compassion for others. Democratic cultures are necessarily egalitarian cultures that promote a sense of equal worth and respect which can really only begin to be lived once the excesses of free-market capitalism have been curbed. There is no simple 'return to' Hoggart, given the need to recognise the multicultural plurality of modern citizens and a more complex account of popular culture in a way that is absent from much of his writing. Here the emphasis of the 'third way' on questions of individualisation and the radical pluralisation of the public sphere remains important. Further, the third way insistence that we rethink education in a global age while seeking to articulate a common citizenship is also significant. Indeed in attempting to link rights and responsibilities third way arguments remain connected to the liberal socialist tradition I am seeking to defend here. And yet despite many of its progressive features third way-type arguments do not go far enough in questioning the damage being done to education by market-driven societies. While the third way sought to redesign education in an increasingly capitalist dominated society it did not pay enough attention to the generation of structural inequalities or how to promote a more democratic or egalitarian culture. It remains to be seen whether third way-type arguments can be repositioned in the future.

4

Critical Pedagogy, Democracy and Capitalism: Education without Enemies or Borders

Raymond Williams (1989) once tried to explain why, despite the social and cultural transformations of the twentieth century, he remained a socialist. The reason for his refusal to adopt the more accommodating language of either industrialism or pluralism was his recognition of the centrality of the struggles of the organised working class. Williams (1989: 71) argued that the struggle of the industrial working class to emancipate itself from capitalism was opposed by a hegemonic alliance that acted as 'a hostile and organized social formation that was trying to defeat and destroy you'. In this respect, Williams is reflecting the often bitter class-based struggles of the 1980s. Indeed since the time that Williams was writing, the organised working class in the European context has suffered a massive and historic defeat. David Harvey (2006) has suggested that since the 1980s there has been a concerted attack on trade unions, the social state, municipal socialism and a reduction in the levels of taxation, leading to enhanced levels of privatisation, commodification and the development of an increasingly individualised and competitive society. In this respect, the key demand we hear now is for the state to adapt itself to the needs of business, promote competition and provide the educational and cultural conditions for the accumulation of wealth. The reassertion of class power on the part of ruling elites has led to a widely reported increase in social inequality with the redistribution of resources away from the mass of the population towards the more privileged classes. These features have arguably played a central role in reshaping the relationship between the economy, everyday life and education.

The development of the cultures of capitalism has not only reshaped access to resources but has also arguably impacted upon the social and cultural well-being of the population more generally. There is now for example a widespread concern about the commercialisation of childhood and the possible negative effects this is having in respect of more educated and cultural forms of development. A recent report highlighted that the UK currently has the highest rate of childhood obesity within Europe (with 35 per cent of boys and 45 per cent of girls between and 11 and 15 being recorded as overweight or obese). This occurs in a cultural context where commercial systems of broadcasting and communication have grown increasingly powerful, seeking to remake children's culture in more market-friendly terms (Compass 2007).

Further, a (2007) UNICEF report on children's well-being sought to measure across the 'developed' world the extent to which children felt loved and supported by their families and wider community. The report focused upon wealth distribution, as well as other measures such as safety, literacy standards and more subjective feelings of well-being. Notably neoliberal UK came bottom of the list with more social democratic nations such as Norway, Sweden and Finland towards the top. Here we need to recognise along with Henry Giroux (2004a) that neoliberalism cancels the possibility of critical citizenship, democracy and social well-being. It is in this context that I should like to reconsider the possibility of a project that links together social justice, democracy and education. If the decline of the labour movement and the rise of neoliberalism has pushed back the possibility of a more just and egalitarian social order what critical resources lie within education to both learn from the past and press for the continued importance of linking questions of culture and democracy?

We need to consider in this context how to devise a critical politics that links questions of educational development, well-being and social justice. After the partial defeat of the labour movement how might it be possible to devise a new ethics of education that seeks to take the development of every child seriously? What kind of critical pedagogy can become mobilised in settings where commercial culture is more readily accessible than democratic culture, and where the 'value' of education is seemingly in decline? How might education become a place for the fostering of a critical literacy beyond the requirements of the labour market without itself becoming authoritarian? What kind of education is best suited to the development of a democratic, educated and participatory society?

Chantal Mouffe (2000) argues that democratic public space depends not upon mere pluralism, but the expression of antagonistic interpretations and perspectives that resist closure. Democratic expression is dependent upon a form of politics that allows space for contested viewpoints. There is in this reading no set of democratic procedures that is capable of completely absorbing alterity. Here Mouffe argues that the democratic process is about the conversion of enemies into adversaries. In other words, in democratic settings cultural politics depends upon passionate forms of agonism, not an antagonistic struggle to the death between enemies. The language of enemies has no place in a democratically constructed public space, as rather than political contestation what becomes pressing is the elimination of the Other. In a post-9/11 world I would argue that educated forms of dialogue have a central role in criticising binary thinking that uses the languages of war and elimination rather than more democratic forms of contestation. Similarly Richard J. Bernstein (2005) argues that Schmittian ideas of friend and enemy or good versus evil pervert democratic cultures that are dependent upon ideas of dialogue, inquiry and that all knowledge is potentially fallible.

These reflections are central to any attempt to reinvent a critical pedagogy in new times. This means that democratically constituted space is threatened by those who would seek to silence opposition, impose authoritarian solutions, argue for a simple-minded pluralism or use the language of friends and enemies. If mainstream liberalism often fails to recognise that the political, cultural and educational relationships are inevitably power relationships then much critical or Marxist inspired thought has overly concentrated upon the idea that public space is constituted through the central division between capital and labour (no matter how important) and an authoritarian mode of politics and culture. However, this does not mean that we should abandon the languages of empowerment, democracy and emancipation. Any critical theory of education, which critical pedagogy claims to be, is intimately caught up in questions of value, critique and the possibility of constructing more engaged and democratic forms of learning.

The struggle for a democratic education is, however, more than the expression of antagonism, and is also deeply concerned with human experience and its potential for transformation. Democratic education cannot be reduced to a learned technique but is more of an art that is less concerned with the transmission of knowledge than it is with authentic learning. Any critical form of pedagogy needs to carefully consider relations of freedom, authority and responsibility in ways that are likely to facilitate the process of learning. As Giroux (2006b) argues a democratic education would seek not only to develop a process of learning that assisted public forms of participation but also to enable students to produce new forms of democratic knowledge.

Here I shall investigate the writings of both Paulo Freire and Jürgen Habermas to look at how they have sought to defend the ideas of a democratic education that is both emancipatory while being critical of the prevailing neoliberal climate within education. The rise of the New Right within education has sought to maintain the debates in terms of a concern with basic skills for the labour market, the return of vocationalism and the fostering of more entrepreneurial attitudes amongst the young. Alternatively a concern with democratic education encompasses the fostering of those human qualities that are required for us to become citizens who are capable of autonomous thought and respecting difference while caring for one another. As Carr and Harnett (1996) proposed, there is no critical citizenship without the ability to think critically and make politically based judgements. In addition, as Giroux (2006b) argues, a democratic education also needs to emphasise the multiple possibilities of agency as well as the hope of living in a more emancipated society. Here I shall seek to explore which education is best suited to meeting these needs. However, notions of critical pedagogy will have to be considerably revised given that it was developed in a Third World context and can only become translated for the overdeveloped West after a considerable amount of reflection. Indeed I aim to demonstrate that the inspirational writing of Pablo Freire was itself involved in a long process of internal critique and reflection, and that his analysis continues to have a great deal to offer critical educators.

Paulo Freire and democratic education

The writing of Paulo Freire has inspired generations of critical educators in the South and North American context. Freire's explicit concern to devise an approach to education and learning that was both democratic and dialogic has meant that his work continues to receive a considerable amount of attention. Freire's radical classic *Pedagogy of the Oppressed* has helped shape the horizons of Marxists, feminists and all those interested in linking questions of liberation and education since it was first published in the late 1960s. His writing does of course need to be understood in the context of a Brazilian Third World society whose social and cultural relations were shaped by the impact of colonialism. In the early 1960s Freire had worked on literacy campaigns for the urban poor before becoming director of the Brazilian National Literacy Programme in 1964. Here he helped set up a plan for aiding the literacy of over two million people, given the estimate of illiteracy rates of over 50 per cent. However this work was soon interrupted by a military coup in the same year, leading Freire to both lose his professorship at the Recife University in Brazil and be imprisoned for 70 days. He was then to take up a visiting professorship at Harvard University before working in adult education in Chile. Another military coup in 1974 meant moving to a post at the World Council of Churches based in Switzerland before eventually returning home to Brazil after an amnesty in 1979 (Coben 1998). Freire was to eventually die in Brazil in 1997 after a life spent seeking to reflect upon the interconnections between critical forms of education, liberation and democracy.

These are not merely biographical facts, but represent the necessary context within which to assess both the intellectual vitality of Freire and an idea of the social and cultural conditions that helped shape his ideas. Any consideration of Freire today is necessarily involved in a process of postcolonial translation. By this I mean that in addressing Freire we need to be aware of the ways in which a colonial history shaped his aim to develop a critical pedagogy within Brazilian society. This offers the possibility of both forging political and cultural solidarities across cultural contexts, and of course focusing on the ways in which talk of Western modernity often seeks to sweep colonialism under the carpet (Young 2001). Indeed Freire's own complex intellectual history (being influenced by many intellectual currents from both inside and outside the West) and the ways in which he has crossed a number of cultural borders invite a careful re-reading of his life and intellectual production. Nevertheless, in this section I aim to draw upon the aspects of critical pedagogy that remain relevant today, while also critiquing those aspects which may have a diminished critical purchase.

As I have already mentioned, Freire's (1970) text *Pedagogy of the Oppressed* remains key in this context given that it brought his work to an international audience. Henry Giroux (1993b: 184) has argued that in interpreting this text we are engaging in a process of critical border crossing that should alert the reader to the fact that Freire is not a 'recipe for all times and places'. Freire argued that educated forms of development offered the possibility of either humanisation or dehumanisation, and that in turn these possibilities would remain tied to the prospect of a revolutionary movement seeking to end class and racial oppression. Human beings who are oppressed and enslaved are compelled to live a life of unrealised human potential. A politics of liberation is required so that both the oppressors and the oppressed are able to live more responsible, autonomous and fulfilled lives. The prospect of human liberation aims to produce the prospect of human beings living more liberated lives. However, Freire was deeply critical of Marxist-Leninist ideas concerning the leading role of the party in the formation of revolutionary consciousness. A critical pedagogy needs to both oppose the strategy of the oppressors who are largely motivated by money and profit and seek to address the dispossessed not as the objects of revolutionary strategy, but as subjects who have internalised their own sense of inferiority as it is mirrored back to them by those oppressors. The act of liberation for Freire cannot be achieved by relating to those participating in the act of revolt as objects, but must instead be engaged with as potentially critical and reflective human beings. The recovery of the humanity of the oppressed can only be achieved by challenging the oppressive relationships that can be found at the heart of traditional forms of education. As Freire (1970: 48) suggested 'liberation, a human phenomenon, cannot be achieved by semihumans'. More specifically a democratically inspired pedagogy should break with the 'banking concept' of education. Freire (1970: 53) argued: 'Education thus becomes an act of depositing, in which students are the depositories and the teacher is the depositor. Instead of communicating, the teacher issues communiqués and makes deposits which the students patiently receive, memorise, and repeat'.

For Freire the legacies of colonialism and capitalism helped reproduce hierarchical civil and cultural relations that actively disallowed authentic learning. If knowledge was something which merely transferred this would disallow the possibility of students participating in their own learning and producing their own knowledge. It was only through the reconstitution of the teacher/student relationship in both more democratic and dialogic settings that the possibility of critical thinking could be reintroduced. Here Freire advocated a form of problem-posing education where the student and the teacher would seek to learn from one another. This should not be an abstract process, but on the contrary involve acts of concrete and critical thinking. At this point Freire had learned a great deal from Sartre and Fanon (who I shall return to) on the idea of the existential human subject who is always incomplete, but when drawn into dialogue becomes aware of their location as a historical subject with certain creative capacities. For Freire there could be no learning or humanisation without the act of mutual dialogue. Yet for dialogue to be transformative it needs to be carried out in relations of love, mutual respect and trust. If the capacity to dialogue offers an alternative to the 'banking concept' of education it does so because it no longer reduces the oppressed human being to the status of a thing or object. As Freire (1970: 82) wrote: 'Only human beings are praxis – the praxis which, as the reflection and action which truly transform reality, in the source of knowledge and creation'.

In Freire's later (1974) work he went to great lengths to stress how a dialogic view of human beings not only broke with the implicit elitism of the banking concept, but also argued that to be an illiterate peasant meant that the world imposed a passive and subjected sense of reality. Freire frequently reminds his readers that to be at the bottom of such a society is to have silence and inaction imposed upon you from above. The anti-dialogic society cannot create the conditions for a participatory democracy where people are free to develop themselves. In a passage that draws upon some of the work of the early Frankfurt school (especially Erich Fromm) Freire (1974: 15) commented:

> Men are defeated and dominated, though they do not know it; they fear freedom, though they believe themselves to be free. They follow general formulas and prescriptions as if by their own choice. They are directed; they do not direct themselves. Their creative power is impaired. They are objects, not Subjects. For men to overcome their state of massification, they must be enabled to reflect about that very condition.

Freire argued that the colonial culture created by the Portuguese had prevented the development of a democratic culture and had also paved the way for a submissive attitude towards the media of mass communication. In this context, he emphasised the liberatory implications for those who had begun to realise after a process of dialogic interchange that they too were cultural creators through the medium of language and thought. To break with the anti-dialogic culture of Brazil when working with the oppressed, Freire and his colleagues sought to persuade the downtrodden that in their everyday actions they were involved in the transformation of the world. This process was then extended into the beginnings of learning to read and write. This deepening of the process of learning and critical reflection is what Freire (1974: 90) often referred to as 'conscientizao'. This should be understood as a process without end rather than as a moment of radical transformation. What he meant by this process was the development of a capacity on the part of the human subject to reflect upon and criticise as well as act upon the world creatively. Here the human subject becomes humanised as he or she begins to realise their 'independent' capacity for interrogating critical thought with purposeful action. The dialogue, then, is a necessary condition of revolutionary action that does not end in reproducing another set of oppressive relations. For Freire (1974: 121), there was 'no oppressive reality which is not at the same time antidialogical'.

Freire, Fanon and feminism

Freire's arguments have since the late 1960s inspired a number of critical debates across the world. Before investigating some of these, I think it is worthwhile pointing out some of the similarities between Freire and the critical intellectual he most closely resembles, Franz Fanon (De Lissovoy 2008). Freire's arguments about the divisions between the colonised and their colonial rulers, the possibility of a revolutionary transformation, the existential capacities of the human being and the internalisation of a negative view of self as Other all find echoes within Fanon. Franz Fanon (2001), like Freire, worked both inside and outside of Western intellectual traditions and contexts, and sought to press home the economic and cultural violence of colonialism especially in the context of France's occupation of Algeria (Stevenson 2007). If Fanon was principally concerned with the ways in which colonialist culture sought to fix certain stereotypes about black Africans and Europeans, then Freire was equally indignant about colonist attempts to a reinscribe a hierarchy that were supported rather than resisted by the education system. The banking system of education is where a colonist sense of superiority and a capitalist need for hierarchy find a meeting point. Further, both Fanon and Freire emphasised the importance of a liberation struggle that would connect cultural spheres, self-images, nations and wider relations of economic dependency and domination. For Freire and Fanon these wider relations of global domination found their expression not only in the human subject but also in familial, cultural and educational relations. These features, I would argue, are crucial for a critical re-reading of Freire's early writing as they connect questions of education to wider concerns about the possibilities of anti-colonial struggle and the desire for liberation.

However this intellectual legacy is not without its own internal problems and contradictions when viewed from the point of view of the present day. The question then becomes how relevant is Freire to an understanding of more contemporary post-colonial societies and post-Marxist frames of reference? Here a number of difficulties seemingly become apparent. bell hooks (1994: 49) argues that Freire's early writing 'constructs a phallocentric paradigm of liberation'. hooks is concerned not only with Freire's (and of courses Fanon's) use of sexist language but also with his lack of concern for relations of gender more generally. Similarly to other Marxist intellectuals Freire has little to say about questions of gender, and is mainly concerned with economic relations and how they become translated into cultural relations. Other feminist critics like Kathleen Weiler (1994) have argued that his opposition between the oppressed and the oppressors fails to take account of questions of cultural difference. There is a notable lack of complexity in the essentialised language that would find it difficult to take account of more complex cultural relations. Further the student and the radical tutor are assumed to be 'on the same side' yet there is little exploration of the inevitable power relations involved in this relationship. The teacher, after all, is granted a certain amount of authority (and responsibility) given the ways in which institutions create hierarchies in education and learning. There is also the assumption that once the student becomes 'humanised' through dialogic processes of exchange 'he' will then want to join a revolutionary movement. Jeanne Brady (1994) states that Freire's writing contains a reluctance to address the complex, contradictory and multiple meanings of human subjectivity involved in a dialogic process. Instead his Marxism presupposes a modernist project that legitimises the passage of consciousness through predefined stages. As Jennifer Gore (1993) points out, the concern here is that the 'liberatory' teacher simply acts to empower students in the interests of a universal humanity. The idea of the 'liberatory' teacher not only ignores more complex realities, but also can easily end up reinforcing a form of dogmaticism where peasants are educated to produce a revolutionary consciousness. These objections of course come close to positioning Freire with the kind of Marxism he was actually keen to criticise. However, the charge from much of the feminist criticism, even when it has been sympathetic to him, has been focused on his inability to reflect upon the ways that his own background and intellectual influences have failed to problematise an unreflective modernist masculinism.

Freire undoubtedly sought to learn from and respond to some of these and similar criticisms in his later writing. Reflecting upon his early writing, Freire (1994) defended a radical politics whereby progressive forces need to be involved in the political creation of unity out of diversity. He referred less to the 'oppressed' and more to the popular classes who were involved in a hegemonic struggle. However, he continued to argue that the dialogic education of the masses in Chile and Brazil was not possible outside of a politics of struggle and a deep interest in the transformative potential of loving pedagogic relations. In particular, Freire argued that he had learned a great deal from feminist criticisms of his work, accepting that it was impossible to be a progressive educator and favour the discrimination of women. In this respect, he pointed out that critical pedagogy needed to invest in a democratic and anti-discriminatory discourse. Freire argued that the point of critical pedagogy was not to produce revolutionary subjects, but what he called 'educands' who were 'capable of knowing' (Freire 1994: 46). However, he (1994: 96) never failed to protest against what he called 'the wickedness of capitalism' in the context of a society where at the time he was writing it was estimated that over 100 million people would die during the 1990s of disease and malnutrition. He was in this context unwilling to abandon the idea of class conflict and the need to combat a neoliberal pragmatism that suggested the world was unimprovable. Freire, then, was able to reflectively rethink his vocabulary in the light of criticism in a way that was not available to Fanon given his premature death. As Homi Bhabha (1994) has argued, if Fanon remains productive for the way he imagined a future free of racialised discourse his use of binary categories and essentialist language continue to trap the way he wrote about the possibility of political and cultural transformation. In other words, despite the attempt to rethink universal categories Freire remains trapped in rule governed foundational thinking that seeks to exclude cultural difference (Bauman 1993: 8–10). Arguably, however, Paulo Freire retained the idea of remaining critical while increasingly subjecting his own language, categories of thinking and pedagogic analysis to rigorous criticism. Indeed, as his work progressed, Freire became increasingly interested in the idea of utopia and its connection to the development of a progressive education. However, despite the many twists and turns of his intellectual development that are crucial in this respect, it is to his final works I now wish to turn.

The late Freire

In Antonio Darder's impressive (2002) study, Freire's work is described as becoming progressively concerned with the act of teaching as being centrally related to the love, care and concern for the other. These motifs do not simply appear at the end of Freire's work but are central to his concerns throughout. If his early work is mostly preoccupied with revolutionary struggle his later writing is explicitly concerned with the ethics and virtues of education in the context of injustice. Freire (2001, 2004), despite this notable transformation, never relented in his criticism of global capitalism and the way it sought to preserve certain pedagogic approaches rather than others. However tack he did change, preferring to defend the importance of a universal ethics that would affirm the need to grant dignity and respect to every human being on the planet. For Freire it was the cynicism of neoliberalism that preferred training to education and adaptation to thinking that meant it was inhospitable to education. Indeed it was neoliberalism's own indifference to globally structured inequalities that led him to argue that teaching and educating could never be a neutral act. Freire, in this respect, still tried to write critically from the point of view of what Fanon (2001) called 'the wretched of the earth'. What is noticeable is that Freire's (2001: 23) hostility was towards a political doctrine (rather than say a class enemy) and that this allowed him to speak from the point of view of what he called a 'universal human ethic' – an ethic of all humanity that seeks to protest against racism, sexism and class discriminations of all kinds. For Freire education was built upon the dignity of others, which meant it could not be indifferent to mass starvation, hunger and unemployment on a global scale.

Neoliberalism thus stands condemned for its cynical acceptance of reality and its failure to speak of 'humanity's ontological vocation' (Freire 2001: 25). By this Freire meant our ability to simultaneously recognise ourselves as incomplete or unfinished beings that are capable of learning and transforming the world by dreaming of alternatives while taking responsibility for the world which we help create. Critical pedagogy necessarily resists neoliberal attempts to convert education into forms of technical training, and instead emphasises critical thinking, dialogic forms of engagement and the autonomy of the learner. As human beings through an ongoing process of critical reflection come to experience themselves as historically and culturally formed creatures capable of learning and transformation they simultaneously begin to dream of possible new futures for human society. If human beings are necessarily incomplete and capable of processes of transformation then the same can be said of the social order.

In terms of the relationship between the student and the teacher Freire consistently rejected turning critical forms of pedagogy into a recipe. For example, many have interpreted his arguments about the banking concept of education as being against lectures and in favour of seminars. However, such assumptions are too reductive. Freire argued that critical pedagogy was less about the mode of delivery (although it was not unconcerned with these questions) and more about the ability of the teacher to engage democratically with the students (Shor and Freire 1987). Here Freire proposed that all critical educational practice sought to develop democratic forms of authority that never lapsed into authoritarianism or an indifferent laissez faire attitude. Democratic teaching was less a matter of techniques or methods, and more concerned with the dynamism of the relationship between students and teachers. If an authoritarian education could be concerned with impressing upon the students the will of the tutor then a laissez faire attitude would fail to engage with the concerns and passions of the taught and a democratic disposition would be concerned with problem posing, dialogic engagement and a politics of the conversation. For Freire what needed to be respected in this process was the freedom of the student to follow his or her own intellectual path. The paradox that he was pointing to is that there is no intellectual freedom without democratic authority. In other words, 'to teach is not *to transfer knowledge* but to create the possibilities for the production or construction of knowledge' (Freire 2001: 30). Within this relationship, he argued that learning required teaching, but did not require a rigid hierarchy, and was stunted by indifference. Democratic visions of learning require the idea that education is about the mutual transformation of the teacher and the student as they seek to engage with one another while mutually respecting their capacity to be both curious and autonomous. The student requires the love and guidance of the teacher, who, to be effective, needs to be continuously engaged in the process of learning. In this relationship the student's own experience and knowledge of the world should be respected. Freire was deeply concerned about pedagogic relationships where 'the truth' belonged only to the tutor, and where participants failed to engage in a shared capacity for critical and utopian thinking. To resist attempts to 'bureaucratise the mind' and communicate a belief in education as a permanently open project in itself resists attempts by neoliberalism to convert education into a mode of training. To educate is both to develop a pedagogic practice that respects the dignity of the other and to also engage in an act of hope by opening up the possibility of change. Authentic education is about the mutual process of becoming. Teaching is an implicitly ethical act that is involved in the opening up of closed questions, listening to others, being responsive, while avoiding a fatalistic acceptance of the status quo. To follow this vision Freire argued that educators had to be involved in a political act that joined together the possibility of a more just future with not betraying the idealism that was necessary to the purpose of education in a democratic social order. Henry Giroux (2006b) argues in this setting that to develop critical pedagogy in modern information-based and technological societies we have to recognise that learning takes place in a multitude of spaces and places. In other words, there is no radical politics that is confined to the classroom, but there does need to be a focus upon up new narratives and sites of learning. A democratic education in this setting is not simply learning about politics but also needs to recover a broader language of civic responsibility in terms of the creation of new public cultures.

The ethical requirements of democratic forms of education suggest certain virtues on the part of the educator. Education is linked to a model of the good society about which the educator cannot afford to be indifferent. Freire's (1998) vision of the good society points out that democratic teaching cannot be sustained in either an authoritarian state-dominated society or the free-market society instituted by neoliberalism. Instead it is the aim of the democratic educator to struggle for a just order where education is protected against the market, and where it is not converted into a site of instruction. The autonomy of teachers as learners and learners as teachers is crucial within this context. A good society cannot be indifferent of the extent to which education is able to develop the curiosity of teachers and students as well as their capacity for discovery through reading, thinking and mutual dialogue. More specifically a democratic education should seek to foster a number of virtues amongst both students and teachers alike. These are humility (the ability to respect the views of the other), lovingness (the ability to communicate a sense of care and connection), courage (the ability to be able to teach whilst facing your own fears) and tolerance (making space for the expression of difference, but not accepting discrimination). These universal human qualities can only exist within a democratically constituted classroom and a wider civic order that respects the right of teachers to funded sabbaticals, autonomy and the ability to criticise the status quo. Indeed if these conditions did not exist Freire argued that teachers would have a responsibility to struggle for the social and cultural conditions that were necessary for the establishment of democratic practice within education. Education (like democracy) is necessarily ideological and cannot hide behind appeals to neutrality. It is compelled to imagine and struggle for a more globally just world.

If, as we shall see, Habermasian critical theory offers a deliberative view of democracy that emphasises the capacity of citizens to come to an agreement by supporting reasonable arguments, then Freire's views are suggestive of a different approach. Critical for Paulo Freire was a democratically orientated society built upon equal rights, an opposition to discrimination, and above all freedom to learn while respecting thinking that contradicts our own. In his work democracy must become a grass-roots lived practice that finds expression within the family, the school, the media and other institutions. In other words, democracy inevitably must be built up from below and unless it becomes a contested practice may wilt and wither away.

Perhaps missing from Freire, given his emphasis upon educational freedom, is a more careful consideration of the responsibilities of both teachers and students. If educators require rights to protect their intellectual freedoms they also need to consider their responsibilities to their students and the wider community. Further, students themselves need to consider their responsibilities to themselves and others. Responsibilities are of course especially pressing in an age of ecological vulnerability, but also apparent in an increasingly global and interdependent world and the wider community more generally. As Geoff Mulgan (1994) has stated the language of responsibility is often denied by the market (usually concerned with selfishness) and the state (more concerned with bureaucratic imperatives). Such reflections also imply that rather than seeking to maximise freedom we need instead to consider the responsibility that society has for the poor, the vulnerable and other members of the community.

In an important essay on Freire, Henry Giroux (2000b) argues that the democratic conception of education reaffirms students and teachers as critical border crossers involved in the taking up of different dialogic positions while deconstructing a number of oppositions that would seek to determine who learns from whom. Giroux points out that despite Freire's increasing insistence on the need to respect the voice and experience of the student he does this without arguing that education should simply act as a form of positive affirmation. Ultimately the idea of education being tied to an emancipatory project is not best served if the educator simply hands authority over to the student body. Such an argument would turn education over to a branch of 'positive' psychology where teachers simply reaffirmed the vision of students. This view would not only negate the role of the critical educator to present the student with alternative models as to how we might live, but most crucially of all from a Freirian point of view, it would also disable the tension between the 'positions' of the tutor and those taken up by students. In other words, the positive affirmation model tends to cancel the critical position adopted by the tutor who works for an educational practice that links the personal to a more emancipated future society. This opens up the possibility of students who will of course disagree with the tutor, but who are nevertheless challenged to think by a different perspective without being compelled to take up this position as their own. A Freirian approach to education is not merely an affirmation of student liberty it includes, the enhanced capacity to dialogue between different positions in a democratic discussion. In addition to these arguments I would also add that both teachers and students have a responsibility to listen. There is, then, no politics of voice without a politics of listening. As I indicated above this sometimes gets lost when questions of voice seemingly take priority.

Critical pedagogy in postmodernity

Recent developments within social and cultural theory have meant that many of the modernist assumptions made by Freire are now increasingly open to question. Henry Giroux (1992) has commented that the idea that the oppressed can be seen as a unitary category and that there is no central unitary agent has led to an increasing focus upon a variety of struggles and movements. As Chantal Mouffe (2005: 51–54) argues such considerations should lead us to rethink the democratic project. If democratic politics is a form of contestation amongst adversaries then the lines of argument and debate are necessarily plural. However, if the Marxist tradition overly concentrated upon the politics of class it still correctly appreciated the importance of capitalism in terms of the structuration of wider social and cultural relationships. In this sense the attempt to reconfigure education within society is inevitably connected to a differently constituted hegemonic social order. Further, much of the current work within cultural studies has sought to emphasise the decentring of a unified and stable subject for a more fluid appreciation of identity that is constituted through language and discourse. Subjectivity is now understood less through a language of critical rationality and reason (or as having the attributes claimed by Freire) and more as appreciative of the ways in which identity becomes constituted through a multiplicity of overlapping and contradictory discourses. In this setting, Usher and Edwards (1994) argue that postmodernism offers a critique of the 'essentialist' idea that education can in an uncontradictory way simply emancipate humanity from ignorance, poverty and backwardness. Here Usher and Edwards seek to emphasise the plural rather than the uniform possibilities of emancipatory strategies within education.

The social theorist who has most consistently questioned the emancipatory possibilities within education was Michel Foucault. As is well known, Foucault (1977) held that schools (like prisons, hospitals) and other institutions that accompanied the arrival of modern society were less sites of potential emancipation than of disciplinary power. Social control was instigated through the introduction of diverse regimes of continuous surveillance. The schoolroom would be organised in such a way as to normalise students into adopting good behaviour, otherwise they would risk a range of punishments and exclusion. Schooling was less about enlightenment than monitoring behaviour and the hierarchical ranking of students via reports, assessment and classification. Education, in this reading, is constituted through the management of bodies, the individualisation of punishment, the normalisation of behaviour and exclusion. Yet, as many have pointed out, Foucault's account of disciplinary power did not really consider questions of experience in respect of the subject and offered a one-sided view of power from the point of view of the institution (McNay 1994). Returning to Henry Giroux (1992) he similarly argues that despite many of the insights of postmodern theory there is a tendency to neglect some of the more critical potential evident within issues related to reason, agency and the possibility of overcoming suffering, all of which have found expression in modernist theory. Yet, as Giroux (2006c) points out, postmodernism remains valuable to any attempt to rethink critical theory in relation to pedagogy for the way it has challenged relations between the centre and the margin and made room for the local and the contingent. Similarly Nancy Fraser (1994) argues that part of Foucault's and postmodernism's critical drive is to argue against essentialist understandings of human nature in favour of how the subject is constructed through social and historical discourses. However, if we are able to more specifically locate the ideas of autonomy and rationality as being historically created we can perhaps defend the capacity of education to develop certain human capacities without falling back on essentialist arguments. Further we can also question postmodernism's neglect of more normative questions by arguing that the tension between realities and norms is necessary to any project that aims to criticise and thereby 'improve' society. In other words, despite the introduction of a more sceptical language in respect of emancipation it is not clear why this should indeed be given up as an aim. If Foucault reduced educational practices to questions of discipline then he was undoubtedly mistaken to do so. This foreclosed the possibility of the ways in which pedagogic relations could be constituted in some of the more democratic ways that Freire suggested. Further, if the attempt to link education and emancipation has less than certain outcomes this is not really an argument for giving up. Here I would argue that Freire had more in common with the idea of critical theory than postmodernism. If the main aim of critical theory is to criticise coercive institutions in order to produce collective forms of self-reflection as to how such beliefs and practices might become revised then these features are central to questions related to any idea as to how we might link education and democracy (Geuss 1982). Yet, as Zygmunt Bauman (2000: 40) comments, the task facing critical theory today is to reinvigorate the public sphere in an age where it is 'increasingly empty of public issues'. We will return to these questions after we have explored Habermas, who has perhaps more than any other scholar pressed the importance of the idea of a vibrant public sphere for democratic societies.

Critical theory, Habermas and education

The idea of contemporary critical theory and its relation to education can only be explored if we take a brief detour through the work of Jürgen Habermas. In this respect, Raymond Morrow and Carlos Alberto Torres (2002) have argued that Freire and Habermas share a number of similarities. These include a dialogic understanding of human beings, the coercive potential of unequal power relations, the argument that human subjects best develop their capabilities in democratic settings, the importance of the connection between ideas of self-reflection and emancipation and, finally, the need to develop a critical understanding of society and human relationships from an explicitly moral point of view. Further Habermas's attempt to rethink critical theory in a resolutely post-Marxist context while addressing the role of universal reason is crucial in our context.

Despite these similarities it is important to highlight the historical and cultural context that has governed the development of Jürgen Habermas's attempt to develop critical theory. Habermas has sought to develop an explicitly post-Marxist critical theory in the aftermath of the Second World War. As a German citizen it is not surprising that after Nazism, Habermas would construct a social theory built upon the emancipatory potential of democracy. This critical context has proved to be crucial for Habermas who is widely known within the social sciences for seeking to resist post-modernism while seeking to draw out the critical potential of modernity. This is not the place for an extensive critique of Habermas's ideas, but at this point we need to recognise that while he rarely discusses education directly his theory of communicative action is centrally concerned with how democratic societies can be potentially learning societies.

For Habermas there are basically two types of action: instrumental forms of action, which depend upon egocentric forms of calculation and strategy; and communicative action, where actors are prepared to commit them-selves to norms that are the outcome of rational agreement. Further Habermas (1981) has been keen to distinguish between 'the system' (the economy, state, institutions) and 'the life-world' (stock of traditions, inter-pretations and intersubjective meanings shared by overlapping communi-ties), which are increasingly separate in late modernity. By this he mainly means that modern systems are becoming more complex and less depend-ent upon the cultural traditions and horizons of ordinary citizens for their reproduction. We might talk here about the logic of the system that is increasingly indifferent to the lifestyles and orientations of its members. In addition, we might also point out that domains such as education are sub-ject to rationalisation (in that they have to be built upon rational principles) while being subjected to what Habermas has called the colonisation of the life-world. This is where the life-world becomes more subject to the instru-mental logic of the system and less anchored in more communicative forms of rationality. At this point, citizens begin to experience a loss of freedom and meaning as instrumental criteria begin to replace the possibilities for com-municative action. Further, as expert cultures become impenetrable through the development of languages of specialisation they begin to be shut off from lay opinion. This enhances not only the fragmentation of knowledge, but also the cultural impoverishment of the life-world more generally. For Habermas the twin processes of cultural colonisation and impoverishment make it dif-ficult for more critical forms of thought to emerge.

In complex Western societies the main way we have of addressing these problems is through an idea of the public sphere. For Habermas (1989, 1996) the idea of the public sphere also has a long and complex history, but he largely argues that there can be no democracy without public spaces that allow for the equal participation of its citizens. Proceeding this we can say that public opinion has been activated once the various interactive agencies of state and civil society are focused on a particular problem. An informed public culture, in this respect, is built upon the complex interaction of a number of different public realms and arenas, from rock concerts to television and popular journalism. The public sphere is not contained within national frameworks, but necessarily links the episodic to the relatively durable, the local to the global, the visual to the literate and popular culture to high culture. Yet unlike Freire, Habermas does not address questions of public learning and transformation in pedagogic terms being more concerned with the expression of rationality.

Arguably given the importance of communicative action to the public sphere these features have implications for the organisation and practice of education and learning. Robert Young (1989), in this context, offers an invaluable account as to how ideas of communication action could be developed within education. Young argues (drawing upon a previous work by Habermas (1976)) that education faces a legitimation crisis. For most of the twentieth century the central contradiction within education was between a pedagogy that emphasised training and one that had a deeper interest in more personal forms of development. The needs of the nation and the economy were potentially in conflict with human needs for the autonomous development of the self. However, this situation has now been altered through the rise of 'civic privatism' where citizens have increasingly adopted consumer-orientated lifestyles while becoming increasingly apathetic about citizenry involvement in democratic systems. Neo-conservatives have sought to emphasise the role of education in the economy and the requirement that it injects citizens with a sense of national loyalty. In this respect, neo-conservatives have adopted three main strategies in respect of education (1) making educational success important for success in the job market; (2) controlling of subversive groups who would seek to utilise education as a space for experimentation in the context of learning; (3) increasing the application of financial and economic planning in education. Young argues in Habermasian terms that the crisis in education cannot be adequately resolved in these ways but requires a resistance to further colonisation through the application of communicative reason. For Young, Habermas's idea of communicative rationality is central to the ethical rebuilding of education given its ability to hold in check an authoritarian attitude towards education that potentially replaces one dogmatism with another. In this respect, early work by Freire perhaps becomes suspect despite its concern for individual development given the presumption that critical thinking would necessarily lead in a revolutionary direction. Habermas's writing contains a key corrective in respect of critical pedagogy in that it need not presume that the application of communicative action necessarily leads subjects to adopt a Left-wing political position. Instead, argues Robert Young (1989: 87), through the application of communicative action we become aware that when 'fully reciprocal communication is achieved it is no longer appropriate to speak of teaching but acts of mutual learning'.

However, Young (1989: 88) is also aware that the application of communicative action to the sphere of education and learning requires us to face a central educational dilemma. This is concerned with the teachers' and educational authorities' role in the setting of a curriculum and power within the classroom and the attempt to develop critical citizens who are capable of making autonomous judgements. There is an inevitable 'tug of war' between the requirements of autonomous learning and the systemic requirements of society that ultimately means it cannot be 'neutral' concerning what children are taught. In this context the idea of open and uncoerced dialogue can act in a counter-factual way whereby the teacher invites the critical questioning of students. This requires the maintenance of an orderly learning environment where both the teacher(s) and pupils are invited to produce reasoned responses within a structured framework. There are further democratic opportunities to influence classroom relationships by seeking to involve students in the democratic running of the school and the discussion of educational questions within the public sphere more generally. These features would seek to make education more meaningful by developing the autonomous capacities of students and making sure that education was developed in accordance with democratic principles. Yet, as Antonio and Kellner (1992) point out, Habermas's writing is overly distanced from more specific historical and cultural contexts that would inevitably have a great bearing on the possibility of developing a radical democracy. However, Habermas has prompted a rethinking of critical theory through his discussion of the colonisation of the life-world (the extent to which money and power serve to bracket off democratic practices and values) and issues related to cultural impoverishment (the increasing dominance of experts). These features have a particular relevance to education given the possibilities for students to learn to question taken for granted assumptions and to navigate a number of complex debates and concerns. Education, in this understanding, is caught up with the wider question of how the public sphere can become constituted. Again, while Habermas has identified some important general tendencies within which the struggle for a democratic education would take place, his account remains limited in certain key respects.

Postcolonialism and feminism: education after Freire and Habermas

As I have already indicated Habermas, more explicitly than Freire, seeks to develop a post-Marxist approach to education. In particular, he has been especially critical of Marxist theories which have failed to adequately distinguish between between instrumental and communicative action. For Habermas (1991) a democratically constituted Left has to give up ideas of overthrowing the system, and is more properly involved with a switch from a market-led to a democratically controlled society. The inability to distinguish between instrumental reason and communicative rationality has meant that sections of the Left remain authoritarian in purpose and application. However, we should also note that Habermas's writing remains explicitly Eurocentric in its inability to appreciate the continued significance of the histories of colonialism in marking much of the contemporary world. As Paul Gilroy (1993) has argued, Habermas's faith in the Enlightenment and the approach to social theory seemingly remains unaffected by the histories of colonial barbarism. Here Gilroy is pointing to the extent that an exclusive focus on the reconstruction of Western rationalism blinds him to the role it has actually played in constructing binaries between culture and nature, the rational and irrational, and men and women, which has enforced the dominance of a Eurocentric and masculinist culture. Further, I would argue that Habermas's concern with the rationalisation thesis means that his writing is overly abstracted from the post-colonial, feminist and socialist struggles of the twentieth century that dreamt of a society free of domination. In this context, what is missing from Habermas's writing is a concern that an educated and learning society can only come about through social and cultural struggle. On this Raymond Williams's (1965: 10) insistence on the fight for democracy remains correct along with his further insistence that a capitalist market-based society is incapable of developing the educative potential of the globe's citizens. More explicitly, as Henry Giroux (1989) maintains, schools need to embrace the politics of voice whereby students not only learn to think across different narratives but also seek to explore their own problems and questions. Here education systems need to become open to the specific concerns of students as they seek to produce a link between the personal and the public. Further, as we saw earlier, Chantal Mouffe (2000) comments that political and educative space cannot exist without inviting contested interpretations. Despite the theoretical advance of Habermas's idea of communicative action too often the aim of such engagements is the production of consensus.

As Benjamin Barber (1989) argues, despite the dominance of a masculinised political theory the lives of actual citizens are shaped as much by affiliation and affection as they are by rationality. Indeed many feminist writers have pointed out that Habermas's exclusive concern with issues related to justice neglects other concerns around the capacity of human beings to care for and have sympathy with one another. In this respect, we could imagine a Habermasian initiative in education to open up a space where students and their teacher calmly exchange reasons with one another. Many feminist writers have argued that such a stance reproduces an overtly masculine view of the subject. Nel Noddings (2002, 2003) speaks in favour of a feminist ethics of care rather than an exclusive focus upon justice. If justice is overwhelmingly concerned with what is right (being an undogmatic teacher that allows for a multiplicity of narratives in the classroom) then an ethic of care is more focused upon what is good for people. In other words, whereas Habermasian initiatives tend to locate the learning context within the cold exchange of reasons, an ethics of care approach stresses the importance of the ability of educationalists to build human relationships that are grounded in love and trust. Here our moral and emotional development is dependent upon the ability to dialogue critically in an atmosphere of care and respect. Indeed the concern is that Habermas's focus upon rationality leads to a model of the public sphere that considerable overstates the ability and necessity of its citizens to reach a unified consensus. We should also recognise that many subordinate groups have historically found it necessary to construct what Nancy Fraser (1993: 527) has called 'subaltern counterpublics'. For example, many feminists, socialists, ecological activists and advocates of radical multiculturalism have attempted to set up alternative spaces in order to develop new discourses and narratives that can formulate oppositional ideas and interests. This has been necessary to the extent that more officially defined publics have sought either to ingest or expel the Other.

And yet I would agree that both Habermas and Freire resist the theoretical pessimism of much postmodernism by demonstrating that the human subject is capable of mutual forms of reconstruction through the dialogic process of learning. Here human subjects are not merely constituted through the practices of discourse but are able to engage in a communicative dialogue about their own needs and issues as related to wider questions of social and public power. Ultimately, however, both Freire and Habermas share a great deal in common given their mutual commitment to human development through communication and the flourishing of democratic practices in the context of everyday life. Indeed, Habermas (2001) has similarly been very critical of neoliberalism for how it has sought to reshape the autonomous development of civil society, the social state and cultural autonomy in favour of a more market-orientated way of life in ways that would find echoes in Freire's late writing.

Despite some of the problems that can be located in Freire's earlier Marxism, I would argue that in his later writing many of these have been resolved. Paulo Freire remains a more significant figure than Habermas in educational debates for several good reasons. First, he consistently sought to speak up for the 'wretched of the earth' who were denied access to educated forms of personal development. He argued that in this respect educators could not remain 'neutral' while many children were denied access to a formal education or suffered the consequences of poor housing, violence or malnutrition that made education impossible. In this context, the United Nations has recently reported that as many as one in four adults remains illiterate and if we took as little as half of what the United States spends on ice cream it would be enough to grant universal access for all children to primary education. Here Freire argued that critical educators and others had a responsibility to struggle for their own democratic conditions of practice and the educated development of all children globally.

But the problem still remains of students and educators who are unable (or perhaps unwilling) to live up to the image of critical pedagogy. What of the student who does not wish to be critical, or wants to stick with what they know? If critical pedagogy does not wish to become authoritarian it would need to be careful it does not become a demand that you must be critical. Critical pedagogy for all its insights perhaps underestimates the violence and uncertainty involved in changing our perspective. Sharon Todd (2003) argues that the invitation to alter our identities is fraught with complexity and difficulty. As education remains for the most part a reciprocal relation we remain responsible for the Other even if our invitation to change is ignored or rejected. In this setting it is the educator's ability to listen to the Other rather than proposing different ways of thinking that becomes important. If critical pedagogy rightly emphasises the need to be critical then equally important here is the ability to respond to difference. At this point we could argue, suggests Sharon Todd (2003), that it is less important to love the Other or rationally argue with them than it is to carefully attend to them. The question of responsibility summons the tutor less as a speaker in a dialogic context and more as a listener. If we would wish to respond to what is often a cruel and unjust society it must be as speakers as well as listeners. That we learn to listen to the alterity of the Other becomes significant in a context where we seek to uphold the right to communicate as well as the responsibility to listen.

5

Pragmaticism and Environmental Education

Up until this point I have tried to defend a democratic conception of education that has largely emerged out of a democratic or liberal socialist tradition. This has been because of the need to defend the practice of education in public spaces that are not colonised by the needs of capital but equally are not subservient to the state. The democratic socialist tradition has played a crucial role historically in seeking to defend a view of education that was potentially accessible to everyone, mixed students from different class backgrounds and granted them autonomy to follow their own interests while seeking to develop a responsible society. However, I have also sought to criticise this tradition in terms of questions that have arisen in relation to feminism, multiculturalism, human rights, and an increasing awareness of global and cosmopolitan questions. Here my argument is rather than jettisoning these diverse traditions of thinking, they need to be carefully rethought in light of more recent times. Therefore I would seek to extend this argument by focusing on the work of John Dewey. As will soon become apparent, Dewey is locatable within a liberal socialist discourse but this time one emerging out of a philosophical tradition called pragmaticism. Dewey remains crucial to the argument that a democratic education concerns the development of public institutions and public reasoning. To illustrate these questions I want to ask how helpful his approach is in raising environmental questions in relation to education. In the context of the environmental crisis and the widespread concern to link education to questions of sustainability these issues are likely to preoccupy educational thinkers for some time to come. As with the previous chapters, then, the approach to Dewey's contribution is marked by a spirit of critical reconstruction.

John Dewey, pragmaticism and democratic education

John Dewey was born in Vermont, USA, in 1859 and spent most of his life working on problems of education and philosophy in the universities of Minnesota, Chicago and Columbia. Dewey was a pragmaticist in that he was sceptical whether philosophy could bring us any closer to 'the truth' but that it could best serve us when it sought to deal with practical problems. In this quest, Dewey was deeply influenced by both Hegel (in that he retained an aversion to static and dualistic models of society) and Darwin (in that he saw human beings seeking to practically adapt themselves to a changing environment). For Dewey, as a democratically inspired American citizen, philosophy was best served dealing with problems rather than searching for utopian solutions. A central category for him was that of 'experience' which arises out of interaction with the world. In particular, Dewey sought to emphasise our shared capacity for experiences in common and to act in an experimental fashion when attempting to solve our shared problems (Bernstein 1966).

John Dewey argued forcibly for an approach to education that was both practical as well as theoretical. His central argument was that education should avoid indoctrination while at the same time recognising that it was impossible to be politically neutral. At the time Dewey wrote American society was encountering a period of intense class conflict and the educational debate was sharply divided between those who wished to train workers for capitalism and those who sought to utilise education for more revolutionary purposes (Ryan 1995). In this atmosphere he was both a liberal educator and a reformer who argued that schooling should help foster democratic identities and sensibilities. In this respect, his views on education come close to those of Aristotle, in that education should help foster the virtues of rationality, a participatory democracy and moral conduct in such a way that this balanced human needs for co-operation and the development of individual talents. As such, the idea of a good education was intrinsically linked to the notion of the good society that was built on the development of the democratic capacities of its citizens. Despite Dewey's championing of reason, rationality and scientific methods of deduction he was under no illusions that it could deliver the values by which we should live (Westbrook 1991: 145).

Notably his proposals to democratise education were resisted by the business community who wished to impress a distinction between elite and vocational training. Dewey argued that by simply training workers to work this failed to recognise that much employment was monotonous and intellectually undemanding. Education, then, should not only awaken in citizens the demand for more engaging forms of employment but should also treat them as democratic citizens with rights to participate in democratic decision making both within their workplaces as well as in the wider community (Westbrook 1991). In the 1920s these ideas led Dewey to found his own school (sometimes called 'the Laboratory school'). He argued that school and education more generally should help create a liberal environment that was suitable for a newly emerging democratic society. In this context, Dewey was critical of traditional pedagogy that emphasised rote learning and the passivity of the student. Instead teachers should convey the spirit of inquiry and life-long learning to their students by adopting a questioning and critical attitude. Educators should also reject the false idea that education produces citizens as a finished item and seek to awaken in themselves and their students the desire for education and learning without end. For Dewey it was indeed the task of the philosopher not to be indifferent to the problems of society nor to dream up impossible utopias, but to consider how a good society could emerge out of the conditions of the present (Wirth 1966: 29). To this end, the fostering of a critical attitude could not deliver absolute certainty, but a scientific and experimental attitude that would help foster the spirit of continuous reform that was necessary for a democracy and help puncture dualistic thinking that likes to separate knowing from doing (Biesta and Burbules 2003).

Dewey's own (1916) contribution to the philosophy of education argues that schooling should provide children with access to knowledge and ideas outside of their original environment. Crucially this means not only preserving the best that 'civilisation' has to offer, but also making sure that schools foster communication amongst people from different class and religious backgrounds. Here schools should aim to nurture individual and collective growth, rejecting a repressive and conformist approach to education. Dewey (1916: 61) believed we should 'surrender our habit of thinking of instruction as a method of supplying this lack by pouring knowledge into a mental and moral hole that awaits filling'. Education would act as a civic space that would enable children to follow their own interests while learning from one another. A democratic school would have to draw children from social groups who might be currently isolated from one another and have little experience of interacting. For Dewey (1916: 99), 'the essential point is that isolation makes for rigidity and formal institutionising of life, for static and selfish ideals within the group'. Such an approach recognises that people of different backgrounds and with different experiences need to learn to live together and that democracy is a way of living in common with others (1916: 101). Such arrangements not only help foster individual talent, but also provide an education where citizens become used to communicating across boundaries. In this respect, Dewey was deeply critical of nationalist attempts to subordinate education to the needs of the state, but argued as well that education that sought to foster the personal development of the individual was necessarily cosmopolitan in orientation (1916: 110).

Here his interactionist orientation benefitted greatly from his colleague George Herbert Mead's understanding of the development of the social self. For Mead (1934) human selfhood developed out of our capacity to view ourselves from the particular and general attitudes of other people. Until an individual is capable of viewing herself from the concrete and generalised standpoint of others we cannot be said to have developed a personality. It is in 'taking the attitude of the other' that the 'me' learns to control actions, attitudes and social expressions. A subject only gains consciousness of itself in the extent to which it is able to perceive its own actions through the lens of the other. This is not a description of moral conformity, but a recognition, by Mead, that the 'self-regarding self' can only handle community disapproval by setting up higher moral standards which 'out-vote' presently held societal norms (1934: 168). When there is a conflict between individual and community, the self is thrown back into a reflective attitude of examining whether the values and norms that are currently held are in need of revision. The necessity of the individual bringing her values to bear upon the community opens up a universalistic morality and lifts us out of our more concrete ties. Similarly, for Dewey, through engagement with the Other we may learn a democratic ethos, while taking a critical attitude towards our current convictions and passions. Dewey (1933: 18) later emphasised that our capacity to engage in a communicative reflective process was indeed what distinguished the 'civilised' from 'savages'. It was, then, through education that the merely superstitious could become critically interrogated without ever of course reaching any final set of truths that were beyond question.

Dewey was a defender of a communicative idea of the subject as well as the scientific method of rational interrogation. Indeed it was through rational thought and thinking more generally that we could be said to learn. For him (1916: 174) we should persuade students to formulate testable hypotheses before we reach our own inevitably tentative conclusions. More practically teachers should also encourage students to become curious about their own experience before subjecting their ideas to the rigours of critical questioning. This would encourage the idea that learning was a form of participatory discovery that could engage both teacher and student. Such an approach could indeed be contrasted to what Dewey (1916: 186) called the 'cold-storage ideal of knowledge' where students were encouraged to accumulate facts.

Procedures of rational interrogation must be followed so students could actively engage in democratic learning. Yet Dewey was clear that there were no unified general method of critical inquiry beyond a step-by-step process of rational interrogation. Above all a culture of scientific questioning would be more concerned with fostering what Dewey (1916: 206) called a child-like openness to the world that encouraged a permanently curious approach to understanding our shared world in common. He describes the democratic mind as the hospitable mind (1916: 206) in that one should continually subject one's understandings, prejudices and beliefs to rational forms of inquiry. Such an approach is likely to help foster useful knowledge that will also help us with our shared problems and aid us in maintaining a reforming attitude towards our shared institutions. In Dewey's terms a democratic education should be forward looking, always seeking to improve upon the past through processes of carefully argued reform.

In making these arguments he was widely interpreted as arguing for a progressive education that had radically broken with the past. However, as I have already indicated, Dewey (1939) was critical of dualistic thinking. If traditional and progressive education is opposed what does become lost is the democratic problem of authority. If traditional education emphasises discipline and obedience then progressive education is more about enabling students to learn from their experience. In other words, we need to be careful that the argument that education should be based upon freedom does not itself turn into a new form of dogmatism. If traditional education simply killed students' passion to learn and ability to exercise their own judgement we need to be careful that progressive education does not become 'planless improvisation' (Dewey 1939: 18). In other words, a democratic education would need to foster a democratic ethos. A democratic education is after all dependent upon student development and growth. Dewey (1939: 31) argued it was education's ability to get the student to learn from his or her own experiences and judgements that would offer the break from traditional education. In particular, a democratic education would need to take account of students' own connection to the host culture and their own experiences before seeking to involve those students in processes of critical reflection and inquiry. There is, then, a need to adapt education to their needs, interests and capacities and not simply treat them as blank slates. As Dewey (1939: 50) commented:

> What avail is it to win prescribed amounts of information about geography and history, to win ability to read and write, if in the process the individual loses his own soul: loses his appreciation of things worth while, of values to which these things are relative; if he loses desire to apply what he has learned and, above all, loses the ability to extract meaning from his future experiences as they occur.

In other words, a democratic education must encourage students to be passionate about their own learning and to learn how to learn from experience. In this Dewey argued that students needed educating in the humanities as well as the sciences as we can learn as much about the contemporary world from a poem as we can from a scientific idea. Both poetry and science are attempts to make sense of the world and can offer us valuable resources for understanding. It is mistaken to think that science is somehow 'truer' than poetry; what matters is how useful they are in helping us respond to the inevitable problems that we encounter in our engagements with our environment (Ryan 1998). Dewey affirmed that the intellectual ground beneath our feet was far from solid, with the scientific attitude being adopted less because it produces certainty and more because it helps us to produce useful knowledge and foster a deep love of thinking (Hickman 1995).

Rorty, education and pragmaticism

Before looking at some of the problems associated with Dewey's idea of a democratic education I want to look at the way these ideas have been translated more recently by Richard Rorty. Unlike Dewey, Rorty has not written extensively on issues related to education although this has been one of his concerns. For Rorty (1991a) a pragmaticist approach to education and knowledge means that we have to accept that there are no universals and that our self-understandings are embedded within specific historical and cultural constructs. We are thus 'condemned' to be ethnocentric in our accounts of the world and Western liberals need to recognise the extent to which their beliefs have been historically formed by the culture of the Enlightenment. Pragmaticists, unlike realists, doubt that science is able to offer a true picture of the world and instead value its contributions because of its ability to practically remodel the world. Science does not produce a true picture of reality, but useful knowledge. Dewey was a challenging philosopher as he argued that everything could be scientific and that the scientist was a figure who could guide the rest of our culture (Rorty 1991a: 63). Pragmaticism, however, is not a form of positivism given that it explicitly rejects the idea that we can accurately capture objective reality. Like Dewey, then, Rorty argues that philosophy can not really bring us closer to reality, the good or truth. For him (1991b: 127) pragmaticism more modestly aims to 'make us happier by enabling us to cope more successfully with the physical environment and with each other'.

Rorty (1989: 73) has developed these views further by claiming that we aim to justify our actions by employing what he calls a 'final vocabulary'. This means that when pushed we will justify our arguments through words such as 'right', 'true', 'good' and 'beautiful'. However, what we lack is a way to finally justify our attachments to these beliefs. For Rorty an educated disposition towards this problem is to become self-consciously ironic; that is, an ironist is 'aware of the contingency and fragility of their final vocabularies, and thus of their selves' (Rorty 1989: 74). In other words, an ironic disposition can be contrasted with our common sense that is largely unaware that in re-describing the world we can alter our own perception. Another way of considering this position is to encourage a recognition amongst ourselves and our students that we believe the things we do because of having been born at specific times, in particular places, and within certain contexts while also having had certain experiences, and crucially, because of having understood ourselves through particular narratives. Hence 'nature' can be variously described as embodying God's vengeance, as a place of brutish survival, or as offering the possibility of healing and rest. The ironist realises that our vocabularies from science to literature are more poetic re-description than objective reality. If the metaphysician is searching for the one correct and true vocabulary then the ironist is concerned about the consequences of becoming trapped in any one mode of interpretative understanding. Intellectual and educated life is inevitably ironic and needs to guard against those fundamentalists who would propose a master discourse that offered a true account of reality. Whereas Dewey proposed a democratic education, Rorty is similarly concerned with the communication of democratic-liberal understandings as this best allows all individuals the opportunity to create themselves. What educators need to guard against in this process are dogmatic doctrines of various kinds that seek to disallow the possibility of re-description and self-invention. Rorty's understanding of the educated self is the ability to move across a range of shifting vocabularies and understandings while recognising that they do not deliver a final truth and that they may become replaced by other descriptions.

While Rorty describes himself as a follower of Dewey the inflections that were described above are undoubtedly his own. However, he (1996) agrees with Dewey that questioning comes from a particular problematic situation and our efforts to resolve certain questions. To aid us in this process we need liberal laws and a liberal society, and should be critical of Marxist forms of ideology critique that depend upon the idea that we can cut through appearances to reveal a singular underlying reality. Here I would accept that many traditional Marxist accounts seemingly disallow the possibility of multiple interpretations and some also have a tendency in this respect to be dogmatic in respect of their descriptions of the external world. With the latter both Rorty (1999) and Dewey sought to promote a liberal model of education based upon the freedom of the individual, tolerance and social equality. In terms of education this would mean abandoning an idea that it was concerned with the liberation of the 'true' self, and to instead promote liberal freedoms and communicative forms of engagement. Rorty and Dewey both hold that democracy is not based upon the 'nature' of human beings, but is instead more an experiment in living together. In this respect, Rorty (1999: 12) argues that a liberal and democratic education has a 'fuzzy' utopian appeal. By this he means the hope that we might learn to live in a freer world in the future has no definite outlines and cannot be connected to any firm base in human nature.

Both Rorty and Dewey remain committed to the official national democratic culture of the United States and argue that universal moral principles are actually the expression of particular national cultures. Both can be understood as promoting a form of liberal-socialism that is in keeping with America's own democratic traditions, and finds an echo in European social democratic thought (Anderson 1992b). In these traditions there is no need for a revolution and the realisation of a democratic education system is more a matter of slow patient reform. Historically these traditions of thinking have maintained a strong affinity with national politics and the idea of the good society. Both Dewey and Rorty are deeply suspicious of Kantian appeals to more universal forms of reason. For them there is no transcultural moral law that can be realised by the use of reason as our sense of morality comes from more local practices and concerns. Not surprisingly Rorty (1998b) has more been connected to debates that have sought to defend a patriotic American Left. He has commented that such a Left should pay closer attention to questions of class inequality than it does to questions of difference and Otherness. Rorty (1997: 176) has also explicitly argued that once we put foundationalism behind us we would need to concentrate upon a 'sentimental education'. Rather than arguing that solidarity can be based upon human rights and so-called universal rational principles, Rorty (1997: 180) proposes that our education system should be geared to enhancing sympathy with others whose lives lack basic forms of dignity and security. It is not the rational recognition of a moral law that will lead to a concern with the oppression and fate of others, but middle-class suburban liberal values such as 'niceness' (Rorty 1997: 184).

While recognising the discursive inventiveness of Rorty's own arguments these do seem to have a number of flaws. Despite his more recent concern with the erosion of democracy by a powerful global capitalist class his liberalism fails to acknowledge some of the critical tensions outlined by Dewey. Richard Bernstein (1992) argues that Rorty actually distorts Dewey's legacy as he simply treats liberal democracy as a unified tradition without inner tensions. Notably he mostly ignores the liberal socialist critique that the structures of capitalism are capable of undermining liberal ideals more generally. This is an explicit concern of Dewey's whereas Rorty's talk about 'our' ideals does nothing to suggest that liberalism has its own internal critics. Further, especially when we come to look at questions of environmental change, we might be able to agree that all knowledge is linguistically and culturally constructed, but this does not mean that some takes on reality are not more convincing than others. As Best and Kellner (2001: 104) point out, Rorty's constructivism does not allow us to distinguish between arguments that claim the earth is flat, creationism or indeed scientific assessments of global warming. This is not to say that what science offers is 'facts' that are not shaped by history, culture and knowledge. However, I would agree with Mary Midgeley (1989, 2001) that we can recognise 'facts' are not neutral while also recognising some descriptions of external reality are better than others, while with Rorty I would share a concern about a form of scientific fundamentalism that suggests it was the only way of understanding reality, and think it is the proper place of any education to offer competing understandings of how different traditions have helped frame our shared understandings of the world. Here we need to be careful of the kinds of intellectual fundamentalism that both Dewey and Rorty sought to warn us against without presuming that we can abandon metaphysics altogether or that we do not need to distinguish between the validity of different claims about reality.

Scientific thinking itself offers us an imaginative means of grasping the world much of which is contested within scientific discourse, but also has inevitably suggested certain visions of 'reality' rather than others. For instance, Dewey's own Darwinism was built upon the idea of relatively successful individuals and societies struggling to adapt to a changing environment. As Raymond Williams (1980) argued many, although not Dewey, utilised Darwin's writing to propagate an ideology that sought both to legitimate free-market capitalism and to deny the more co-operative features of human and animal conduct. Williams I think sought to make us aware of the idea that our understandings of 'nature' are constructed and possess an inert material quality that we disregard at our peril. Here my remarks are not intended to bring these debates to an end, but to point out that Rorty's postmodernism pushes the argument on social and cultural construction further than it needs to go. We can agree then that human beings construct their understanding of the world through different discourses, while also recognising that we are relatively vulnerable biological creatures that depend upon nature for our survival.

Education, tradition and the environment

One of the main criticisms of Dewey's approach to education has been his neglect of issues related to tradition. On this critics point out that such was Dewey's desire to break with so-called traditional methods in education that he offered an overly individualised and child-centred approach to learning. The sociological theorist most closely associated with emphasising the role of tradition within the context of education was of course Emile Durkheim. Notably Durkheim (1956) placed his emphasis upon the inter-nalisation of culture by the individual and not on the liberal freedoms of the individual. Education is centrally concerned with the inculcation of a number of ideas, habits and sentiments within children. It is primarily a socialising mechanism that adapts a child to the particular society within which he or she is going to live. Especially in these terms is the need to curtail the egoism of the child by instilling a sense of self-control, duty and responsibility in the wider community. More recently certain strains of communitarian thinking have sought to revive some of Durkheim's princi-ple ideas in respect of a sense of duty. Much communitarian thinking stresses the need to curtail a sense of the social and cultural breakdown that has usually been associated with the rights-based culture connected to the radicalism of the 1960s. In these terms, communitarians argue it is the job of teachers and education to instil within children a sense of right and wrong and the moral order more generally (Etzioni 1997). However, this strain of thinking can be related to a form of moral repressiveness in that there is a concerted attempt to deny any of the democratic sense of author-ity that we find within Dewey. If he was concerned with balancing the needs of the individual and the community in a democratic context, Durkheim more explicitly concentrated on questions of moral breakdown and the decline of a traditional social order (Sadovnik and Semel 1999). At this point my argument will be that there is no decent solution to the environmental crisis facing global societies that is not at the same time democratic in orientation. Rather than returning to some of the more mor-ally repressive features of Durkheim's legacy as some (although not all) of the communitarian critics have tried to do, I would wish to point out that unless children are brought up in a democratic context they are unlikely to exhibit the civic freedoms necessary to address a number of public questions, including the ecological crisis.

There does, however, seem to be grounds for arguing that despite many of Dewey's qualifications he went too far in rejecting the role tradition should indeed play in children's learning. Anthony O'Hear (1991) has argued in this context that Dewey's emphasis upon problem-centred learn-ing neglects the role of past traditions in communicating to us our own self-understandings and the meaningfulness of our current identities. Indeed, if that emphasis is placed upon children being encouraged to think through problems for themselves there is a tendency to neglect the way similar problems have been faced in the past, and further, that in facing 'our problems' we undoubtedly draw upon the wisdom inherent in past cultural traditions and generations. Dewey's emphasis upon 'present' problems seems to presuppose that the past could only be of any use if it helped us right now. This rather instrumentalist approach to learning does not offer us very good reasons as to why we might become interested in a novel, historical work or scientific idea from the past unless this could be directly related to some of the problems being faced by our society today. This view is less a Dukheimian argument about moral cohesion, and more a concern that the study of past ideas, imaginings and perspectives is relevant if education is to remain tied to questions of individual curiosity. Indeed Rorty's own (1999) critique of Dewey partially concedes this point by arguing that a good education should guide us through different traditions of knowledge and learning. We can perhaps agree with Dewey's critics that, while he was not a positivist, by focusing education so exclusively upon the role of problem solving he did not pay enough attention to education's role in communicating complex intellectual traditions of learning and inquiry.

At this point we need to look more closely at the critique of Dewey offered by C.A. Bowers. Bowers' main (1993, 2003) argument with Dewey (as well as with Freire) is the extent to which they both represent a modernist capitalist culture that has little respect for traditional ways of life, and thereby reproduces the dominant values of the system of abstract rational thought, competitive individualism, profits and efficiency. It is lifestyles based upon economic competiveness and hyper-consumption that are threatening planetary survival. In particular Bowers wishes to develop an education system that is more tailored to our ecologically vulnerable times. This involves questioning many of the assumptions that seemingly lie behind many of the claims made by Dewey and Richard Rorty. Bowers, like some of Dewey's other critics, is worried about the extent to which his proposals would undermine the transmission of inter-generational knowledge. In an ecological context this argument is given added force in that many indigenous and tribal societies have been able to sustain knowledge and practices that have been less harmful to the environment than Western modernity. Like many in the ecological movement Bowers (1993) is keen to explore the possibility that pre-modern lifestyles could indeed offer alternative sources of knowledge (1993: 185), and has argued that actually a deep engagement with 'ecologically successful cultures' could indeed highlight our own taken for granted assumptions. Western liberal thought by emphasising individualism and our capacity for self-creation simply presumes that we can take from nature. By contrast many traditional cultures recognise that they need to build a reciprocal relationship with nature if they are to preserve their way of life for future generations. A more sensitive recognition of the natural implies that educators could by encouraging students to explore more traditional cultures seek to highlight the extent to which human beings have a necessarily inter-dependent relationship with the natural world. In particular, given that many traditional cultures have a circular view of time, this emphasises the extent to which the past is never really left behind. Western modernity and much liberal thinking by contrast tend to be future-orientated, drawing upon a linear sense of time and a powerful myth of progress.

More specifically, in addressing the contributions of John Dewey, Bowers (2006) argues that Dewey was ethnocentric in that he built his model of education on an idea of rationality that positioned traditional societies as 'Other'. This was especially notable through Dewey's championing of scientific reason as the dominant culture of Western elites, thereby closing his mind and those of others to alternative ways of knowing. For Bowers (2006: 77) such arguments represent a form of 'cultural colonisation' given that he universally assumes a model of the good society that is based upon the dominance of the United States. This would seemingly not only further enhance the violent repression of indigenous cultures like the Native Americans, but also disallow similar possibilities in other contexts where some of Dewey's ideas have been adopted. While Bowers recognises that Dewey's liberalism was indeed sharply critical of the lack of democratic ethos apparent within the kinds of industrial training being insisted upon by elites, he acknowledge he did so in such a way that this further impressed the exclusion of non-Western cultures. This is indeed the problem with insisting the ideal of critical reflection has a natural alliance with thinking that problematises ethnocentrism. As Bowers argues (and Dewey is a case in point) an insistence upon critical reflection can indeed be mobilised to justify a cultural binary between so-called enlightened democrats and savages.

Indeed, what counted as progress for Dewey was not the revival of different kinds of inter-generational knowledge, but ideas of critical rationality and the continual subjection of tradition to critical forms of inquiry. Here Dewey was complicit with the culture of capitalism as it seeks to banish the memory and skills of less consumer-orientated lifestyles as it increasingly subjects everyday life to its imperatives. In these two respects, then, traditions and skills that are associated with less consumer-orientated lifestyles and knowledge about ecologically sensitive cultures are important features in arguments for a sustainable education.

For Bowers traditional knowledge and practice can be a crucial resource in the educated struggle for a sustainable and a respectful world. Indeed Dewey's insistence on the virtues of experimentalism serves only to legitimate the dominance of the market given the link between technological innovation and the search for new markets that will provide the basic driver for capitalist expansion and ecological ruin. Rather than upholding the global importance of democratic learning, Bowers seeks to conserve traditions and practices of inter-generational learning that would practically help citizens reduce the size of their ecological footprint. Instead of the hegemony of the market and the development of new technology, he argues that it will be the ability to sustain less consumer-dependent ways of life that is most likely to guide us in the direction of a sustainable society. This will involve both preserving traditional skills to enable us to develop forms of living that are less dependent upon cash payment and adopting non-Western beliefs that can act as a means of critical reflection.

Similarly Bowers (2003) is also critical of Richard Rorty's attempt to reinvent pragmaticism in more contemporary contexts. Bowers argues that Rorty's brand of postmodern liberalism entirely ignores the environmental crisis. It is within this context that we should judge Rorty's aim to defend everyone's right to individual forms of self-creation. The maximisation of the ability of individuals to become ironic about 'final narratives' is deeply reactionary in the context of global environmental degradation. By contrasting claims from metaphysics and liberal ironists, Rorty is actually reinventing notions of progress whereby a life of continual doubt and contingency is considered superior to that which rests upon claims to ontological certainty. The liberal ironist is deeply concerned with escaping from the confines of tradition while also embracing a more rootless less certain culture of continual questioning. Like Dewey, Rorty seemingly makes a virtue out of both newness and an experimental approach to knowledge, thereby neglecting the insights of traditional culture.

Finally, and in my view most powerfully, Bowers argues that the emphasis placed upon the necessity of self-creation fails to recognise the importance of an ethic of self-limitation that is central to environmental ethics. Here he highlights perhaps the major flaw within Western liberal culture in the context of the environmental crisis. Our concern with the liberties and democratic freedoms of the individual fails to recognise his or her inter-dependence with and integration into the earth's ecosystems. In the context of widespread environmental erosion and some of the risks that have been associated with global warming any ecological ethics would clearly need to involve questions of self-limitation in the context of Western lifestyles built upon hyper-consumption and unsustainably large carbon footprints. And in such a context neither an insistence upon an ironic attitude towards final narratives nor one harping on the virtues of tradition is likely to be of much help. Instead I shall argue that a renewed attempt to link an idea of the good society with issues related to human rights is much more likely to lead the debate on the environment and education in the right direction. Before proceeding with these arguments, however, I think we need to consider some of the broader, more sociological features within which the debate on education and sustainability inevitably takes place. As we shall see, these features have been almost entirely ignored by the philosophical writing of both Rorty and Bowers.

Individualisation and post-democracy

Individualisation means a disembedding of industrial society's ways and the reinvention of new communal ties and biographies. For sociologist Ulrich Beck (1992) as more areas of social life become less defined by tradition the more our biographies require choice and planning. We are living in the age of DIY biographies. Under the conditions of welfare industrialism 'people are invited to constitute themselves as individuals: to plan, understand, design themselves as individuals and, should they fail, to blame themselves' (Beck 1999). The disintegration of the nuclear family and rigid class hierarchies means we are all released from the structures of industrial society into the uncertainties of a globalised society. This profound sociological shift means that tradition has become increasingly open to question and forces individuals to plan their biographies and make choices about their lifestyles. In our context, however, I doubt we are as post-traditional as Beck and some of his followers like to claim. Traditions if they are to stay alive have a habit of reinventing themselves in the context of the present. Further, others have argued in the context of class societies that not everyone has access to the cultural and material resources for reflexive individualisation. For example, Beverley Skeggs (2004) comments that under individualisation the idea of being middle class becomes coded as normal whereas sections of the working class are seen as an Other. It is perhaps in this context that we can best understand the rise in Britain of a so-called 'chav culture'. This widely employed and derogatory term is used predominately by the middle classes and the respectable working classes to distinguish themselves from a seemingly poorly educated and tasteless underclass.

If processes of individualisation produce an Other it can also be linked to the commodification of the self. Richard Sennett (1998) has argued that global capital has promoted an uncertain culture based upon short-term contracts, insecurity, risk and superficial communal relations. The self fostered by neo-liberalism is both open to the culture of the market, while fostering a pervasive sense of insecurity and a longing for community. As the market spreads into different areas of social life citizenship arguably becomes increasingly defined through different kinds of social conduct. The market's view of the citizen is through the individualised ability to be able to 'maximise his or her lifestyle through acts of choice' (Rose 2000: 99). The market, under the guise of freedom and autonomy, acts as a mechanism regulating norms and instilling certain forms of behaviour. The commodified struggle for the lean and slender body and the Othering of the fat body can be understood in these terms. The plastic individualised body is dependent upon reflexivity, access to cultural and material resources and of course the idea that anything disagreeable can be avoided with the flash of a credit card. If we are in the age of plastic bodies we can make a similar argument about the self. As Mary Rogers (1999: 143) has put forward, under consumer capitalism we are condemned not simply to perform or to realise the self, but to endlessly tinker with it. Consumer capitalism requires that we are not only constantly dissatisfied with our appearance, but that who we are must also be constantly updated, overhauled, and if necessary disregarded.

We might as well add that despite Dewey's faith in democratic progress modern societies might be more accurately described as entering into a post-democratic age that complements the individualised and commodified self. While democracy as a set of institutional practices is still in evidence behind the daily televised spectacle of political clashes it is overwhelmingly subject to control by business rather than citizens' interests. As Colin Crouch (2004) has argued, the period when we could be optimistic about the progress of democracy (perhaps culminating after the Second World War) is over. In this reading the decline of labour and trade-union politics has simply handed over control of the political process to powerful political elites and the interests of global capital. If individualised consumers have grown wary of political definitions of the good life this situation has been complemented by the erosion of explicitly egalitarian democratic projects. Neoliberalism has not only triumphed over the fantasies and engagements of ordinary people it has also just as crucially increasingly handed control to the interests of corporations. Democratic citizenship begins to wither on the vine as the wealth gap between rich and poor grows, the welfare state is privatised and run down, people do not vote and the case for redistributive taxation becomes harder to make.

These features undoubtedly give those who have any sympathy for Dewey's arguments in respect of democratic schools reason enough for pessimism. Yet we need to be careful not to bend the stick too far as individualisation does contain within it more progressive features. Individualisation cannot be wholly encompassed by questions of Othering and commodification but is an *ambivalent* social and cultural creation. Alberto Melucci (1996) argues that globalisation (rather than commodification) has meant that we are able to experience greater levels of inter-connection with the lives of spatially distant others, and multiplied possibilities for what we might become. The ethical side of individualisation is less concerned with what we might possess, and more with ethical and global questions. If globalisation is intimately connected to neoliberalism it is also concerned with the development of more cosmopolitan identities and concerns. While these questions are undoubtedly marked by the politics of class and resources they do suggest other perhaps more hopeful political agendas beyond the fears of mass commodification and democratic indifference. These arguments can be related to what Anthony Giddens (1992) has called 'life politics'. That is the idea that the rise of feminism and green politics is an attempt to ask questions about the choices we must make rather than simply seeking to struggle for increased autonomy. If we are to recognise our vulnerability and interdependence upon the earth then we will need social movements that will prove able to promote different understandings of our shared human condition. Further we need to be careful not to suggest that neoliberalism has simply 'made over' the cultural domain. The idea of a liberal education has a long historical legacy and has not been entirely defeated in our admittedly increasingly market-driven times. On this we need to remember that, even though I was largely critical of the idea of the third way, it at least try to address educational disadvantage even if the way it did so was mostly instrumental. In the final section, I want to explore the kinds of implications these arguments will have for the idea of democratic schooling in more global contexts and, in addition, to ask how ecological questions might best proceed in these terms.

Democratic schooling, human rights and ecological ethics

In the context of individualisation I think that Bower's arguments about the role of tradition miss the point. In a rapidly individualising society tradition is increasingly subject to critical scrutiny. It may well be that the ecological imaginations of the young could be stimulated through an engagement with 'ecologically successful' cultures, but that this is best done in settings that are democratic and allow for curiosity as well as critical questioning. In the context of individualisation a Durkheimian emphasis upon tradition could easily lapse into a reactionary form of moralism. If individualisation has an ethical core as well as being potentially a form of social exclusion or way of commodifying the self the educative challenge is clear. The question for educators is how to enhance and develop ethical individualisation. In the context of environmental change a democratic schooling can no longer simply be linked to the realisation of the individual self. Dewey's argument carefully recognised that individualism needs to be balanced against forms of a social co-operation understanding that individuals are cultural creatures. Rorty, as we also saw earlier, sought to develop an ironic liberal self that would be continually sceptical about final narratives. However, as Bowers claims, the main problem with these positions is that they have very little to say about an ethics of self-limitation that would be necessary within an environmental argument. An ecological ethics could indeed learn from 'successful' ecological cultures that took their responsibilities to future generations and the environment seriously. Here, it seems to me, we need to readdress the role education can play in seeking to develop and foster more ethical forms of individualisation rather than, say, Rorty's views on the ironic self or indeed Dewey's reliance upon the experimental self. This is not to say, however, that the liberalism of Dewey and Rorty does not provide important ethical resources in respect of the environmental debate, merely that their respective arguments need to be substantially recast.

Against Dewey and Rorty I would suggest that a democratic and environmentally informed education needs to be based upon a respect for fundamental universal human rights. If Bowers worries that the human right to an education might undermine the capacity of indigenous societies to reproduce themselves, then Dewey and Rorty contest that a universal morality could never be the product of a disinterested rationality. If I could take the latter claim first I would argue that in the context of increasingly interconnected global societies this argument makes little sense. As Norberto Bobbio (1996) has argued, we can uphold arguments in respect of human rights not because they are based upon an understanding of human nature or a sense of innate rationality, but because since the 1948 declaration on human rights we now possess a valid way by which we might judge global humanity. Since 1948 there has emerged a global consensus on human rights not as a reality, but as an ideal that should be pursued. That many people across the world (both inside and outside the West), particularly after the end of the Cold War, have sought to claim their human rights means that these have become an important part of an emergent cosmo-politan dimension. This is not, of course, to deny that claims to human rights are dependent upon the will and developmental capacity of nation-states, but it is to argue that they are less a philosophical question and more a concern of politics and social struggle. The other view that to grant eve-ryone a human right to an education potentially universalises the culture of the West and thereby homogenises the globe's capacity to sustain cultures of difference is also questionable. Seen from the global perspective of chil-dren's human rights such a view fails to recognise the ways in which vulner-able and poor children are exploited as a source of cheap labour, in sex industries and used as soldiers in military conflicts. As Manuel Castells (1998: 159) has argued to talk of children's rights recognises not only the disintegration of traditional societies, but also the downward pressure being exerted on children's rights in mature industrial societies as a result of pri-vatisation and a deregulation of the global economy. In the context of the break-up of the family, the decline of tradition and commodification the struggle for children's global human rights (including the right to an educa-tion) arguably takes priority over the defence of particular traditions. The struggle to recognise children's right to a democratic education, then, should be seen not only as a form of empowerment, but also as a powerful universal normative claim. The recognition of this human right inevitably takes the debate beyond Rorty's concern with educating the sympathies of middle-class Westerners, to include the right of children everywhere to learn to speak in their own voice (Spivak 2002). Ours is a world where the language (if not the practice) of human rights has become universal. As such we need to give up the practice of seeing human rights as opposed to the idea of the good society, and instead argue that in our world the local and the global and the right and the good become connected through human rights. Dewey's argument that the task of the philosopher is to work on the idea of the good in the context of a specific bounded human society therefore needs to be radically rethought in the context of our increasingly globally interconnected world.

Further, I also think that Rorty's patriotic pragmatism is unnecessarily exclusive in the context of arguments in respect of a global civil society (Kaldor 2003). While the idea of a global civil society is still an emergent debate it undoubtedly relates to the ways in which concerns about human rights, the environment, gender, peace and a critique of neoliberal economics can only be thought of as overlapping rather than as exclusively national concerns. Educational debates at this level will undoubtedly need to become concerned with questions of cultural difference in ways that are largely absent from Dewey and Rorty. If globalisation pushes humanity together then it will be our ability to negotiate across cultural boundaries that will become important in such a way that this is underpinned by basic human rights. The process of multicultural translation is no longer exclusively concerned with national societies, but takes place in between different cultural locations. Finally, following Noddings (2002), Dewey's emphasis upon critical and reflective thinking overstates the extent to which rational inquiry will necessarily produce humane results or indeed lead to conclusions which will manage to reconcile the interests of 'our' community with others. Democratic conversations are necessarily governed by a commitment to certain universal principles such as the right of all peoples to a good environment. Such commitments would necessarily prevent not only our dumping of environmental problems upon our neighbours, but would also recognise the interconnected nature of ecological questions in a global world.

However, while these are important principles, the environmental ethic of self-limitation requires more than the recognition of human rights: it asks us to re-imagine the relationship between human and non-human nature. Vaclav Havel (1998: 81) proposes that such concerns need to recognise 'a metaphysical anchor, that is, a humble respect for the whole of creation, and a consciousness of our obligation to it'. Our question then becomes one of how to reconcile a liberal ethics of self-creation and freedom with that of responsibility and self-limitation. Here I would argue that rather than abandon liberal traditions and principles these need to be radicalised. In Dewey's context he was well aware that liberal principles without an emphasis upon equality and the need to keep the market out of education would lead to these very principles being undermined. Historically this has provided the basis for much intelligent socialist critique that sought less to replace liberalism and more to extend the practice of freedom to everyone within the community. As Terry Eagleton (1996: 83) argues, democratic versions of socialism promise to make available to each the material (and cultural) resources to allow individual liberty to become a serious prospect for most people. Similarly, the ethics of self-limitation only becomes possible if people are encouraged to think of themselves as responsible citizens.

David Orr (1992) points out that the environment is a major educational challenge requiring a fundamental change in our mind-sets. Despite Rortyian irony, environmental questions are also irredeemably metaphysical and cultural questions that suggest we need to rethink ourselves in relation to the natural world. In this respect, if industrial civilisation required the domination of nature, then a different set of attributes is required to 'heal' the earth (Orr 1992: 1). This point meets with a genuinely liberal education concerns on the fostering of human beings with a wide range of capacities and qualities. Orr argues that we should learn to distinguish between 'the clever' and 'the smart' and 'the intelligent'. Whereas cleverness is specialised and offers short-term knowledge, intelligence is more concerned with a wider view that considers questions over a longer time-frame.

It is not surprising that many institutions now value 'smart' thinking because of its instrumentality; however, ecological intelligence demands a different ethical set of concerns about limits, unpredictability and responsibility. This will inevitably lead to a questioning of systems driven by profit, consumerism and individual self-realisation. An ecological education not only needs to raise questions of civic responsibility, it should also critically question the idea that the good society is the consuming society. The best way to pursue this without becoming dogmatic or moralistic is to ask whether a society of hyper-consumption is actually compatible with the development of complex and imaginative people. Here the ethics of self-limitation becomes not a form of puritanism (as many often seem to think) but perhaps a more 'authentic' way of becoming. We need to uncover different ideas of what it means to be a 'successful' person.

The existential psychotherapist and Holocaust survivor Viktor Frankl argued that to thrive and to give meaning to our lives we have to discover (not invent) what is good for ourselves (Frankl 1964). We can only do this effectively (and dare we say healthily) if we manage to live in the present while keeping a firm grasp on the future. If we can turn existence into an inner challenge and a place of hope then we can live meaningful lives. If a resolutely liberal education points to the importance of both becoming ourselves and learning to communicate with others, such a venture needs to be undertaken with a sense of responsibility and limits. Happiness is not so much living a life of calm, but of struggling to discover our vocation and what gives our lives a sense of purpose. Here my argument is that lives of relentless labour and hyper-consumption are not only bad for the planet, these are also more often a failure to discover inner meaning. Victor Frankl (1964: 134) famously proposed that the Statue of Liberty on the East Coast should be joined by a Statue of Responsibility on the West Coast. A more ecologically sensitive education requires not only that children are encouraged to realise their own projects, ideas and interests but that they also do so in a way that is responsible. Just as socialism sought to awaken liberalism to questions of equality in the twentieth century, now in the twenty-first century, ecological ideas need to rejoin issues of liberty to an ethics that recognises our dependence upon the natural world. Education in this setting becomes less about the preparation for upward mobility and becomes more one of the few public spaces available where different ethical choices can be deliberated upon. In this venture we are still reliant upon the possibility of schools acting as genuinely public places where different ethical languages can be interrogated. Dewey remains relevant in this quest to the extent that he sought to reconcile the principles of liberty, equality and solidarity within institutional contexts. However, as I have indicated, the development of capitalism, the environmental crisis and the erosion of democracy all mean that we need to move beyond his optimistic pragmaticism in order to adopt a more critical language.

6

Education in the Consumer and Information Age

What are the implications for education of living in a consumerist and information-based society? In the previous chapter we looked at how the rise of a mass consumer culture and ecological questions pose problems for a liberal and democratic approach to education. Might the same be said about the arrival of the information age or knowledge economy? This is significant in terms of the argumentative strategy of this book as most of the critical paradigms in respect of education were developed before the full emergence of this society. If the 1950s and 1960s saw the development of a new phase of capitalism due to the emphasis placed upon the stimulation of new markets and identities through the explicit use of images and symbols to sell products then later transformations have intensified this process. Jonathan Rutherford (2005: 43) argues that despite the considerable amount of hype from government and business about the 'knowledge economy' there are still considerable long-term trends which articulate a shift as profound as the Industrial Revolution, where capitalism is seeking to reshape the activities of universities and schooling while deregulating and creating new markets through new technology. In the shift away from the industrial into the knowledge-driven society the economy requires a supply of operatives who can work in a sector that is increasingly reliant upon the manipulation of culture and symbols. Sociologist Manuel Castells (1996) argues that the emergent 'information society' is primarily being born out of the changing relationship between global capitalism, the state and new social movements. In this new economy it is the application of knowledge and technology in customised production that best ensures economic success. Here the technological level of the enterprise is a much better guide to competitiveness than older indices like labour costs. The rapid development of informational technology in the 1970s in Silicon Valley, California, enabled capital to restructure itself after the impacts of a world-wide recession. The information-driven society has allowed organisations to achieve increasing flexibility in terms of more knowledge dependent and less hierarchical structures.

If human societies are being increasingly penetrated by the logic of capital and consumer culture more generally what implications can we say this has for learning? This becomes a pressing question in light of this book, as while Hoggart and Williams were writing during the initial development of such a society both Dewey and Freire were working in different contexts. Zygmunt Bauman (2007a: 35) has recently captured the dominant ethos of the consumer society which he argues is characterised by an increasing intensity of desires and the arrival of 'the 'nowist' life'. If in a consumerist society we are encouraged to quickly consume and just as quickly discard skills, concepts and frameworks of knowledge then what indeed are the implications for human communication and development? If yesterday's hopes and desires are likely to become tomorrow's discarded refuge, and if we become transfixed by the ways things look or seem, what does this mean for the quality of our public and private lives? Bauman's (2007a: 92) judgements are harsh on the kinds of ethical and moral life that are likely to flourish in such a society. The consumerist society is not so much a society of communal orientation where we learn to take responsibility for the Other, rather it tends to foster a responsibility for oneself at the expense of others. Such features, as we shall see, have deep implications for questions of well-being and happiness and also for the dominant ethos of society's cultural institutions. To begin with I want to explore the main contours of this relatively new society before looking at some of the human qualities that are promoted by consumerism. I shall investigate the extent to which the ethos of consumerism and education could be said to come into conflict, and ask whether education can indeed uphold different models and understandings of human well-being.

Before I do this, however, I think that we need to explore the emergence of the consumerist society whose dominant logic was captured sometime ago through Guy Debord's (1994) notion of 'the spectacle'. While Debord is rarely mentioned in critical debates within education he has a considerable amount to contribute towards our understanding of some of the dominant features of this consumerist age. In particular I aim to recover a language about educated development that seeks to recapture an idea of the common good. This alternative ethic would not attempt to replace capitalist-consumer society with a completely different kind of society but would instead try to speak in favour of what Raymond Williams (1985: 248) called a society of 'common wellbeing'. In the case of Williams we may remember that such an ethic was not arrived at through a violent revolutionary transformation, but was reached via a complex struggle against the logic of Plan X. Plan X was ultimately the dominant rationality of the capitalist system which had seeped into education, the media and sections of the labour movement that had traditionally been conceived of as oppositional. Plan X was quite simply the logic of strategic advantage without reference to the language of the good society or mutual responsibility. What became eroded in such a language was a sense of responsibility for the whole common good.

Education and the good society

In more liberal or social democratic writing, however, it is not that the spectacle is likely to be replaced but that it could be restrained through democratic initiatives. It is this tradition that still offers some possibility of being revived in the context of Western capitalist societies. In the context of the failure of state socialist societies, the increased presence of the capitalist spectacle and the partial collapse of the labour movement, it is with the revival of these traditions that the best hope of restraining a society of hyper-consumerism is to be found. Here the language that needs to be recovered is that of the common good and of democratic forms of community. Alasdair MacIntyre (1981, 1998) states that in this context our understandings of the good life and society are inevitably bound by certain traditions. Whereas liberalism argues that I am what I choose to become, MacIntyre argues that if the self is to discover a set of moral co-ordinates it can only do so within the extent to which it is connected to wider narratives, communities and traditions, all of which help define a version of the good. Important within this relationship are the political and cultural traditions we inherit from the past that will suggest certain practices like working within education have a history that tries to define what this ought to involve. However, given the previous arguments I made about the capitalist spectacle, our sense of an historical connection to the struggles and imagination of the past is increasingly difficult to make. Further, MacIntyre suggests it is a deeply mistaken belief to hold that what it means to say by have a good education can be discovered through disinterested reason. What we mean by a good education will only make sense once we have an understanding of some of the arguments that have characterised education, and how these were then connected to certain political traditions and projects. MacIntyre is aware of course that traditions change and are reformulated, but that the search for the good is defined by a sense of reinvented traditions. Conversely it is partly the responsibility of education to make us aware of different ideas of the good and how they are reshaped across time and space. As Schumacher (1993: 72) points out, if education is to matter then it should help us understand our fundamental beliefs and demonstrate the ways in which different ideas of the 'good' can assist us in shaping our convictions and horizons.

In this respect, I think we can outline a neoliberal education that largely views education as a form of training for the labour market, and has been mainly concerned with converting the practice of education into an obsession with standards, discipline and the passing of exams. This view is of course preferable to totalitarian ideologies that have sought to indoctrinate children more directly, but it remains the case that neoliberal versions of education do a great deal of violence to its practice. Under neoliberalism education is measured by results and is simply the means for getting a job. In the context of consumer-orientated societies good results are the means for earning high salaries and achieving high-status careers. This is education for spectacle, as what is emphasised is a society of atomised competition and the ability to be able to live a life of hyper-consumption. We might also mention the ways in which neoliberal initiatives are progressively privatising education, where students become customers and educational organisations seek to become 'brands' while the market value of knowledge becomes more important than its capacity to be critical (Giroux 2003). Further, we need to recognise how instrumental and market initiatives are undermining the humanities more generally. If 'our' only concern is economic growth and jobs this will inevitably undermine an appreciation of the arts and critical thinking more generally (Nussbaum 2010). Not surprisingly, perhaps, these ideologies that value market forms of competition above all else have a major role to play in shaping the way that education is practised and understood within modern society. All of these initiatives along with various others tend to undermine the meaning and purpose of education.

There are intellectual traditions derived from liberal and more radical currents that argue to become educated is a common good. Here the emphasis is more squarely placed on the ability to learn and open up complex questions. These traditions are also more driven by the happiness of children and questions of common well-being. In this vein Bertrand Russell (who I take as contributing to this tradition) wrote: 'The spontaneous wish to learn, which every normal child possesses, as shown in its efforts to walk and talk, should be the driving force of education. The substitution of this driving-force for the rod is one of the great advances of our time' (1926: 34). This tradition has at its heart the ability of all members of the community to become learning beings. However, whereas democratic liberals have tended to emphasise the importance of individual freedom socialist traditions have stressed the importance of community and the human relationships that are involved in learning and education. These critical debates are central to what MacIntyre (1981: 222) described as a 'living tradition', the extent to which it contains within it conflicts and competing strands rather than a unified whole. There are, then, particular disagreements about the meaning of education. Yet, what both strands of this argument share is the need to engage with the question notably almost entirely absent within neoliberalism as to what we mean by education. Schumacher (1979) argues that in answering this question we are inevitably seeking to answer questions about what it means to be human, and what it is good to become. These, he argues, are not questions that a culture dominated by instrumental and scientific rationality will find it easy to respond to. It is my contention that however modern citizens choose to answer this will differ from that of traditional societies, but will also inevitably draw upon different political traditions and ideas of the good society.

Education, the good and well-being

There is increasing concern that a society built upon individualised competition, privatisation and consumption fails to contribute to a shared sense of well-being. As a number of studies now claim to demonstrate it seems that the link between human well-being and economic growth is less than certain. It is not only that beyond a certain point that increased wealth seems to add very little to human happiness, but also that there is some statistical evidence which suggests that the numbers of those who would describe themselves as happy are in decline. As Clive Hamilton (2003: 34) has put it, 'happiness is less a matter of getting what you want than of wanting what you have'. In particular there is now a growing literature on the misery of those who seem to think that happiness lies in the external goals of wealth, celebrity and personal appearance (all of which are culturally dominant within the society of the spectacle) as opposed to the relative happiness of those more concerned with personal relationships, self-development and involvement in the community. In this respect, as the spectacle gains in dominance there is growing anxiety within a number of quarters about the levels of mental illness and depression amongst affluent populations (James 2007). In particular, and this is a point I wish to return to, there seems to have been an increase in social isolation and a lack of connection to more communally defined activities. We have it seems become societies that are now obsessed with individualised models of success and correspondingly high levels of consumer spending at the expense of other human qualities. If citizens today are experiencing themselves as caught in endless cycles of consumption whereby the economy fashions new products (quickly seen as needs rather than wants) and if rising incomes come with the cost of spending less time with significant others then it is perhaps not surprising that many people are richer if not happier (Layard 2005; Rustin 2007b). Further, there is also evidence that more social democratic societies that have maintained more equal distributions of income are also healthier and happier than those societies that are more driven by the capitalist spectacle (Wilkinson and Pickett 2009). What is being emphasised here is that education and family systems should become less geared towards enhancing the standards of performance and more concerned with well-being and creativity. This is not an argument for poor standards, rather that educational priorities are better served by developing human qualities other than those required by a competitive economy and consumer-orientated lifestyles. In this respect, a good school will be judged on its ability to be able to maintain high exam performance and discipline rather than on its ability to be able to help foster critical, reflective and emotionally secure young people.

To say that consumption and materialism have a tendency to drive out the features that are required if we are to live more meaningful lives is not a new thing. Erich Fromm (1978) commented that we need to distinguish between two different modes that he characterised as 'having' and 'being'. As Fromm identifies it, the con trick performed by capitalism and state socialism was the view that the achievement of privatised lifestyles, wealth and comfort would lead to human happiness. In the 'having' mode unlimited consumption, private property and possessions define our prestige and status. This, Fromm argues, can only provide an illusion of happiness as it is likely to create considerable anxiety should we either fail to keep up with others or lose 'everything'. Similarly Zygmunt Bauman (2007b) states that the terror of the individualised society is no longer that we will fail to conform to society's rules, but will more likely to be motivated by a fear of failing to keep up with a fast-moving society. It is 'the terror of inadequacy' that haunts modern society (2007b: 94). The successful life is one where busyness, consumption and being permanently on the move become some of its defining features. Returning to Fromm, in 'being' mode we are less concerned with frantic activity and a concern for outcomes and more focused on the quality of our experience more generally. Hence in the 'having mode' students learn to memorise the required material to pass an exam or module in such a way that this clearly does not engage them. Learning, we might say, has a very different quality if students come to lectures or seminars with their own problems and questions (Fromm 1978: 29). As they learn to engage with new material in these lectures, seminars and through their own reading they will formulate new questions and problems. Therefore in 'being mode' knowledge is brought to life through critical engagement rather than by mechanical forms of reproduction. If this 'being mode' stresses the joy and wonder of learning then the 'having mode' is more concerned with the end result. On this point I don't think that Fromm means to imply that we could have an education system without both of these modes: what is more significant is which of these distinctive orientations dominates the process.

If these critical debates question the extent to which education can ever become disconnected from questions of personal authenticity and meaningfulness, then there is another set of debates that tries to connect civic involvement with well-being. Robert Putnam's extensively debated (2000) thesis is that it matters greatly to our shared sense of well-being whether communities are able to connect with one another through a variety of civic associations. The problem is that since the 1960s and the rise of the home-centred and communally disconnected lifestyles, civic organisations have gone into decline. Socially disconnected people who have few friends and ties to the community in which they live are less likely to do well at school and more likely to suffer from psychological problems and low self-esteem. This dangerous trend Putnam says has a multitude of causes which includes the increased number of hours people are expected to work, the expanded numbers of women in the labour market and of course the number of hours people spend in an isolated interaction with technology. Educational institutions (irrespective of social class and a number of other sociological factors) that operate in areas where people have relatively high levels of civic and community engagement will experience lower behavioural problems and higher levels of parental support. While Putnam's work has been criticised for its crudity and for overstating the evidence of civic decline he does seem to have a point (Kenny 2004; Elliott and Lemert

2006). Yet his proposals for reversing these features (including part-time hours, civic education and renewed forms of urban design) do seem worthy if also somewhat weak given the sheer scale of the problem described. Indeed, if my arguments have been followed thus far the attempt to revive more communal forms of involvement is unlikely to find much success unless politics finds a way of both restraining the capitalist spectacle and seeking to find new and creative ways to reconnect people with one another and civic institutions. This would require a renewed democratic politics that not only sought to foster a different politics within schools, but that also placed a break upon some of the powerful features of capitalist modernity, including fewer hours spent working and in individualised consumption, increasing income equality, reversing the decline of neighbourhoods, and introducing slower, more convivial forms of living and more places where we can mix with people both alike and unlike ourselves. We should not underestimate just how hard this will be to achieve, and yet nor should we pessimistically conclude that it is beyond the realms of possibility.

As bell hooks (2000a) has argued, neoliberalism has encouraged both consumerism and societies built upon increasing class polarisation. This has meant that the 'American dream', despite class divisions, offers a vision to both rich and poor alike which suggests that a happy life is a consuming life. Much contemporary celebrity culture an induces an identification with the wealthy and privileged classes whereas the poor are seen as moral failures. This is a society where even the well-off or privileged have a sense of something 'lacking'. The consequence here is that the poor and working-class populations are encouraged to gain status through consumption rather than by campaigning against greed or injustice. These features perhaps become even more troubling if we consider the extent to which children's culture has become a commercial culture.

Children's culture and the spectacle

There has been growing interest in how children are now growing up in a corporatised and market-driven culture that is historically unprecedented. However, the extent to which commercial forms of culture turn children into passive unthinking consumers and whether consumer culture actually offers children a place of exploration, autonomy and pleasure, possibly in ways that parents don't always approve, are matters of some controversy. This argument within cultural and media studies has been going on for some time and is unlikely to end in a consensus. While this is not the place to rehearse this debate it inevitably has implications for the dominant ways in which we understand the culture of the capitalist spectacle (Stevenson 2001). For instance, whereas Kellner (2003) views much of the cultural production associated with popular music as promoting an obsession with the body and with image rather than with more substantial political positions, Fiske (1989), on the other hand, argues that the use of popular media cannot be proscribed without investigating the often creative ways that audiences make sense of popular media cultures. In this reading, the idea of the society of the spectacle and the extent to which it converts us into consumers is potentially overstated. However, many of these debates often fail to produce a necessarily historical perspective. Children's culture has indeed been transformed through the development of commercial media strategies that are keen to sell toys, magazines and other 'spin offs'. In the British context public broadcasting has rapidly expanded its coverage of children's television and, while it seeks to present an 'innocent' image to parents, programmes are used to sell toys and other commercial goods. In the United States, radical educationalist Henry Giroux (1999) has argued that large corporations like Disney are a threat to civic values and more democratic identities. What might to many parents look like harmless entertainment is actually a concerted attempt to both commodify the desires and tastes of children and deny wider understandings of justice, history and the possibility of critique.

Under corporate domination cherished values like democracy become the freedom to consume. In this respect corporations promote selfish individualism and consumerism. The aggressive marketisation of children severely limits the range of discourses, concepts and ideas that seem to be suitable for children. Hence children's learning in a capitalist-driven society is not simply about what goes on in the classroom and interactions with carers but is also hugely shaped by the interests and imperatives of commercial mediums. For instance, it has recently been estimated that 70 per cent of British three-year-olds are able to recognise the McDonald's symbol whereas about half will know their surname (Compass 2007). This is a fairly typical finding in a society which is becoming increasingly commercialised and subject to the pressures of the spectacle. The neoliberal solution to the increasing marketisation of children's culture, to put it crudely, is simply to blame the parents. Here there is a call to reinstate authority (usually male) in the home and to question the value of so-called liberal or permissive parenting in the private realm. The home is imagined as potentially acting as a barrier against some of the excesses of a culture increasingly driven by a liberalised market. Evidently this response moves the emphasis away from questions of regulation and corporate responsibility and ends up seeking to pathologise parents who are unable to order and discipline the home (Kapur 1999).

However, some of Ellen Seiter's (1999) research attempts to question some of the assumptions embedded in the research viewed thus far. Missing from the arguments about blanket consumerism is the ability of different social classes to shield themselves from the effects of commercial culture. Seiter's research uncovers the ways middle-class parents use their economic and symbolic capital to keep commercial culture at arm's length and how working-class parents seemingly have a more 'relaxed' attitude towards children's commercial pleasures. In particular she suggests that the fact that many children become experts in popular culture is often experienced by parents as threatening. Seiter suggests that the middle classes should worry less about the 'effects' of commercial popular culture and put greater effort into seeking to improve the education of working-class youngsters. The effect of this study is to turn middle-class parents into a group seeking to pass on educational advantages while distinguishing themselves from the lower classes. However, we could equally interpret Seiter's research as suggesting that it is the lack of economic and cultural capital available to working-class parents that makes it difficult for them to shield their children from corporate concerns. Evidently young people gain a great deal in terms of a sense of identity and pleasure from commercial culture, but equally we need to remind ourselves of the main imperatives behind its distribution and production. The argument here is not for educators and parents to ban or seek to crudely isolate themselves from popular culture, but rather that we need to take account of the dominant interests that shape much popular culture, and think of more imaginative ways in which children might become democratically involved in the discussion surrounding popular culture.

Education, Bourdieu and class

The question of social class is central to the ways in which we understand the debate concerning the commercialisation of children's culture and education. In this respect, the French sociologist Pierre Bourdieu (1984) provides a key insight into what he calls the arbitrariness of culture. By this he means that there is no intrinsic reason why upper-class tastes, aesthetic preferences and cultural judgements should be taken as indicative of 'high' culture. A love of abstract art, classical music and other cultural styles functions as a form of social distinction. What a society takes to be innovative, creative and culturally valuable is largely determined by the social structure. Hence apparently disinterested practices like an appreciation of fine wine, visiting art galleries or indeed preferring Stravinsky over Chopin are used to gain what Bourdieu calls cultural capital.

For Bourdieu the social world is structured by different forms of capital that can be accumulated, gained and lost in a number of different social fields. While fields are the site of constant social struggle they are also the places that distribute and determine access to different kinds of capital. Economists and crude Marxists are mistaken in that they can only account for a narrow set of motivations that will immediately lead to the pursuit of money and wealth (economic capital). Such a definition of capital ultimately colludes with artists and intellectuals who have sought to mystify their practices by presenting them as the pure pursuit of either art or knowledge. Indeed Bourdieu's (1996) work traces the historical emergence of a bohemian view of art that opposed both the industrial bourgeoisie and so-called bourgeois art while developing an aristocratic attitude towards consumption and sexuality. In other words, economists are mistaken in the extent to which they can only recognise economic forms of capital as opposed to the forms of status or capital that can be the result of adopting a particular lifestyle.

99

Cultural capital in Bourdieu's (2004) analysis can exist within three forms. The first form of cultural capital exists within an embodied state or in what Bourdieu also describes as the habitus. The habitus is a set of cultural dispositions passed on through the family that become literally second nature. These embodied dispositions are a way of speaking, standing, walking, thinking and feeling. The habitus is largely structured through the opposition of different cultural characteristics found in different social classes. While it can become transformed by entering into a different field or more generally through social mobility it situates the body in ways that are largely unconscious but relatively durable. By virtue of the habitus individuals become predisposed towards certain cultural preferences and tastes. Hence it makes a good deal of sense to talk of consumer lifestyles in terms of both cultural and economic capital. Those who are able to define taste, vulgarity and discernment are able to impose these definitions on subordinate groups. For Bourdieu (1984) it was the new *petit bourgeoisie* (school teachers, artists, academics, etc.) whose aesthetic lifestyles meant that they became the new arbiters of good taste. Taste was determined by those who are high in cultural rather than economic capital. The new cultural bourgeoisie were able to distinguish themselves from industrialists (high in economic but low in cultural capital) and the working class (low in both economic and cultural capital) by seeking to expand the autonomy of the cultural field. Whereas the transmission of cultural capital through the body is the most efficient given its hereditary nature, it can also be reproduced through material objects. Cultural capital can exist in an objectified state through art collections, musical instruments, objects of art and jewellery. We can also talk of cultural capital in a third sense, the institutional confirming of educational qualifications. This confers on the holder a legally guaranteed amount of cultural respect and level of cultural competence. These three forms of cultural capital can of course all be converted into economic capital. In this sense Bourdieu is able to speak of symbolic as well as material profits due to its relative scarcity, from which its holders are able to benefit. In addition to economic and cultural capital we can also talk of social capital. Social capital depends upon the networks and connections that an individual is able to maintain.

Pierre Bourdieu and Jean-Claude Passeron (1977) study into the functioning of the education system discovered that working-class people tend to exclude themselves from the education system as they recognise that they do not have the appropriate levels of cultural capital. Elsewhere, Bourdieu and Darbel (1991) sought to link these concerns to the cultural capital required to visit a museum or art gallery. These institutions were chosen as they are often (although not always) free at the point of access and emphasise a form of cultural self-exclusion. The study concluded that the best predictor of whether or not someone was likely to attend a formal gallery or exhibition was family background and educational qualifications. Working-class people who lack the necessary cultural capital to make works of art meaningful are forced to make sense of them through more restricted repertoires of interpretation. Working-class visitors are 'condemned to see works of art in their phenomenal state, in other words as simple objects' (Bourdieu and Darbel 1991: 45). Those without the appropriate cultural capital complained of feeling out of place and were in constant fear of revealing their lack of knowledge. Further, they also displayed most interest in art that had an obvious social function (such as furniture). This lack of affinity with the world of art was compounded by educational institutions that only sought to transmit a limited understanding of artistic works. Familiarity with a wide range of artistic and aesthetic practices was more often transmitted by the bourgeois family. For Bourdieu a cultural democracy (or in our case cultural citizenship) can only be achieved by educational institutions seeking to make up for the lack of cultural capital available within the working-class family. Cultural equality for Bourdieu cannot be sought by either celebrating a working-class populism or by leaving artistic taste to the private discernment of individuals. Unless educational resources make some attempt to reverse the flow of cultural capital transmitted in the home the end result will be enhanced forms of cultural inequality. Populist strategies that either seek to convert working-class culture into the curriculum or try to create more opportunities for working-class children to visit galleries are unlikely to have much effect. The question is not so much one of crude populism, rather of how the transmission of aesthetic taste proceeds by habit, learning and exercise. Bourdieu and Darbel (1991) powerfully argue that the only way to short-circuit assumptions of working-class barbarism is to disrupt the idea that taste is naturally rather than socially reproduced. An inclusive cultural citizenship requires an intensification of the presence of learning institutions within working-class people's cultural lives.

More recently other sociologists have sought to develop Bourdieu's writing on education by attempting to investigate the ways in which the education system reproduces a class society. Much of this work has adopted different methods to those employed by Bourdieu who has mainly relied upon large-scale social surveys and been more explicitly concerned with investigating the 'lived' nature of class (Skeggs 1997). Many of these studies articulate the powerful affective dimensions of class and look at how the experience of the education system for many young working-class people can become a site of everyday humiliation (Reay 2005). Here the education system stands accused of inflicting upon young working-class people a sense of inferiority for not having the appropriate cultural capital. Terms like 'cleverness' or 'brightness' have class-specific uses. Further, those relatively rare working-class students who do progress in the education system are plagued by feelings of self-doubt, of being out of place and of not belonging. Indeed, many working-class people in higher education tend to choose 'local' colleges of higher education not simply because of economic reasons, but because they seem safer and there is less chance of being 'found out' (Reay 2004). In contrast, the middle classes are able to use their economic and cultural capital to pass on educational opportunities to their children (Vincent and Ball 2007). The child in middle-class circles is often viewed as a 'project' to be developed and improved by making sure they have access to a number of learning experiences and a variety of after-school activities. This investment in the cultural capital of children is clearly a middle-class privilege which is unavailable to the working classes. Here, to know what is 'good' demands both the capacity to be able to invest in the self as well as the ability to display the right kind of taste. Middle-class children are able to exhibit the 'right' kind of cultural capital thereby making themselves attractive to the 'good' schools. In this respect parenting involves marching children from one activity to the next and intensifying their supervision. If middle-class families ensure that their children are able to participate in a variety of musical, sporting and other cultural activities the working class tend to see their children as displaying a more 'fixed' set of characteristics (Reay and Ball 1997). In middle-class life parents spend a considerable amount of time seeking to 'equip' their children to compete in increasingly unequal societies, whilst many working-class children 'give up' on account of the extent to which the system is stacked against them.

The preceding arguments reaffirm the extent to which the field of education is actively involved in the reproduction of inequality in an increasingly competitive and class divided society. Such perspectives, as I hope I have demonstrated, are crucial if we are to think about the ways in which society might become more equal. However, as Henry Giroux (1983) has remarked, structural and functionalist accounts of education tend to emphasise the extent to which it operates in the interests of dominant social groups. What is often missing from these perspectives is how education might be transformed to make it both more democratic and in keeping with ideas of the common good. Such views while important tend to neglect the extent to which education and schooling have the potential to act as places of transformation and critique. As Nicholas Garnham and Raymond Williams (1986: 130) argue, sometimes Bourdieu (and certain of his followers) have a tendency to overstate the extent to which culture is simply a site of reproduction, thereby also understating 'opportunities for real innovation in the social structure'. In addition Garnham (1993) has questioned the extent to which Bourdieu's work can be said to articulate a political project. A problem arises if education is simply a space which reproduces the symbolic power and cultural preferences of the dominant class and leaves little room for alternative or more democratically motivated visions. It is probable that any progressive movement for change is likely to trade upon the cultural power of the middle class, but this should not be allowed to erase the difference between a democratically inspired project that aims at the common good and one that seeks to press for the neoliberal dominance of capital. Further, we might also be concerned about the extent to which Bourdieu's work comes close to reproducing a working-class deprivation thesis. Schooling for working-class people seems to focus on overcoming their lack of cultural capital. This then seems to cancel any possibility of more dialogic or indeed democratically involved forms of education that try to take the interests and capacities of the student seriously.

Beverley Skeggs (2004) has highlighted to how the rise of neoliberalism has partially displaced these concerns. The neoliberal subject assumed by many of the government reforms in education is overwhelmingly middle class. The idea of the choosing and self-managed subject that is central to the marketisation of education is dependent upon middle-class forms of cultural capital. Correspondingly the working classes are seen as unruly and lacking in 'educated' taste. In an increasingly global society it is the middle classes who are able to articulate their cosmopolitan tastes as legitimate with the working classes occupying the place of the Other. Class struggle in this reading is a form of cultural struggle over definitions of taste and legitimacy. However, critical work also needs to articulate a vision beyond the ways in which culture becomes classified and to engage in a democratic politics that seeks to articulate an idea of the common good. Neoliberalism is not principally concerned with questions of taste but can be more accurately represented as a project that is deeply hostile to democracy as it seeks to erode shared civic values and places of experimentation for a culture that is principally concerned with the accumulation of capital. Neoliberalism in the sphere of education has sought to replace a shared culture of questioning with one including training and spaces of reflection and learning with an entrepreneurial ethos. This of course is not to underestimate the extent to which neoliberalism also trades upon class divisions which will inevitably favour those in positions of cultural power. However, as some of Bourdieu's later (2003) writing seems to suggest, we also need to be aware of the extent to which its overwhelmingly instrumental focus also downgrades middle-class professions like teaching. These questions aside, studies inspired by Bourdieu are crucial in the extent to which they move the debate about schooling away from economic inequality towards social and cultural inequality. This connects with the liberal socialist tradition I am trying to defend that emphasises the importance of working-class children gaining access to a broad range of cultural and artistic experience beyond the narrow confines of vocationalism. The experience of inequality itself acts as a barrier to many working-class children, disabling them from expanding their repertoires and engaging in cultural experiences outside the confines of their class backgrounds. In the next section, I aim to explore the ways in which a neoliberal agenda has increasingly led to the instrumentalisation of education and learning.

Education, Foucault and technical reason

If some critics are concerned that education in the society of the spectacle helps foster a culture of hedonism and consumption rather than responsibility, and as we have just seen class division, then others are similarly concerned that education itself is being increasingly governed by a technical form of rationality. In a world where schools and individual children are set explicit targets that are then measured by a battery of bureaucrats and statistical experts, there is a growing anxiety that education is seen to have little value in itself. The knowledge economy of the twenty-first century requires workers with high levels of educational attainment if it is to remain competitive in the face of global competition. Here education becomes less about learning and more about an audit culture producing league tables and measuring the performance of institutions, schools, teachers and children (Ball 2004; Fielding 2006). If, as Darder and Miron (2006) argue, the new business agenda in schools is being captured by narrow agendas of standardised testing then it would seem anything not measured by these scores is being dismissed as unimportant. Concerns about civic identities or indeed child development are ultimately reduced to ways to improve test scores. Learning in this rubric is defined by teachers' (or, as a New Labour policy document called them, 'curriculum deliverers') ability to prepare firmly packed formation that must be absorbed by students in order to pass standardised tests.

Michel Foucault was the educational sociologist generally held to have best understood the dehumanising effect of these and similar processes. Foucault argued that liberal ideals of education that were based upon the autonomy of the individual had failed to take account of the more specific practices that had helped constitute education in the modern era. Education, rather than being based upon lofty liberal ideals, was actually organised through specific technologies of domination. Foucault (1977) noted the extent to which education, punishment regimes and prisons, hospitals and other institutions all resembled one another. These institutions did not so much spell the freedom of the individual but were to be understood through the arrival of a new form of power. Education was constituted less through the development of rational freedoms, as many of the Enlightenment philosophers had argued, more by being connected to the rise of the disciplinary society. The organisation of classrooms in this respect sought to create the conditions for an operation of power that did less to induce rational reflection and more to shape behaviour.

According to James D. Marshall (1996: 111), Foucault demonstrated the extent to which the practice of education was 'concerned with defining and controlling the conduct of individuals, submitting them through the exercise of power to certain ends so as to lead useful, docile and practical lives'. Disciplinary power in the context of education will organise bodies into specific years, timetables, ability streams and develop certain skills and applications rather than others. More specifically, power will work on the body through processes of hierarchical judgement and observation, the operation of micro-penalties that punish lateness, a lack of attention or poor behaviour and other aspects of a non-conformity to the rules of the institution. One of the main ways the disciplinary society operates is through the rewarding of 'good' behaviour and the punishing of bad behaviour through exclusion or poor marks. Ultimately, Foucault was pointing here to the extent to which educational practice rather than the Enlightenment ideal of schooling was normalising by rewarding conformity to externally imposed rules. Finally, the examination is another means of disciplinary control through which pupils are invited to judge their 'performance' against others. All of these disciplinary mechanisms are focused upon the individual rather than the collective that in turn helps convert each student into a case or set of documents that will monitor and scrutinise the 'progress' of that student. For Foucault, disciplinary power operated by introducing a regime of monitoring and internalised self-surveillance. Foucault's analysis of education pointed to weaknesses within traditional liberal ideals of education that failed to see the ways in which power operated in more micro-settings. The disciplinary society was left under-theorised by liberal ideals of the good society that actually served to mask the ways in which power operated within institutions. The idea of a liberal education served to conceal the ways whereby education can be constituted through disciplinary practice.

Foucault was recommending that we give up on liberal ideals where individuals can become increasingly autonomous through their education. The argument being suggested here is that disciplinary society actually fashions docile and conforming human beings through the threat of exclusion and the careful monitoring of behaviour. In this respect, Foucault offers an important corrective to some of the idealism of liberal notions of education. Yet Foucault did not outline a more emancipatory education. This was because he was seeking to describe and outline the ways in which power and knowledge could work within a disciplinary society, not point to a utopian transformation. However, his later work did try to highlight certain 'technologies of the self' that suggested ways in which individuals could be said to experiment upon themselves. Here Foucault (1984a) argued that rather than seeking to define ourselves in our essence (as we might 'become' many things) we are invited less to 'know the self' and more to 'care for the self'. If the desire to 'know the self' had ended with the rise of the disciplinary society that sought to regulate and control the body through disciplinary institutional procedures, then the idea of 'caring for the self' is not so much a matter of technical know-how and rather one of pleasure and a more poetic sensibility. Here the Enlightenment should be viewed as a particular event located at a certain point in the development of European societies. Rather than follow Kant and define human subjects as rational beings, Foucault (1984b) adopted the poet Baudelaire and suggested we should give up all talk of an innate human nature and seek to experiment with the self. There was no utopian desire to push society beyond the disciplinary society although this would inevitably invite resistance as well as the possibility of a new ethics of the self. Here Foucault was anxious that the invitation to 'care for the self' may become a new set of disciplinary rules. As Edward Said (1988) commented, Foucault was less interested in how 'the rules' could be changed and more with developing an ethics of otherness that resisted domestication. The danger here of course is that this leads to the politics of the permanent margin.

Foucault's writing inevitably offers a particular challenge for liberal ideals of education. However, despite the provocative nature of his work, I am unconvinced of the extent to which this could be said to have eclipsed this particular tradition. Charles Taylor (1989a: 489) argues that Foucault's ethics of the self is caught in the process of reconstructing itself in an 'utterly self-related freedom'. Despite Foucault's many defenders his argument fails to offer an idea of what the good (or simply better society) might be and his view of the self seems entirely cut off from any sense of an intersubjective tension with the other. Here I would say that the objection that education is increasingly subjected to a form of technical rationality is hard to sustain outside of an idea of what education might become or should be. For all of Foucault's brilliance in warning against the blind spots of liberal discourse he confused the need for normative values with the dangers of normalisation (Eagleton 2003). In this respect, Foucault failed to outline what a more democratic pedagogy might look like and how education is inevitably involved in human relationships. That deep dangers to the 'humanity' of educational relationships will surface should these be reduced to technical exercises involved in the setting of 'targets' is obvious. However, that we are unable to argue against such features unless we can propose alternative models and frameworks for education seems to escape Foucault and his followers. We might agree that more democratic models of education do not so much address the permanent capacities of the subject as they are dependent upon the development of a particular tradition of thinking. However, this need not either lead to a form of relativism where we cannot judge some societies or education systems better in terms of the ideals that are articulated. That there are no neutral or impersonal standards does not mean there are no beliefs that cannot be justified by appealing to certain traditions and historical and cultural standards (MacIntyre 1998).

Arguably what Foucault did describe was how lofty educational ideals can co-exist with disciplinary practices (Donald 1992). This does not of course mean that the ideals are themselves entirely bankrupt, but rather that we need to think more carefully about the relationship between educational values and the domains of practice. What is also missing from Foucault's writing is a concern with how the normative ideals of democracy that have a long history within Western modernity might be more effectively mobilised in different educational contexts. As we have seen in previous chapters, a democratic education is actually dependent upon rules and procedures that seek to transform the relationship between the educational institution, the teacher/lecturer, and the student. A more democratic education does potentially allow for the expression of human qualities that are different from those defined by more authoritarian forms of education. On this I remain unconvinced that we can simply give up 'metaphysical' discussions of what indeed constitutes 'the human', and at this point I now want to turn to Martin Buber whose work seeks to ground a more arguably emancipatory vision of what education might mean.

Martin Buber: a dialogic education

If we look at the work of Martin Buber (1947) arguably a different educational logic becomes possible, one that resists the language of instrumentality while arguing that the self learns through its relations with others. For Buber we only became truly human once we entered into a dialogic relationship with the other. Hence dialogue was not the means to realising a more demo-cratic form of education, but was the central purpose of human existence (Sidorkin 1999). Buber remains not just a significant philosopher of educa-tion he was also a significant religious figure, being centrally concerned with the Zionist movement in the early part of the twentieth century. It was not until after the First World War that he looked towards less overtly spiritual and more worldly concerns. Buber's philosophical interest in the centrality of dialogue seems to have been sparked by the visit of a young man seeking spiritual guidance (Friedman 1982). As a major religious figure associated with Jewish Hasidism, this event was not unusual; however, Buber reported that during this mystical phase of his life he was somewhat removed from reality and failed to open himself and be receptive to the young man. Buber was to hear of his death in the war a few weeks later, and while the incident stopped short of his suicide he felt a deep responsibility for the young man's sense of despair. This incident it seems strengthened his sense of the impor-tance of human dialogue.

It was during this period that Buber wrote his philosophical classic *I and Thou*. Early in the text (1970: 69) he argues that 'in the beginning is the relation'. For the human infant this is not simply a way of making sure their biological needs are met but that as humans we become ourselves by relating to other beings. The relationship between an I and a You or an I and a Thou means that human beings are creatures not of the solitary I, as has been presumed by much of Western philosophy from Descrates onwards, but beings who from our first hours on the planet require interrelatedness (Adams 2007). This view of the human subject has a close family relation-ship with some traditions within psychotherapy, and more specifically object relations. Sue Gerhardt (2004) has recently merged much of the psychotherapeutic and scientific information in an account that argues that the quality of our earliest interactions with our main carers as human infants goes some way towards forming us as people as well as the shape of our brains. The quality of our interactions seemingly shapes our levels of stress and happiness as well as our shared capacities to be able to relate pleasurably to other people. Notably our capacity to relate and care for the Other has also played an important role in helping to form some of the feminist literature in respect of the importance of care relationships (Ruddick 1989). These features emphasise that when building an idea of education and the good society a great deal will depend upon how we see the human subject.

Buber's poetic masterpiece makes an important distinction between interrelationships based upon I–Thou and I–It. I–Thou relationships are primarily concerned with a sense of mutuality, authenticity and directness in relation to the other. On the other hand, I–It relations are more instru-mental and turn our relations with the other into those between a subject and object. The worlds of I–Thou and I–It are separate but it is not possible to live exclusively in one sphere. Yet in our relations with nature, other people, and more spiritual relations Buber is deeply concerned with our capacity for different kinds of human relatedness. He writes (1970: 62): 'The basic word I-You can be spoken only with one's whole being. The concentration and fusion into a whole being can never be accomplished by me, can never be accomplished without me. I require a You to become; becoming I, I say You'. Human beings are creatures who are capable of forming loving, caring and reciprocal relations with the Other, and of also forming more manipulative and objectifying relations. This is less an essentialist account of human nature than one which talks about the twofold nature of the self. That we are dialogic creatures was to have important implications for Buber's writing on education.

For Buber (1947) children needed to be educated less in how to become isolated individuals and more in how to be able to relate to the other. This is an important corrective to the liberal imagination that focuses upon the rationality or creativity of an individual irrespective of her relations or ties with the other. As Buber wrote (1947: 107) 'independence is a footbridge, not a dwelling place'. For him the opposite of traditional forms of learning was not individual freedom but came through more explicitly relational forms of education. Simply to assert that education is about freedom will end in a fragmented society where we need to learn how to relate to and be responsible for the Other. The dialogic relation means not only our ability to talk but equally our capacity to listen and where appropriate to become silent. Pedagogic relations are intrinsically relational and if these become too one-sided they lose their balance. This of course does not mean that they are symmetrical relations as where the educator can experience the pupil learning this process is not easily reversible. Further, it is likely that the necessary authority of the educator will be a source of ambivalence that he or she must learn to observe. An important part of this authoritative relationship is that the experienced educator has to consider what the student needs in order to grow. As an educator does this, he or she will inevitably be thrown back on what they are able to give and what they cannot provide. In other words, the educative relationship is profoundly concerned with how the educator learns about his or her own sense of limits. For Buber (1947: 123) education had to be concerned with 'the person as a whole, both in the actuality in the way that he lives before you now and in his possibilities, what he can become'. All education is concerned with the character of both the educator and the pupil. This is not a matter of seeking to legislate for the way a student 'should' be as this is likely to resisted. Instead the educator needs to remember that he or she is likely to be one influence among many and thus maintain a sense of humility. For Buber (1947: 125): 'Only in his whole being, in all his spontaneity can the educator truly affect the whole being of his pupil. For educating characters you do not need a moral genius, but you do need a man who is wholly alive and able to communicate himself directly to his fellow beings'. An educative relationship is less about instruction and more about the ability to be able to build trusting human relationships. The educator needs to be able to handle a considerable amount of ambivalence while also being able to provide 'healing ointment for the heart' (Buber 1947: 128). Like Freire, Buber affirmed the importance of a sense of care for the other in pedagogic relationships. Whereas neoliberal initiatives in education seek to emphasise a technocratic language of measurable outcomes, results and training, more democratically inspired initiatives inevitably trade upon the capacity to be able to learn from the Other in relationships that are authoritative rather than authoritarian. Further, while Buber remains a marginal figure within the liberal socialist tradition he deserves to be reappropriated. Unlike many other educational writers he emphasised the virtues of human relatedness and the responsibility of the educator for the development of students: this pushed the argument beyond the need either to pass on cultural capital or to enhance more technocratic forms of competence.

The good society and educated politics

An increasingly individualised society will find it difficult to admit to notions such as the common good or the good society. The society of the consumer spectacle tends to be immediate and to offer a view of the good life as geared towards consumption, egoism and individual choice. In such a society there is no common good, just individuals free to define their own notion of the good and external rules of behaviour that are required to regulate our actions. In the liberal imagination it is individual autonomy that best preserves freedom and the external laws that ensure moral behaviour. The problem with this formulation is that it ultimately leads to a form of relativism where we are unable to judge what we mean by a good education (or it is simply left for the individual to choose) and it further allows for the domination of corporate definitions of culture. If the individual is simply free to choose what is best for them without any normative underpinnings then such a situation is bound to favour those who have the most power to shape and influence our common environment. However, if the way in which we understand 'the good' is more connected to particular historical and political traditions such a view arguably changes the intellectual landscape. For example, rather than making the individual a sovereign chooser, how does this situation change if we start not from abstract rationality, but from the desire of each of us to live democratic and virtuous lives in a particular social and cultural context? As environmental educator David Orr (1994: 12) argues, 'the planet does not require any more successful people'. By 'success' he means citizens who feel compelled to live a life of relentless upward mobility and hyper-consumption. In this vision education is simply a means of accumulating knowledge and expertise. Indeed since the arrival of the Internet this has expanded the vast amount of up-to-date information that I have at my fingertips, and we have also seen the increasing specialisation of knowledge into smaller sub-areas. There would it seems be no subject area so specialised that it would be unable to demand its own journal or area of 'expert' study. Yet, as Mary Midgley (1989) points out, perhaps what we require is not so much knowledge but wisdom. Wisdom is less about what we 'know' and more about how we might live. Education in an increasingly global and interconnected age encompasses how we seek to live together as well as how we might do so while leading a good and ethical life. There are of course likely to be many different ways to answer this question, but this suggests that education has to become more than simply giving training in an academic or vocational specialism. We need to spend our lives continually asking two questions: what is the right way to live and what is it good to become?

Here we are likely to need to be guided by, as well as transcend, our common traditions. If in the 1960s it was commonly feared that individuals were being reduced to being cogs in a gigantic machine, radical educators' emphasis was placed upon individual freedom, criticism and happiness. A.S. Neil (1962), founder of the Summerhill school, emphasised the need to break away from authoritarian schooling and uphold the right of the individual to follow their own unique creative path. Without seeking to deny individuals' need to be able to creatively follow their own interests and passions, perhaps in the midst of our information and consumerist-driven society what is now required is somewhat different. If the idea of education as a form of authoritarian training is still with us I do not think the ethical question of 'how we are to live' can be adequately answered by just emphasising autonomy. If the 1960s feared rigid conformity then our society is explicitly concerned with the production of mobile and flexible people in the face of uncertainty. As Zygmunt Bauman (2005) has emphasised, it is the fragmentation of human lives, the gradual disappearance of social state and the need to be constantly on the move that now shape the dominant ethos of our society. Bauman's point is that education under the sign of consumerism is more likely to value flexibility than the step-by-step learning of particular disciplines. Education and knowledge using this set of descriptions have to make an immediate impact, be consumable and be quickly digested – and perhaps just as quickly be forgotten. What is then feared in a world where citizens and consumers are constantly on the move is being left behind and rendered obsolete.

The erosion of old-style communities of obligation and the rapid individualisation of society have meant that as with consumerism this is a world that emphasises constant change. If education in the past declared that to transform yourself was a slow process that involved the accumulation of knowledge before moving onto the next stage what is promised, today by a consumer culture is instant transformation. The act of buying a product is often associated with the thrill of becoming someone new without having to wait. Education under the sign of the spectacle seeks to advertise itself to prospective students not as a learning experience but more in terms of the market worth of the particular brand on offer. In an age of mobility, atomisation and image it is becoming increasingly difficult for young people to build a coherent narrative of self and an understanding of the histories of their communities and intellectual traditions. If through education citizens are to build a more authentic sense of self then it will need to become a place not only of individual realisation but also, as we have seen, of dialogic encounter and responsibility to the wider community. Education is charged with linking together a relatively egalitarian ethos, a respect for difference and an appreciation of our rights, as well as a sense of responsibility. These broader questions of citizenship can of course only take root in a culture that values the practice of education. In a short-term and disposable society there must be spaces where the young can discuss what it means to live a good and meaningful life and the kinds of people they wish to become. The fragmented world of image and short-term advantage needs to recover the prospect of asking itself, 'How shall we live?' These educative spaces are necessary if we are to encourage a reflection on those questions the domi-nant consumer society seeks to sideline. Here my concern is that the society of the spectacle is instrumental, has little that is substantial to contribute on matters of pedagogy, and deepens contemporary feelings of atomisation and disconnection from any wider sense of purpose. These issues can only be dealt with by formulating an alternative educational ethic in a way that is poorly grounded in both Bourdieu and Foucault, but as we have seen was at least partially grasped by Martin Buber. The problem with Buber is that his argument was never really developed into an alternative vision of an education for a democratic society. He was, however, very perceptive about the intersubjective dynamics of teaching and learning. Further, it is noticeable that his writings talk about dialogue mostly in terms of face-to-face interaction. While these are still important arguments we would need to recognise that within the postmodern knowledge economy much interac-tion is mediated by computers (Kellner 2000, 2003). If an alternative edu-cational ethic is to be developed it could only be done so by taking account of the rise of technological forms of communication (Moutsios 2008). I now wish to explore these features further.

Lyotard, postmodernism and education

Jean-François Lyotard's (1979) definition of the 'postmodern condition' is worth revisiting in the context of recent debates about the knowl-edge economy. In his terms (1979: xxiii) modernism was a meta-discourse that sought to legitimise itself in respect of a grand-narrative such as reason or emancipation. We can argue that we are living in a post-modern society in the extent to which we are currently encountering a crisis of these very narratives. The collapse of the meta-narratives of sci-ence, Marxism or other features is a by-product of the development of knowledge and an enhanced awareness of the plurality and diversity of lan-guage games. This development and awareness alters the status of knowl-edge within contemporary societies. In the context of a technological and knowledge-driven society knowledge is produced less for its own sake or for an insight into 'the truth' and more because it is useful. In the context of the development of the economy, knowledge is increasingly an important component in the expansion of production and has become as vital as access to raw materials or cheap labour. As the state grows less powerful what is then key is the production of knowledge and its ability to play a part in the development of multinationals, computerisation and the performativity of the system. In this re-definition of knowledge we can see a breakdown in the older distinctions between instrumental and critical knowledge. What becomes significant is who has access to knowledge outside of corporate and political leaders and experts, and how this is utilised in practice. In this situation it is not access to critical perspectives that is important but knowledge as a form of practice in relation to a number of practical questions. Knowledge in this new society becomes less about discovering its essence or thinking of new possible worlds, and more about competence. As knowledge loses its role in providing grand narratives of progress or decline it gains a new role in a plurality of language games and becomes increasingly pragmatic and geared to the continued performance of the system.

The collapse of the hierarchies of knowledge legitimated by industrialism and imperialism has ushered in a greater awareness of and attentiveness towards local language games. These 'networks of inquiry' lead to a breakdown not simply in the role of knowledge as a means of legitimating systems of inquiry but also in the boundaries between different areas of knowledge (Lyotard 1979: 39). If science can no longer guarantee 'progress' it has also asked questions about the boundaries, say, between machines, animals and humans. New areas of inquiry disappear whereas others emerge as knowledge increasingly questions its ability to legitimate itself and the boundaries between different areas of inquiry. There is, then, no universal meta-language that is able to regulate the production of other forms of knowledge; instead there is simply a diversity of language games. This ushers in a new pragmatism where each discipline or sub-discipline evolves its own languages and means of pragmatically pursuing its interests. These language games are more attuned to making efficient and effective moves in terms of their own rules of the game than they are to announcing universal truths. Yet these games do not operate on an equal footing, with capitalism funding the research best able to make an efficient impact that in turn helps facilitate the corporate norms being input into educational institutions. As Lyotard (1979: 46) argues, 'the goal is no longer truth, but performativity – that is, the best possible input/output equation'.

This redefinition of knowledge has implications for the transmission of knowledge or education. The knowledge economy increasingly demands certain skills, especially at the middle-management level, and it is the job of the university to make sure these are transmitted. Notably, as the post-industrial economy grows it will require higher education to 'create skills, and no longer ideals' (Lyotard 1979: 48). Learning, Lyotard predicts, will increasingly be driven by a number of pragmatic features that will train people in the appropriate skills sets while also developing increasingly instrumental agendas. There is no role for a democratic or civic university in the future as higher education will become focused on training the managers and computer operatives of the future. Lyotard envisages one where universities no longer teach students en masse but increasingly serve 'à la carte' knowledge to those already working on seeking to update their skills for promotion (1979: 49). Further, there is likely to be a decline in the experimentation available within education as the system has to orientate itself more pragmatically towards the development of useful knowledge. Lyotard at this point in the analysis imagines the university classrooms of the future where lecturers have been replaced by computers, learning aids and other technological features. This would not necessarily mean a decline in the quality of pedagogy, but 'students would still have to be taught something: not contents, but how to use terminals' (1979: 50). Indeed, it is only in the context of the assumptions of emancipatory theory, Lyotard reasons, that these and other proposals become objectionable. In such an environment what matters is not that something is 'true' but that it can be put to 'use', is 'efficient', and be 'sold'. This is knowledge without illusions that requires 'the renunciation of fables; it demands clear minds and cold wills' (1979: 62).

For Lyotard any move to close the plurality of language games and re-order them under a new meta-discourse should be regarded as a form of totalitarian control. Postmodernity represents not only the exhaustion of modernity, but also a proliferation of language games that are propagated largely to serve the interests of commerce rather than the state. As we grow increasingly sceptical about emancipation pedagogy, education is centred on the pragmatic development of skills sets and transferable knowledge. In the information society, as the state goes into decline so too will the narratives and any hopes of liberation as the population increasingly becomes enmeshed in computers, flexible labour markets and global competition.

There is, then, no longer any pretence of a universal language that can adjudicate between the different claims being made in a diverse language games. Enlightenment arguments based upon disinterested and rational inquiry that are able to make such judgements are rejected in favour of a heteronomous postmodern plurality. If education can no longer be legitimated in terms of bringing our minds closer to 'the truth' or 'reason' (as there are lots of 'truths' and 'reasons'), then we are asked to tolerate a plurality of narratives that are often incommensurable. It is our ability to create new local narratives as educators that is the best sign of creativity. If higher education has seen a rapid expansion in the number of specialist journals and in niche-marketed subject areas Lyotard's response to this would be to welcome the possibility of new micro-knowledges, point to their connection with a wider culture of performativity and view any attempt to judge one area as more significant than another as potentially authoritarian. The problem he misses is that such a situation could increasingly lead intellectuals into debating specialised and sometimes pointless distinctions in increasingly niche journals with little thought of their public relevance.

Lyotard is, however, worried that an emphasis upon performance could well act against the plurality of narratives on offer. Postmodernism is not a new form of conservatism as it may require us to respect and protect the incommensurable (Peters 1995). We might also point out that the collapse of grand narratives and the development of more micro-discourses and disputes represent a grand narrative. Presumably students still need to be taught about the power and historical importance of grand narratives so that they can learn to deconstruct them while using their new computer skills (Nuyen 1995)? Lyotard's agenda for education involves the fostering of a cool scepticism in educational attempts to seduce students into a belief in totalising narratives while picking up the skills they need for the global market place. Indeed, in his (1988) work he is particularly keen to argue that we should stop seeking to force cultural differences into the meta-languages of liberalism and Marxism. Again there is no 'reason', only reasons and multiple language games which should flourish without end after the collapse of grand narratives and intellectual investment by the culture of modernity (Peters 2006).

Reading Lyotard today it is hard not to be aware of how closely he maps some of the transformations that have taken over higher education. Whatever we think of the postmodern condition it is hard to argue that it does not have a certain descriptive relevance in respect of some of the dominant changes that have taken place in higher education since Lyotard produced his famous text. Bill Readings (1996), a scholar much influenced by Lyotard, argues that the university is currently caught between a world that was organised on the basis of nation-states and a more corporate global order. If the role of the university has been to preserve the elite culture of nation-states and national traditions this function has gone into decline as universities have begun to become relatively independent and increasingly globally organised bureaucracies. If in the past they legitimated themselves through ideas of 'culture' today they are more likely to use the language of 'excellence' and a range of performance indicators. If universities were once built upon the superiority of culture they now prefer the bureaucratic measurement of performance. This might include regulating the number of first-class degrees awarded, the results of quality assessment, exercises on research or teaching, performance-related pay or the results from student feedback forms. Universities by seeking to measure the performativity of their staff and students also seek to quantify and measure 'excellence'. As Readings points out, missing from this rhetoric are questions of value and ethics. Indeed he argues that rather than viewing education as a site of emancipation we should see it as a location of ethics and obligation. Offering a less technocratic language than some of Lyotard's original reflections, he suggests that teaching should build dialogic forms of engagement with students while dispensing with the idea that the tutor is the final authority and refusing to reduce pedagogy to training. His point is not that such dialogues could expect to be emancipatory, but that they should aim to be thoughtful while being ethical. Indeed, Readings argues that the call that universities should seek to produce more radical students does not so much undermine the system as fit into a performative logic that requires more and more students irrespective of what they are taught. The performativity of the system is not undermined by critical or different kinds of knowledge, it is only undermined by more ethical relations of obligation that are in excess of the business inspired logic of the system (Readings 1996: 164). If students do not require liberation from an oppressive system they do require guidance and the thoughtful exploration of difference.

Frank Webster and Kevin Robins (2002) argue that a more complex understanding of university culture is required. Readings offers (perhaps like Lyotard) a partial understanding of the university and its relationship to the knowledge economy. First, during the era of the nation-state, universities were not simply elitest but did counter a considerable amount of pressure to broaden access and were not just involved in the reproduction of the national culture but also often became the place for more cosmopolitan dialogues. However, Webster and Robins do agree that universities have indeed adopted a more corporate ethos that has also seen a rise in new subject areas, especially in business, management, marketing and information studies more generally. Furthermore, the emphasis on transferable skills, the encouragement of entrepreneurial orientations amongst academics, branding and performance-related criteria has produced a more corporate style in higher education. Does this mean that higher education is now inevitably caught in a process whereby it progressively becomes a large corporation that gives up any wider civic purpose it might have had? Gerard Delanty (2002) wisely cautions against such a conclusion when he says that the idea of the university continues to have a potentially critical role to play in wider public debates. Such a position is arguably different from one that simply values the proliferation of knowledge and difference for its own sake, instead seeking to emphasise the role that critical intellectuals can play in forming a wider culture of criticism. It is to these matters I now wish to turn.

Education and civic ideals

Much of Lyotard's work on postmodernism is an explicit attack on Habermas's ideals of reason and rationality leading to the possibility of consensus (Holub 1991). This is evidently also an attack on the idea that the university can have a civic role by opening up critical questions and feeding them into wider forms of public discussion in the public sphere. Habermas (1983, 1987) has sought to defend the Enlightenment project, the emancipatory potential of knowledge and the civic purpose of the university in the wake of postmodernism. Modernity has witnessed the development of three separate areas of knowledge (namely science, public forms of morality and politics and art), all of which have their own separate criteria of assessment. It was the project of the Enlightenment to develop an objectively based science, universal morality and autonomous art. In particular many Enlightenment philosophers maintained the idea that through the rational control of nature and understanding of politics this would deliver moral progress, just institutions and individual happiness. After the twentieth century these ideas are difficult to maintain. Instead, the increasing specialisation of knowledge has created a culture of expertise that is distant from the fabric of everyday life. This cannot be overcome by simply seeking to make science more accessible to the public or by returning to a pre-modern world that seeks to unify the domains of science, morality and art. Instead, Habermas argues that we should seek to reconnect these different domains through argument and debate, utilising the public sphere more generally as a place to engage the wider citizenry. In these terms, the idea of the university as a place that potentially seeks to close the gap between expert cultures and everyday life would seem to have an important function to play in the future. It can perform this role if universities are able to guarantee certain academic and civic freedoms. For Habermas (1987) the self-image of the university continues to be connected to ideals of critical self-reflection and emancipation as it attempts not only to revise previously held 'scientific assumptions' but also to critique modern culture and politics. This is inevitably a communal process that involves the critical scrutiny of scholars, participation within wider and overlapping academic communities and the practices of argument and persuasion. Despite the increasing commercialisation of the university, the fragmentation of knowledge and the dominance of instrumentality Habermas maintains he can see no good reason as to why the university should give up its civic function. Indeed he (1985) had closely identified postmodernism with neoconservative attempts to turn away from more radical democratic traditions. While I think Habermas misrepresents some of the conceptual arguments in respect of postmodernism he is rightly concerned with some of the more conservative implications of writers like Lyotard who would seek to turn their backs on the emancipatory potential evident within democratically based arguments. The maintenance of difference is in the end of lesser importance than the sustainability of intellectual and civic freedoms that will potentially allow scholars to make critical and informed judgements in a democratic context. Indeed, if Lyotard seemingly privileges paralogy (language which is lacking in logical sequence), Habermas upholds the importance of agreement through reason. Yet while the latter's arguments, as has been widely suggested, overstate the importance of maintaining a rational consensus, Lyotard's focus upon questions of difference has little to contribute to the continued normative potential of education.

This said the argument that postmodernism is simply conservatism in disguise is not very convincing. Many postmodern arguments are explicitly concerned with drawing attention to the elitism and authoritarianism evident within both modernist and Enlightenment cultures. By attacking the boundaries between high culture and more popular domains of expression and experience certain versions of postmodernism have made to unsettle narratives of emancipation as either male dominated or ethno-centric. The attack upon grand narratives seemingly provided opportunities for women, ethnic minorities and others to point to the extent to which dominant cultures were inscribed with dominance (Wolff 1990). Yet in revealing the extent to which the Enlightenment and modernism had been culturally constructed, some postmodern arguments push for the abandonment of normative arguments altogether. As Nancy Fraser (1994) argues the need to give up philosophical foundationalism (the recognition that ideas of rationality, autonomy and democracy are socially created) does not entail that the ideals themselves should be ditched. While I shall return to this point below, I do think that the idea of postmodernity poses particular problems for a sociology of intellectuals. Arguments about postmodernity and the potential abandonment of civic ideals and purposes obviously have a strong connection with the role that they can be said to play in the wider society.

Zygmunt Bauman (1992) has argued elsewhere that the condition of postmodernity is more complex than arguments about the displacement of democracy would have us believe. Postmodernity articulates a particular crisis for intellectuals who have suffered a period of relative displacement. First, they are unable to offer authoritative answers to questions of truth and the normative claims of justice and taste. Their ability to influence modern society can be said to be in decline. If during the modern period the state required intellectuals to articulate a cultural mission based upon civilisation and cultural distinction this is no longer the case. The state's role as a 'collective teacher' sought to shape and legislate the identity of its citizens. Intellectuals in alignment with the state established their right to be able to shape behaviour, convention and taste. Largely Bauman contends that with the arrival of a consumer society the state has been less concerned with regulating the reproduction of 'culture' and more concerned with ensuring the reproduction of consumers. That the new ruler of the cultural domain is the capitalist market is a fact hugely resented by intellectuals more generally. Stripped of their cultural mission to ensure loyalty to the state, intellectuals turned on the market and accused it of fostering a low and debased culture. Yet attempts to legislate 'culture' on their part are likely to become an increasingly frustrating enterprise given that they now lack the older means of enforcement. In this respect, Bauman suggests that intellectuals must adopt a new role by becoming interpreters of knowledge rather than legislators of new social systems. A recognition of the inevitably pluralistic features of modern life disrupts universal claims and introduces questions of relativism into the production of knowledge. In Bauman's (1992: 22) terms 'knowledge has no extralinguistical standards of correctness': this means that its production, interpretation and reception are always contextual. These arguments not only convert pluralism into a permanent feature of our everyday life they also offer intellectuals a new role as interpreters between inevitably different branches of expert knowledge and more lay publics. The postmodern mind is aware that modernist attempts to 'improve' the condition of humankind can end in genocide, racism and more authoritarian forms of control. The postmodern condition is best represented as a form of disenchanted modernity. For Bauman (1997) the role of universities in the postmodern age is recognising that they no longer hold a privileged position given the plurality of new spaces and centres of knowledge that have come about with the rise of the Internet and new media more generally. Indeed, in the postmodern era they need to become less sites of emancipation and more places where different thought styles and languages can flourish. There is no way back to the hierarchical relationship between intellectuals and publics, and rather than mourning their decline in status intellectuals are urged to dust themselves off and adopt a more modest interpretative role in the culture more generally.

Some of the points about the undesirability of meta-narratives and problems with modernist assumptions have been more generally well taken. Only with the most extreme forms of cultural repression can we pretend that the social and cultural conditions of intellectuals have not been transformed by some of the changes that have swept through education and modern culture more generally. Just as postmodernism has tried to challenge claims to 'know better' intellectuals are becoming increasing dethroned as their traditional basis for autonomy (namely the university) has been transformed. If intellectuals and academics do have new freedoms in terms of what they teach this is because they are no longer required to legitimate the status quo. Yet, as I have indicated, Lyotard and his followers pay too little attention to questions of democracy and the public sphere more generally. This might be because ideas of 'democracy' can start to resemble a meta-narrative, but this need not be the case. The idea of democracy is not an 'essential' expression of our shared humanity, but a set of historically defined practices that have a certain history. Nor do I think we can simply say that the idea of the public sphere and democratic institutions is a technocratic set of practices that require specialist treatment through journals and articles. It is noticeable that Bauman's account ignores the role that intellectuals might play in the context of a democratic society. His argument that intellectuals resent the dominance of the market is well made, but he neglects to mention that many New Left intellectuals during the 1950s and 1960s sought to argue that the market society was anti-democratic and made a number of important public proposals about how it might be improved. And, even within a consumer-driven society intellectuals continue to have a crucial role in questioning, legitimating or imagining alternatives to our current society. If universities and education more generally are no longer quite as dominant in shaping these processes as they were in the past I remain unconvinced that we have become as post-ideological as Bauman seems to claim.

Democracy, if it is to mean anything, has to be a practice that involves criticism, listening, and above all the development of robust civic values and identities. Gone, it seems from postmodernism, is any of the language of democratic practices or associated ideas of the common good. We should note that while these concerns about the public sphere are evident in Bauman's later (1999) work they are largely absent from his reflections on intellectuals. If Habermas bases his theory of democracy on the communicative competence and rationality of the human subject at least he does so in such a way that it recognises the centrality of democratic practices and experience in the context of Western modernity. These aspects are too quickly dismissed by the postmodern critics of modernity.

More to the point for our purposes is Richard Rorty's (1985: 174) essay that seeks to 'split the difference between Lyotard and Habermas'. By this he means that any retreat from meta-narratives is interpreted as neoconservativism by Habermas and any attempt to uphold the importance of a rational consensus is read as totalitarian by Lyotard. For Rorty we do not need meta-narratives to underwrite our belief in democratic criticism and practice or universally valid reasons to be concerned about the need to uphold liberal freedoms and equality. Instead it is better to be what Rorty (1985: 166) calls 'frankly ethnocentric'. From this point of view we may understand the Enlightenment, science and democracy as a set of practices that are historical inventions rather than 'essences' waiting to be realised. For Rorty (1985: 168) we do not require meta-narratives to press the need for liberal virtues such as 'tolerence, irony, and a willingness to let spheres of culture flourish' without thinking that this commits us to a particular view of human nature or ideas related to essential features of modernity. Yet he sides with Habermas in his critique of Lyotard and other post-structuralist writers in simply celebrating plurality for its own sake without addressing a wider language of emancipation. Indeed it is post-structuralism's disconnection from public questions that frustrates Rorty. Its inability to speak the language of solidarity (or 'we talk') in the hope of making the world a more democratic or indeed a better place is a serious limitation to its ability to operate as a public philosophy.

While Rorty agrees with Lyotard that we should indeed abandon meta-narratives and talk of trans-historical universal visions of humanity, what is missing in Lyotard and others is a wider sense of the connection to a liberal politics and political ideals. Here I would broadly agree with Richard Rorty's critique although I think his description of democratic and liberal values is inadequate and could have been made in a less conservative way. More helpful in this respect is Cornelius Castoriadis (1991, 1997b) who, similarly to Rorty, emphasises the extent to which democratic cultures and procedures should be considered to be less the result of rationality and more the product of an imaginative creation. A need to defend democratic public spaces where the common affairs of ordinary members of the public can be discussed allows us to make informed choices about how we wish to live and the kind of society we want to inhabit. The maintenance of democratically orientated public spaces is built upon a shared civic commitment to participate in a dialogue with others. The public sphere can never be simply a matter of legal freedoms alone, it requires active forms of participation. A democracy asks that we recognise that our laws, traditions and common customs are not based upon a foundation but are historical inventions that may have to be revised in the future. Democratic debate and discussion requires dialogic forms of participation where different arguments are engaged with rather than swept away.

What is missing from Lyotard's analysis is a concern with the role that universities and institutions of higher education might still play in the construction of the democratic imagination and wider civic values. Despite the arrival of the knowledge economy universities still have a critical role to play in the formation of public spheres. Here the argument is not that all academics should operate as public intellectuals, but that if universities simply become businesses and academics serve their functions as experts in certain areas then their capacity to be able to facilitate wider forms of public debate will go into decline. Part of the civic role of the university is undoubtedly under pressure – to facilitate public criticism while also emphasising the importance of democratic cultures and criticism to its students. If this is indeed the case what implications do these features have for the specific role of intellectuals in the wider culture? If intellectuals are indeed to have a role beyond acting as specialist or as functionaries training knowledge workers then what might this be in our admittedly increasing fragmented and complex times? Here I think it is necessary to join together notions of modernity that continue to recognise the importance of democracy and civic values, and those of postmodernity that have more acutely focused upon the fragmentation of knowledge and the partial displacement of intellectuals. It is, however, worth remembering the public role that many intellectuals continue to play in providing the wider narratives and discourses which frame many of the key intellectual debates of our time.

Intellectuals and public cultures

In the recent writing on intellectuals many have tried to claim that they are either in decline or disappearing from the public stage. Frank Furedi (2004) argues that the claim that there is no singular truth and the spread of relativism more generally have encouraged a widespread cultural philistinism and disrespect for intellectual pursuits. In particular he highlights the growth in what he calls 'elitist populism' that has sought to undermine more traditional intellectual pursuits while insulating children from the challenge of ideas and complex perspectives. The reason we no longer have intellectuals of a high status is due to a culture that celebrates the ordinary and banal and a feel-good populism that has given up on being judgemental and critical. The end point of this process is the infantalisation of a culture that propagates low expectations, an obsession with personal experience and the protection of ordinary people from elitism. These arguments are, however, somewhat sweeping and poorly contextualised within broader historical developments. Furedi's celebration of intellectualism seemingly disallows the dialogic engagement of others and at times seems to champion a culture of authoritarian masculinity. From a postmodern point of view it has been the role that many intellectuals have played in some of the more authoritarian movements of the twentieth century which has led to the need to rethink their part. Democratic cultures require disagreement and a scepticism about attempts to define 'the truth', but can well do without the idea that they are a priest-like class. A more sophisticated view along similar lines is presented by the sociologist Bryan S. Turner (2006a), who argues that British sociology (which might have been expected to produce robust intellectual narratives in respect of the post-imperial decline of British society) has generally failed to produce a public culture of critical engagement. Under the influence of cultural studies much contemporary sociology has produced a 'decorative sociology' that has become increasing concerned with topics such as identity, fashion and lifestyle. Here the conclusion is that the British have failed to foster public intellectuals, not so much because of a wider public investment in philistinism as argued by Furedi, but because we lack a vibrant public culture that has been influenced by critical philosophy or social theory. Despite their differences, both Furedi and Turner argue that the anti-intellectualism of British culture and passive consumerism have meant that public intellectuals have no decisive role to play in British society.

These arguments, were they not misleading about the impacts of cultural studies or populism more generally, overstate their respective viewpoints. Both sets trade upon a highly influential set of debates about British intellectuals and public culture produced by Perry Anderson. Anderson (1992a) famously stated that British society lacked a robust public intellectual culture due to historical and cultural reasons. The development of a feudal and only partially democratic state that was not challenged by revolutionary ideologies meant that both 'traditionalism' and 'empiricism' had taken hold of English intellectual life. That British society remains deeply class ridden (an over-hang from the feudal era with its associated ideologies of rank) and also deeply suspicious of ideas more generally has helped produce a philistinism towards broader philosophical ideals. This argument would explain both the conservative nature of British life and its general distrust of intellectuals. In Anderson's view it is not surprising that critics like Furedi and Turner have failed to discover a robust intellectual culture thriving within British society as it has historically failed to produce revolutionary ideals that would challenge deferential social relations, ideologies of rank and a suspicion towards ideas.

At the time, the historian E.P. Thompson (who became a significant public intellectual in his own right) subjected Anderson's argument to a robust critique. While this is not the place to explore these arguments in depth, Thompson (1978a) argues at some considerable length that historically intellectuals associated with social movements have helped forge a radical culture. He (1978b: 109) once described himself as 'the last of the great bustards, awaiting extinction of my species', recognising perhaps his uncompromising nature and of course his considerable civic courage. Thompson's view of the public intellectual is one that is more closely concerned with questions of public duty and participation within democratic movements than university politics. Indeed, he wrote a savage satire in 1970 on a species he called 'Academic Superciliosus', who knew very little of life outside the university but a great deal about how to get on within it. Edward Said (1994: 17) similarly described the role of the critical intellectual as 'someone whose whole being is staked in a critical sense, a sense of being unwilling to accept easy formulas, or ready made clichés, or the smooth, ever-so-accommodating confirmations of what the powerful or conventional have to say, and what they do'. Critical intellectuals are not so much outsiders always clinging to the margins to avoid accommodation by the powerful, but requiring considerable amounts of courage in making a stand in public outside of the more comfortable routines of academic criticism. Whereas Bryan S. Turner (2006a: 172) rightly recognises the romantic flavour of these ideas they do perhaps describe a mythology that is sometimes necessary for those who are willing to say what the public may not wish to hear.

Similarly, Stephan Collini (2006) points out that the attempt by Anderson and others to argue that Britain fails to produce 'proper' intellectuals continues to work under the assumption that it is their role to guide and direct the masses into becoming a different society. This, as I have argued, is something public intellectuals, as many of the writers influenced by postmodernism recognise, could well do without. Indeed Collini (2006: 192) goes so far as to argue that what is actually characteristic of British society is not a lack of intellectuals, but 'hostility towards what are alleged to be the *intellectual* traditions of the county'. It is not that the public role of intellectuals is disappearing but that some cultures are hostile to the idea that they both need them and that they have helped construct and influence different traditions of criticism. Equally, in more contemporary times, I might have mentioned Stuart Hall, Angela McRobbie, Bernard Crick or, of course, Anthony Giddens as figures who have moved between some of the more specialist debates engaged in by academics and public questions and controversies. However, there is an argument that the ability to move between universities and more public debates is currently being squeezed as they have increasingly sought to adapt themselves to the performance-related criteria that leads academics to spend their time cultivating more professional identities and specialised debates (English and Kenny 2001; Gamble 2005). It is arguably these features along with the gradual introduction of performance pay, the development of increasing amounts of bureaucracy, the long hours culture and the rise of niche-marketed journals that make it more difficult for academics to take a public role. These features are perhaps more important than either the development of a philistine culture or the historical failure to develop a suitably radical culture in placing barriers between universities and the public realm.

My argument is not that universities can simply turn their backs on the knowledge economy and set themselves up as civic institutions, but that what is required is a more critical and evaluative language supplied by democratic movements for change rather than postmodern pluralism. If universities are to maintain a role other than the more instrumental one required by the economy while also recognising there is no returning to the social and cultural elitism of the past, then this is likely to come from an ability to contribute to more democratic self-understandings and criticism. Against those who have claimed that critical intellectuals have largely disappeared from the public realm we might do better to point to the increasingly complex and multiple realms within which intellectual activities now take place. As Henry Giroux (2006d) argues, intellectuals have a responsibility to engage students in the possibility of living and learning in different ways. However, he asks less for a rebirth of the universal intellectual of the Enlightenment or the postmodern facilitation of difference and more for the ability to link critical debates to more personal forms of experience. Further, intellectuals and academics need to be encouraged to write at a number of different levels for different kinds of public. In this Giroux (2006d: 209) optimistically points to the possibility of being able 'to bridge the gap between higher education and the broader society'. To be able to do this maintains the possibility of democratic criticism as a permanent option in the context of an information-based society.

Education, democracy and cultural citizenship

The arguments about the disappearance of public intellectuals have been found to be considerably overstated while there are more convincing grounds for seeking to explore the different ways in which intellectuals can continue to make a contribution to public debates. Gramsci (1988: 304) once remarked that everyone was an intellectual, but 'not all men have the function of intellectuals'; this points to the idea that the role of the public intellectual has an institutional basis. Through the notion of the 'organic' intellectual Gramsci argues that much of the cultural production of intellectuals through newspapers, on television and within the wider culture is not as 'independent' as it might at first seem. The role of public intellectuals in Gramsci's analysis becomes important in articulating hege-monic and potentially counter-hegemonic ideals and visions crucially informing public dialogue and engagement in a democratic context. These can no longer, as they were perhaps at the time Gramsci was writing, be simply divided on questions of class, but can help define a public ethic while seeking to articulate what we might take to be in the public inter-est. The development of the Internet and electronic forms of communi-cation more generally has transformed the basis upon which public intellectuals and civic actors can become involved in our culture as a whole. The development of blog sites, activist web pages, e-mail cam-paigns and Indymedia (www.indymedia.com) has arguably altered the relationship between intellectuals and publics.

These features offer new possibilities both for public-spirited intellectuals and wider publics. As Hardt and Negri (2000: 289) point out, the informa-tion-based society is developing 'a new mode of becoming human'. The world of just in time production, computer screens and fast communication fosters an environment where 'we increasingly think like computers' (2000: 291). Historically, the idea of a democratic education was built upon certain presumptions. The work of John Dewey, Paulo Freire, Richard Hoggart and Raymond Williams has argued that whereas capitalism needed labouring bodies democratic forms of participation required the long-term educated development of the self. The desire 'to better' the self was linked to the desire of workers to become more than simply people who engaged in physical or indeed mental labour. The argument here was that democratic forms of participation required different vocabularies of critical understanding, literacy and sociability that were in excess of the forms of symbolic expression that were required for work. The need to 'educate' the working class was as much about self-fulfilment as it was a political aim to allow people to express themselves in a mass democracy. This particular project is now in need of revision. Our new knowledge economy requires a mass of working population who can engage in symbolic, emotional and computer literate labour. This has seen the introduction of a new educational agenda that seeks to drive up standards, publicise league tables and transform education along more overtly entrepreneurial lines. If this agenda is no less instrumental than previous formulations it does at least insist upon a basic working knowledge of computers and associated skill sets. If the knowledge economy requires educated labour then recent transformations within universities and schools are also connected to this agenda. If universities in the past were elitist institutions that sought to preserve elite knowledge and tastes then they too are in the process of transformation. In a rapidly globalising and interconnected world it is perhaps the computer terminal that is becoming the dominant symbol of our age.

Arguably the development of interactive websites and web forums evidently expands the possibility for critical dialogue as well as the organisation of democratically orientated campaigns. Of course, we need to remember the web is not simply 'virtually democratic': it offers similar opportunities to fundamentalists, authoritarians and those who wish to close down democratic spaces or simply insist upon the dominant neoliberal form of common sense (Kahn and Kellner 2004: 90). Evidently much of the information on the Internet is either entertainment based or promotes values which are not really democratically informed. In this respect, those seeking to promote democratic forms of education cannot afford to become technophobes, and should instead use the Internet as a place to encourage the development of different literacies and perhaps most importantly opportunities to engage in educated dialogue and reflection on the key questions of the day. If, as radical educator Henry Giroux (2008: 156) argues, the dominant common sense of neoliberalism is 'the discourse of self help, personal responsibility, and self-reliance' then citizens require spaces and places of critical reflection that will allow them to explore its limitations. In making this move critical and public intellectuals must avoid the trap of viewing new technology as a form either of salvation or damnation and instead explore the undeniably exciting critical possibilities that it seems to offer (Kellner 2005).

If the ways in which the knowledge and information society are currently being conceived depend upon only minimal forms of democracy and the operation of the market this can only be resisted by activated citizens and more democratically orientated states. As Henry Giroux (2008) has argued, education, despite the deep dangers of neoliberalism, consumerism and the instrumentality of the information society, still offers the possibility of the introduction of other logics and more challenging ideas as to how we might live. Yet how greater numbers of educated public spheres are to be opened in our increasingly neoliberal times is a vexing question. Henry Giroux (2007) suggests that the recent corporate reshaping of the university that aims to produce the entrepreneurs and consumers of the future has increasingly squeezed the possibility of critical forms of intervention. He sensibly urges academics both to contest corporate power where possible internally and to help in the construction of counter-public places outside of the university. Here Giroux underlines the continuation of the civic possibilities of education even within these instrumental and consumer-orientated times. These will remain important considerations for those who would seek to pursue the meaning of education in a world where knowledge is increasingly being shaped by global consumer economies.

I have argued in this chapter that within the context of a consumer and information society democratic and civic forms of education in respect of the common good remain a distinct possibility. However, the room for manoeuvre that more critical forms of education have within a computer-literate and consumer age has been reshaped. Refusing either technological optimism or radical pessimism I have also pointed out that critical and public forms of debate remain possible even within an increasingly instrumental and capitalist-driven society. Here I have argued that there is a distinct need to reconfigure the progressive values of citizenship in new times. In the final chapter I shall seek to consider the possibilities and challenges that can be associated with a democratic and civic education.

7

Education, Hope and the Politics of Fear: The Resilience of Democracy and Cultural Citizenship

That the world post-9/11 is entering into a new phase has become increasingly apparent to many. The challenges of fundamentalism, war, religious hatred and intolerance, corporate power, increasing inequality, widespread consumerism, financial collapse and ecological devastation all suggest a new educative politics. Previous generations of critical educationalists, including Hannah Arendt, Martin Buber, John Dewey, Paulo Freire, Jürgen Habermas, Richard Hoggart and Raymond Williams, have offered ethical visions that connected the moral development of the self, the idea of education as a public space, and the need to develop critical and democratic citizens. These visions are still urgently needed if educationalists are to develop critical perspectives that will meet the needs of the present. All of these authors were deeply sceptical of education that had been reduced to vocationalism, training or standardised testing. Broadly speaking they spoke up for a broad concept of education that was less concerned with defending its neutrality and instead sought to foster a moral and ethical understanding about what human beings could become in particular social and historical contexts. We are, of course, the direct inheritors of these visions, which not only require careful attention but also critical revision in light of the different social and cultural conditions that confront us today. This said, all of these thinkers hoped that education could become connected to an understanding of the social, cultural and emotional dimensions of being human and the idea that as teachers and educators we are fostering the horizons of future democratic citizens. This meant a responsibility to criticise dogmatic assertions and help foster dialogic relationships with our students, while encouraging individual curiosity, an empathetic concern for others and responsible forms of civic engagement. If Arendt was troubled by indoctrination, Buber concerned about instrumentalism, Dewey worried about the failure of democratic virtue, Freire indignant about the banking concept of education, Habermas cautious about the colonisation of money and power, Hoggart angry about the rise of vocationalism and Williams hopeful about the possibility of an educated and learning democracy, it was because they all maintained different if overlapping ethical visions that linked a concern for 'humane' development with the realisation of a substantive democracy. In education we are not simply reproducing the class structure or performing as technicians, passing on competencies and skills, but potentially acting as educators seeking to foster civic responsibility, respect and a public orientation.

However, the world in which critical forms of education have to operate is in certain respects different from that of previous generations. If democratic ideals and visions were challenged in the 1930s by the rise of fascism and communism and in the 1960s by the fears of a mass society, today we are caught between the dominance of global corporations and fundamentalism of quite a different sort fostered by racial and religious intolerance. We cannot assume in this setting that democratic virtues and sensibilities will survive the pincer movement of power being transferred upwards into the hands of global conglomerates and politically disenfranchised populations who are increasingly turning to extreme nationalism, racism or other forms of fundamentalist thinking. Further, as the influence of consumerism and more pragmatic attitudes towards education has spread through civil society education is being permanently threatened by instrumentality. As radical educationalist Henry Giroux (2004a) argues, the rise of state authoritarianism and the attack on civil rights in the context of the war on terror and the enhanced power of corporations further close the possibility of intellectuals posing radical alternatives to the present. In this respect educators have a vital role to play in creating space for democratic discussions and controversy. Democracy and the public space in this reading are not simply a matter of participating in elections or of maintaining passively held rights, they also depend upon the intervention of a critical and active citizenship. As E.P. Thompson (1980) never ceased to remind us, in becoming civic actors we need to be guided by a sense of the democratic struggles of the past and of the different political traditions and visions of the good society that have helped forge our identities. The idea of democracy being remade by the struggles from below of common people is a necessary counter-weight to the appeal of fundamentalist ideologies and the perversion of the democratic process by corporate control.

The idea of a participatory public sphere and democracy is still connected with the ability of ordinary citizens to learn through dialogue and develop critical forms of agency. Democratic institutions and ideals institute a way of life where education is not simply a matter for schools but is part of a daily experience of living in a democracy. Democracy in this understanding is never a given, it needs to be continually renewed in public spaces constituted through the media, education and other places that handle questions of public controversy.

In this regard, the idea of a deliberative democracy remains important given the emphasis it places upon participation, active discussion and plurality. The deliberative ideal calls for the construction of civic places where citizens have an equal opportunity to express themselves while listening to the multiple voices of others. Here the idea is that we can engage with one another, work through our differences and eventually arrive at the common good. Rather than a cold exchange of views, notions of deliberative democracy at their best recognise, along with Iris Marion Young (2000: 50), that processes of communicative engagement should include the art of listening and persuasion, as well as solidarity and responsibility. Yet on this point I would like to emphasise the importance not only of our ability to dialogue but also those questions related to respect. In particular, issues related to cultural citizenship have emphasised questions such as whose voices are heard, who is disregarded and disrespected, and who becomes converted into an Other (Stevenson 2003). As Axel Honneth (1995) argues most social and cultural struggles historically have been ignited by a sense of unfair treatment and a demand to be recognised as fully human. Struggles for respect and recognition not only work at the collective level, they are also bound up with an individual's sense of self-respect and well-being. To be disrespected or rendered invisible not only damages wider societal levels of solidarity it also erodes individual feelings of self-confidence. Democratic societies demand public cultures that are based upon vibrant forms of critique and dialogue as well as trying to secure a common sense of respect for all citizens. The question that emerges is whether public institutions are able to encourage a sense of active dialogue under conditions where most people are able to feel valued and also maintain a reasonable level of esteem. In this sense democratic citizenship is not just a matter of legal frameworks, it is also more explicitly concerned with building a democratic culture in common.

Finally, the right to a voice and the need for respect should be part of the requirement for responsibility. Here society cannot afford to be 'neutral' on whether or not its citizens have an internal sense of connection to its democratic institutions, traditions and responsible forms of criticism. On this my argument is that citizens not only need to be personally responsible they should also recognise a sense of responsibility towards society as well. Citizens need to be willing to assume responsibility for one another through everyday actions and common institutions. The extent to which they do this for the wider society will have an impact upon their willingness to participate more generally as well as engage in wider debates in respect of their common citizenship.

Of course it is not the job of educationalists to 'convert' their students into being democratic activists, but it is vital that education operates as a place of critical inquiry, knowledge and tolerance. Bernard Crick (2000), who helped write the British Labour government's report on citizenship education, makes an important distinction between the citizen as a subject who obeys the law and the citizen who plays a part in the affairs of their city or state. In this respect, Crick argues that children need to learn to act responsibly, have the potential to become involved in their communities and understand how to take effective public action. However, democratic models of education also need to criticise the view that schools and educational institutions should simply hand down democratic virtues to their students without also creating public spaces that are dependent upon the expression of difference and the absence of cultures of normalisation (Carlson and Dimitriadis 2003). The danger of simply impressing values on the young (or at least attempting to do so) is that this may well suffocate any possibility of more critical languages and sensibilities emerging. Here one of education's central concerns is how to foster a sense of personhood that facilitates learning. This is unlikely to be the outcome of authoritarian public spaces, but of democratically conceived human relationships that are prepared to struggle, to encounter ambivalence and a degree of frustration as each learner seeks to become themselves in relation to others (Salzberger-Wittenberg 1999). As Bernard Crick (2000) recommends, the idea of citizenship has to tackle a pervasive culture of civic indifference. This can only be achieved by communicating a sense of how democracy 'works', its importance in shaping our identities, and also how we are each responsible for its functioning. Unless citizens share a sense of the importance of public involvement and developing common cultures of criticism the practice of democracy will inevitably fail to stand the test of time. If we take questions of rights, respect and responsibility together and connect them to the need to create a common culture of democracy this is what I broadly mean by developing a citizens' culture of citizenship.

The war on terror and the education of citizens

It is currently difficult to write about the desirability of overlapping cultures of democracy, respect and responsibility without also registering a profound sense of public crisis. The decline of the labour movement and welfare state along with the globalisation of neoliberal capitalism has meant that national democratic politics have become increasingly undermined. If the state has lost power in relation to the global flows of information and finance it is not surprising that national politics and democratic participation are in decline. More recently, in the European context, we have seen the rise of a form of anti-politics that combines neoliberalism with an anti-immigration agenda. If the struggle for a democratic and culturally inclusive society is threatened by this turn of events then the so-called 'war on terror' has legitimised the passing of a number of illiberal laws in the face of the terrorist threat. As many critics have recognised, America's war on terror is the coming to fruition of the idea of the 'New American Century' that predates 9/11 (Rogers 2008). The idea of a globalised free-market economy and liberal democracy is a vision that gained prominence amongst influential neoconservative thinkers after the collapse of Communism. This was primarily conceived as a strategy whereby the United States would not become overly weighed down by multilateral agreements and would be able to face down what it had identified as the 'axis of evil'. Many radical critics have sought to argue that the war can also be connected to either a 'new imperialism' or a more coercive American empire (Harvey 2003; Mann 2003).

Whatever the outcome of the debates in respect of America's global power there can be little doubt that the neoliberal state seeks to create a 'good business climate' that includes the free mobility of capital, tax reduction measures, the curtailment of trade unions, a minimal state and the promotion of the values of entrepreneuralism and consumerism. As Naomi Klein (2008) has persuasively argued, American-style capitalism has been increasingly imbricated within a pathological culture that, while talking the language of democracy and human rights, also uses torture, intimidation and war in order to extend its frontiers. If the American empire, as Klein suggests, seeks to profit from disaster then it does so without necessarily injuring its ability to see itself as upholding the values of 'civilisation'. Central to the neoliberal reinvigoration of capitalism has been the role of educators and in particular the public role of Milton Friedman and the Chicago School of Economics who were instrumental in the spread of free-market doctrines from the fall of the Allende government in Chile on 11 September 1973 and then across the globe. The administering of a free-market 'shock' treatment not only seeks to quickly eradicate more collectivist and social democratic achievements but just as crucially it also presents neoliberal restructuring as if there were no alternative. While this doctrine has become intimately connected to human rights abuse, Klein holds that neoliberalism acts as a public pedagogy seeking to both intimidate and persuade populations into accepting a more market-orientated public life and ethos.

In this respect, as Susan Buck-Morss (2003: 103) has commented, the cultural domain takes on a new significance that is just as important as economics. The imposition of a liberal Western democracy in Iraq through the privatisation of assets, development of a free market and flat-rate taxes is just as important economically as it is culturally. If neoliberalism produces intensified forms of inequality within and between nations, then such features are likely to produce a reconfiguration in culture and the production of subjectivity more generally. Lisa Duggan (2003) has argued in this respect that one of the many ruses of neoliberalism is to try and pass itself off as purely a form of economic policy. Neoliberalism not only attacks the public domain in favour of profit-making institutions, it also does so in ways that are not neutral within the definition of public space. For Duggan (2003: 12) neoliberalism not only aims to fashion market cultures but its effects can also be traced through its two principal concerns of privatization and the promotion of personal responsibility at the expense of responsibilities towards a wider public. As bell hooks (2000a, 2000b) recognises, the politics of neoliberalism and class division promotes a greedy and competitive social order where endless cycles of consumption come to replace a sense of compassion for the poor. Neoliberalism is an educative project that is as much concerned with the remaking of institutions as it is with social and cultural identities. In particular, it seeks to shut down the possibility of education as a form of public politics by cancelling democratic initiatives and seeking to manufacture pro-market identities. Neoliberalism is not simply economic policy, it also has a specifically 'educational' agenda of its own.

A good illustration of its attempt to refashion education in the light of the newly emerged knowledge society can be glimpsed through the academies' programme in Britain. This strategy has met with fierce opposition from local groups of parents, from the teaching unions and also sections of the labour movement. The academies' programme is an explicit attempt to both undermine local forms of democracy by removing schools from public control and to hand the education of young people over to private interests, thereby promoting an entrepreneurial culture (Beckett 2007). Similarly the desire to enhance 'faith' schools is worrying from a democratic perspective. While these measures are complex and supported by some critics in the name of 'equality', they arguably do little to promote multicultural schools based upon a diversity of lived experiences and religious cultures. Rather than promoting a greater number of faith schools, a more democratic position would have been the promotion of explicitly secular schools that allowed plural spaces for different religions and faiths to both co-exist and respectfully interrogate one another. Further, faith schools often perpetuate class inequalities as they operate systems of selection that in practice tend to discriminate against children from poorer families. In the British context, schooling is currently being remodelled by the cultures of faith and business in such a way that this is pushing out a more democratic ethos that could have been developed from the notion of the public comprehensive school that has traditionally emphasised a liberal education and a 'mixed' intake.

The politics of fear

If the 'war on terror' is undoubtedly linked to the progressive marketisation of the cultural domain it has simultaneously sought to undermine the legitimacy and practice of democracy. As Henry Giroux (2004b) argues, the fact that the 'war' on terror faces inwards as well as outwards has meant in practice that the liberal democratic order is becoming progressively dismantled in the name of fighting terror. In the United States this can be seen in cuts in the domestic funding of education, health care and other public services, and a rapid increase in military spending. In 2007 it was conservatively estimated that the cost of the Iraq war stood at $2.5 trillion for the United States and £5 billion for Britain. These figures do not, however, include the war in Afghanistan or indeed the long-term care that is likely to be required for combatants with either physical injuries or mental-health needs (Stephen 2007).

This is of course not the first time historically when critical educationalists have sought to warn us about the destructiveness of an educational agenda driven by capitalism and nationalism. Adorno (1998) argued that the central demand for education after Auschwitz must be that it should not happen again. This should not be a matter of 'idealist platitudes' but a need to address the dangers to humanity that are evident in aggressive forms of nationalist thought and practice (1998: 192). The only real guarantee against the return of hateful forms of nationalism is an education that encourages forms of critical reflection and autonomous self-development. In particular Adorno was concerned about the psychic cost required from the individual who attempted to identify with the authoritarian forms of collectivism demanded by nationalism. He sought to unsettle masculine notions of hardness and an indifference towards pain and vulnerable others that is often traded upon by nationalism. Unless education can encourage citizens to develop more individual forms of reflection they will remain potential victims, both of a nationalist logic that encourages the self to treat the other as 'an amorphous mass' and an aggressive bureaucratic rationality that exhibits a form of ethical blankness by focusing upon procedural criteria (1998: 198). These seemingly different personality types revel in a cult of hardness while exhibiting a form of 'reified consciousness' (1998: 199). The form of subjectivity that needs to be countered by education emphasises a view of humanity that is cold and distant but above all defined by the inability to love. Adorno (1998: 2001) writes that 'if people were not profoundly indifferent toward whatever happens to everyone else except for a few to whom they were closely bound and, if possible, by tangible interests, then Auschwitz would not have been possible, people would not have accepted it'.

If for Adorno nationalism produces the desire for homogeneity which kills critical thinking then market-driven capitalism is responsible for the fragmentation and reification of the self. Central to this loveless and masculinised world is the market's ability to produce competitive forms of individualism. It is ultimately the dominant culture of competitive advantage that drives out more generous feelings of solidarity and helps foster indifference towards the other. Here Adorno is explicitly not arguing for children to be protected from the harsh realities of the world for as long as possible or for teachers to be 'compelled to love' their students, but rather for the fostering of critical forms of understanding along with a sense of solidarity with the other.

Henry Giroux (2004c) has revisited Adorno's essay and believes that it continues to have much to teach us in the context of the American-led war on terror. Education in Adorno's hands is partially a means of social reproduction, but also a space for critique and contestation. Indeed, Giroux argues that schooling and education more generally are being instrumentalised and privatised precisely because they have the potential to operate as alternative public spheres where students can become more critical citizens. Following Adorno, he points to the hegemonic culture of hardness that has flourished within American civil society after the atrocities of 9/11 both to legitimate the aggressive forms of nationalism and masculinity required by the war on terror and to underwrite neoliberal moves to attack the social state and welfare programmes. In calling for education to develop alternative discourses to those of empire, Giroux calls for a critical politics of memory. This is the recovery of counter-narratives and political formations from the past that might spark the imagination in terms of a search for alternatives. As with Adorno, it is critical forms of knowledge and autonomous forms of thinking that may have a potentially emancipatory effect in the face of capitalism and nationalism. Crucially Giroux and Adorno recognise the need for compassion for the other alongside the development of civic identities and democratic practices. In doing this both also recognise the necessity of developing an alternative ethics of identity.

From a feminist point of view the idea of an exclusively autonomous individuality is based upon an intrinsically masculine view of development. This not only disallows the ways in which the 'individual' remains connected to the social through a number of complex bonds and networks (as if it were ever possible to entirely detach the self), it also calls into question the dominant masculine ideal of the self-sufficient individual. Jessica Benjamin (1990) argues that the hegemony of the idea that we should all be our own 'self-creations' still persists in a world of gender polarity. The idea of nurturance and responsiveness eventually giving way to independence is less universal, and more usually dependent upon masculine forms of personal development. Critical educationalist Heidi Ross (2003: 34) also argues that education is not simply a matter of reasoned dialogue or critical discourse, but what she calls 'relational thinking'. As I have said throughout, a genuinely culturally inclusive education would need to recognise the relational needs of citizens and not simply reduce dialogue to the cold exchange of reasons. This move, however, becomes difficult in the culture of fear fostered by neoliberalism.

Here we might remember that earlier I discussed the attempt to rethink liberal socialism through the third way. The problem with this approach is that it failed to offer a substantive critique of poverty and inequality and promoted an instrumental account of education driven by the requirements of the knowledge economy and the need to promote a culture of business, aspiration and upward mobility. More positively, the third way did secure a major investment in educational infrastructure, improve some 'failing' schools and upgrade teacher's pay. However, Anthony Giddens (2008: 82) estimates that this still leaves about 30 per cent of pupils without basic forms of literacy. As I have indicated, these aspects along with a growing sense of instrumentality within education concern many educationalists. Richard Pring (2005) comments that education is a moral practice whose principal aim is to establish a connection between the 'impersonal world' of ideas, concepts and knowledge and the 'personal world' of those seeking to learn. His concern is that over-emphasising the performativity of students (the ability to achieve high grades) does considerable violence to this practice. Education's growing focus on metaphors drawn from the world of business potentially threatens its ability to act as a moral practice. I think this is right but perhaps does not go far enough. Here I would argue that to teach is to act as a critical translator, moving between the horizons of texts, theories and the taught. In this practice we need to bracket off who is going to learn from whom as the educator seeks to develop an extended conversation while drawing upon the principles of dialogue, respect and responsibility. On this my concern (which I share with many others) is that I am not convinced that this practice is aided by the growth of either marketisation or authoritarianism within places of learning or the wider society. Generally speaking for the practice of teaching to flourish it requires relatively liberal institutions, a more equal society, a politics of voice and an ability to listen to the Other.

Zygmunt Bauman (2006) has similarly described the pervasive culture of fear and authoritarianism as marking the transition from social state to security state. If neoliberalism has helped propagate an increasingly competitive, atomised, market-driven society then the state under such circumstances requires a new ideology. According to Bauman (2006: 148), if the state no longer talks the language of welfare and collective solidarity it has then increasingly sought to legitimate itself through issues related to security. If the state at one time tried to protect its citizens from social degradation while offering them a share in the benefits of a 'civilised' culture today the compact between citizen and state is rather different. The security state having removed much social protection now seeks to defend its citizens from threats posed by terrorists, the underclass, teenage 'hoodies' and other less than dutiful citizens. The attack on civil freedoms, marketisation and enhanced forms of social inequality shows no sign of being addressed in the near future (Lister 2008). Currently it is estimated that about a fifth of British children live in poverty (Toynbee and Walker 2008). This means children growing up with no access to a home computer, holidays and birthday parties in a celebrity culture that increasingly celebrates wealth. At the other end of the scale it has been estimated that tax avoidance costs Britain £25 billion annually, with only £3.4 billion required to halve child poverty by 2010 (Toynbee and Walker 2008: 16). If we add this on to a context where the top rate of tax since 1979 has been progressively reduced from 83 per cent to 50 per cent then it is not surprising that many are becoming increasingly concerned about the effects of class inequality. The idea that everyone should strive to become rich has been normalised by a host of television talent shows or programmes that have more overtly sought to promote entrepreneurialism. In this regard a mass celebrity-based culture encourages individualism, cancels a sense of solidarity with the poor and promotes a feeling of shame amongst economic 'losers'. The culture of class resentment pushed forward by these developments cancels any possibility of what bell hooks (2000a: 79) has called a 'democratic vision of prosperity'. This would involve a community where everyone could live abundantly and have access to a liberal education, and where the principles of sharing are privileged over those of greed.

The new politics of class polarisation is such that Zygmunt Bauman (2007b: 90) has coined the phrase 'mixophilia' to describe the reluctance of citizens to come together in urban places across class boundaries. If the global elite are increasingly placeless as they move through rather than interact with localities then the poor have maintained much thicker ties to the local. Concerns about personal safety and security become translated into adopting a lifestyle that keeps the poor at a distance. Urban politics on this reading are subject to a class driven attempt to occupy spaces and places that hope to keep questions of difference at arm's length. The fostering of communities of sameness is not simply one way of keeping out otherness it is also of itself deeply undemocratic. As Bauman (2007b: 88) recognises, if citizens in their daily encounter within public spaces are not called upon to negotiate understandings and meanings they are likely to be frightened by things they don't recognise. The politics of fear in this setting both minimises the possibility of unexpected encounters and also closes the possibility of constructing hospitable public spaces where meanings and experiences require artful negotiation.

Returning to Dewey (1916), the democratic school is crucially the intermixed school that provides a complex cultural space where citizens from different communities can intermix and interrelate. The idea of the democratic school as a place where people from different backgrounds can come together trades upon a democratic model of the life of the city. Richard Sennett (1970) argues that the city is continually caught between a retreat from diverse forms and entanglement and a more democratic urbanity that embraces different points of contact. The democratic school (like the democratic city) would be marked less by a social and cultural hierarchy than it would with less ordered and sometimes more discordant social relations. As Richard Pring (2007) has argued, Dewey's account of the common school is increasingly under attack in an educational climate where the wealthy are educated in different settings from the poor. As Pring points out, the case for the common school is moral as the personal growth of the individual and the community is dependent upon citizens learning to converse and live with one another. For Pring, Dewey feared that if rich and poor were not educated together this would not foster the necessary social solidarity where they could recognise mutual common interests in community and citizenship. Without daily forms of reciprocity in the life of a community more generally it was likely to become subject to sectional interests without any substantive sense of fellow feeling. We are all the poorer in a society where social and cultural differences are feared and communication across barriers is being diminished. However, in an educational agenda that is driven by an anxious upward mobility these features are rarely mentioned within public debates.

As James Beane and Micheal Apple (2000) highlight the notion of democratic schooling has been undermined in Britain and the United States through an increasingly centralised curriculum, performance management, the deskilling of teachers and an increasing emphasis being put on the marketisation of schools. To become a democratic school education would need to involve young people in questions of governance that put an emphasis upon the voices of the young, co-operation within the wider community, and the welcoming of difference and Otherness. For the education of the young to be considered democratic it has to question the narrow approach to what counts as knowledge while seeking to empower the voices of those who have been traditionally marginalised by the dominant culture. The idea of democratisation is not simply linked with questions of mixed intakes, it would also involve cultural politics issues about whose cultures and ways of life are reinforced, contested or negotiated as part of the curriculum.

In order to sustain a more culturally inclusive education this necessitates a number of different cultural strategies, including a critical discussion of children's popular culture and developing an emphasis on dialogic forms of engagement. In this respect, Henry Giroux (1999) has emphasised both the power of popular culture to act as a form of public pedagogy and the extent to which the language of the market and consumerism is seeking to replace that of democracy. As democratic ideas wither on the vine the ideas of the good life become defined by commercial culture. Yet despite this powerful warning it is of course important that popular culture is not simply dismissed as the site of instruction for corporations and hyper-consumerism. The domain of the popular often contains a number of more ambivalent features and is also often a site for children's learning, passion and transgression. A democratic education therefore should lead to a criti-cal discussion of popular culture that neither dismisses it through a culture of condescension nor simply celebrates its popularity, but instead subjects it to critical forms of analysis. Popular culture remains an important site for children's and young people's learning that is often unnecessarily pushed out of classroom conversations. If discussions of popular culture need to be welcomed into classrooms so should more 'real world' concerns. For example, critical forms of education that aim to challenge discrimina-tory attitudes and political agendas are not best served by turning a blind eye to unacceptable attitudes and practices. In the British context a key document in this respect remains the Parekh Report (2000b: 149), pro-duced by a number of critical educationalists and academics to inform public policy discussion on questions of multiculturalism. Here they clearly state that a genuinely anti-racist education can only be promoted by focusing on questions of human rights, issues of equality and the skills of deliberation. It is only through processes of deliberation that children will learn to criticise the prevailing local culture, while seeking to articulate alternatives. A genuinely engaged and non-discriminatory culture would mean not only addressing the fear that popular culture is somehow not appropriate for educated discussion it would also allow young people the space and freedom to engage in open-ended forms of dialogue.

There is also in this context the emergence of a new politics of belonging that increasingly stresses the importance of integration and nationhood. If the multicultural project refers to the possibility of reimagining boundaries between previously differently conceived groups so that they might learn to live together, then in our post-9/11 and 7/7 world a new politics is begin-ning to appear. Multiculturalism tried to emphasise the 'mixed' quality of our shared lives and identities and the heterogeneity of citizenship. Such an argument sought to forcibly disrupt more traditional liberal assumptions that counter-posed civic neutrality and the 'particularism' of the claims of so-called minorities. As Stuart Hall (2000a: 229) comments, the educated politics of multiculturalism aims to reveal the extent to which national forms of citizenship can be understood through social and cultural codes in ways that were mutually inclusive as well as exclusive. If citizens belong to a diversity of overlapping communities and occupy numerous forms of identification in that process then education as well as the wider public sphere becomes an important place where these codes are negotiated, respected, displaced or indeed marginalised. Nira Yuval-Davis (2006) has argued that the politics of multicultural citizenship is concerned with questions related to issues of belonging and inclusion. Recently British political parties declared multiculturalism as dead, with a renewed emphasis upon integration and the imposition of common understandings of belonging rather than their careful negotiation. If there is a new language that highlights the common culture of nationhood it is also noticeable that there has been a re-reading of the virtues of the British Empire as a civilising mission that can undoubtedly be linked to Britain's role in support of the 'war on terror'. If, as Ruth Lister (2007) points out, the inclusive potential of citizenship depends upon marginalised communities finding a multiplicity of voices in the policy process then the recent abandonment of the idea of multiculturalism is a cause for considerable concern, especially given some of the successes in these areas in respect of schooling.

Education, ethics and citizenship

If the ideals of a democratic and culturally inclusive education remain central to preventing the further erosion of public sensibilities on the vine of authoritarianism, consumerism, extreme nationalism and fundamentalism, then these also remain dependent upon an ethical vision of what we might become. If cynicism about students, technocratic procedures and a renewed focus on the homogeneous cultures of nations is a permanent threat to more dialogic forms of engagement, then education needs to be guided by a more genuinely democratic ethos. Pablo Freire's (2007) radical vision of education continually outlined the importance of hope and the need to keep one foot in the real world while carefully placing the other in other possible futures. This also meant keeping alive the conversation about a society where education was not being reduced to training and where neoliberal cynicism was a matter for intellectual challenge. Freire as ever continued to affirm the possibility of social and cultural change within contexts that would drain hope from even the most optimistic. The responsibility of critical educators to offer dreams and aspirations that are counter-hegemonic without lapsing into either a laissez faire approach or dogmatism is at the heart of the idea of a democratic education. Freire (2004: 35) often spoke of the idea of human beings as creatures who were permanently 'unfinished', meaning that they could never be completely determined, but that their ontology also predisposed them towards curiosity, learning and the possibility of making their own decisions. For the progressive educator this meant dialogic forms of encounter and a keen interest in protecting the autonomy of the learner. Democratic families and systems of education and learning are thereby compelled not to micro-manage children or adopt a liberal permissiveness but to help them to become themselves. This is less what is now called 'liberal parenting' and more the development of democratic forms of dialogue both within the home and the school. Such a sensibility requires courage, non-violence, the capacity to live with difference, and perhaps above all, to recognise that human beings will ask for respectful forms of reciprocity.

An intersubjective and democratic account of human development is not simply a feature of Freire's writing, it also connects with other currents within phenomenology, hermeneutics and existentialism more generally. Martin Buber's (1970) emphasis upon 'I and thou' and Hans-Georg Gadamer's (2001) assertion that all education is conversational offer us an ethical and dialogical model of the human subject. The education of the self is dependent upon the quality of our human relations with others and our society's capacity to recognise the importance of human autonomy and liberty more generally. To talk of active citizens as being caught in endless cycles of learning and dialogue that never reach completion displaces more cynical understandings of what education could be about. Cornelius Castoriadis (1997b: 129) sums this up well when he argues that the point of education 'is not to teach particular things, but to develop in the subject the capacity to learn'. The difficulty here is that for education to aid the possibility of self-education it can only do this by instituting a set of complex social relationships between the teacher and the taught. Education aims to assist students to become autonomous, capable of self-reflection and dialogues with others. Here we need to emphasise not only a politics of voice but also a responsibility to listen. We then have a wider responsibility in turn to be careful not to press our views upon others, but to communicate our intellectual traditions and recognise a wider sense of public service to the community. In addition, in our ecological age such a vision needs to be coupled with an understanding of ourselves as vulnerable beings who are dependent and interconnected to webs of life. If a democratic understanding of education requires that we recognise human beings' capacity for liberty as well as responsibility then we also need to talk of human fallibility and vulnerability (Orr 2004). Alternatively we could simply surmise that democracy and civic values are unlikely to survive in a planet driven by hyper-consumerism and wars over resources such as oil. In this respect, democratic self-understandings need to be joined with a citizenry that have developed an understanding of their own limits.

In this setting to talk of hope means rejecting cynicism and authoritarianism in favour of an education that seeks to dialogically engage the sensibilities of young people. It means utilising education as a public space where different ideas about the good society can be interrogated, thereby not giving in to a form of fatalism that would suggest either that everything is either getting worse or better. If, as Stuart Hall (2000b: 45) argues, the so-called 'neutral' liberal state is 'deeply lodged in culture', then an alternative ethic necessitates citizens who will be able to move within multiple public spaces that will be intersected with questions of cultural translation, difference and Otherness. This would also mean critically interrogating neoliberal ideologies of market fundamentalism that talk of the responsibilities of the poor but not of the rich and of fundamentalist ideologies that make simple divisions between the West and the rest. The idea of an education that enables the crossing of borders is built upon an ethical vision that respects the complex languages of cultural difference (Giroux 1993a).

Having said all this, liberal approaches to children's education are now under attack. Stephen Law (2006) holds that there is now a widespread belief that society is in the grip of a moral breakdown, all too evident in under-age drinking, teenage pregnancy, gun crime and various other features as the young now lack the moral guidance that they once had. We might add that currently there is a discussion about 'the broken society' that many right-wing critics attribute to the erosion of moral certainties by relativistic liberal thinking. This has led to the progressive abandonment of the idea of Enlightenment notions that children are themselves capable of moral thinking. Critics of liberal ideas of education argue that such progressive thinking ends with moral confusion and a pervasive culture of selfishness whereby young citizens have little sense of personal responsibility. These arguments are most familiar in the debates around faith schools that are valued for upholding morality, authority and discipline in a culture that is characterised as nihilistic. Rather than seeking to socialise the young into particular social and cultural beliefs, Law argues that a liberal education would as far as possible present young people with different choices and seek to encourage the value of critical thinking and personal reflection. The liberal tradition puts its emphasis on personal freedom and seeks to encourage young people in using their own ability to reason and form their own judgements. Further, rather than dismissing such an education as relativistic we should appreciate how this liberal freedom to reason remains connected to responsibility. If a liberal culture of free inquiry and debate is often characterised as celebrating a culture of individual selfishness then nothing could be further from the truth. Through the practice of critical debate and argument participants learn to take responsibility for their judgements and also learn how others might become affected by them.

In these authoritarian times much of Stephen Law's (2006) arguments are to be welcomed. In particular, he provides a crucial defence of liberalism against the charge of relativism, given its defence of liberty and freedom of speech and conscience. However, Law's tough defence of liberal ideals has a number of flaws, although none of these are fatal. The first is that liberalism itself has a history and many competing strains within it. If you like, liberalism is a diverse set of traditions which cannot be seen as occupying a 'neutral' position. In standing up for freedom of opinion and thought liberalism remains a vital resource in our own times, but we need to be historically aware of its blind spots, evasions and the diverse ways in which it has been applied. Liberal thought is less the view from 'no where' and more a set of ideas with their own histories, cultural categories and internal tensions. Further, as I have argued, democratic socialist modes of thought have historically sought to extend a liberal culture to everyone. Democratic socialist thought has argued that the culture of liberty only becomes meaningful in a world where the basic needs of citizens are met and we are not having to spend too many hours labouring to earn a living (Eagleton 1996: 83). Here we might extend this argument and suggest that liberalism is not only a tradition but also that if it is to be meaningful it needs to become an institutional practice that is supported and accommodated by a wider society.

As Freire (2004) argued, freedom is a careful balancing act between authority and autonomy that depends upon the democratisation of human relationships. He was careful here (1996: 154) to distinguish this position from authoritarianism and permissiveness. This is not simply letting the student make up their own mind, rather it is an attempt to present the learner with alternatives in the context of dialogic criticism. Education, in bell hooks's (2000b: 43) wonderful phrase, should be about 'renewing the vitality of life'. In this sense it needs to move beyond learning as either training for the market or an indoctrination in fundamental beliefs that are unable to admit to further questioning, and instead become a process that admits to learning without end. Education through its ability to foster complex forms of literacy and understanding has a particular role to play in times of clashing ideologies and the intensified appeal of simple binary logics.

Such features are also evident in what Freire (2001: 102) described as 'the bureaucratizing of the mind'. What Freire meant by this is the constant struggle against stereotypical thinking, the need to keep the mind subtle and alert, and of course the requirement that critical intellectuals do not simply end up submitting to the dominant society as if it were a natural fact. Freire was pointing here to the view that freedom has a psychological dimension. Like Erich Fromm (1941), he understood freedom not simply as a question concerning 'external' domination but as the project of making space for critical thinking that implies citizens must be unafraid of being out of step with others. Fromm (1941: 209) warned of educators allowing themselves to be turned into automatons who would rarely depart from the 'received' thinking on a particular subject. This is indeed a crucial and difficult subject to address, as how can you be sure you are not thinking as you are in order to please others, gain favour or simply to make your life easier? The short answer of course is we can't. However, the question itself is an important one to pose, even if it is perhaps impossible to answer. For Fromm (1941: 288) one guide in this respect is to be on guard against thinking that has become overly rigid and formulaic. In particular, Fromm valued the ability to be genuinely spontaneous. The repression of critical thinking in this regard ends up in a kind of pseudo thought where we simply offer up those ideas and perspectives we have been handed. This manifests itself in childhood when children begin to mimic the insincerity of the broader culture. For Fromm the education system often sought to foster compliant people who were fearful of strong feelings and the more permanently tragic features of human life like suffering and death. Such aspects simply flatten human experience and lead to the adoption of inauthentic patterns of thinking. Children's sense of wonder becomes displaced through a fearful and conformist culture that is scared of difference. While this culture has many sources, Fromm paid particular attention to the market where human happiness seems to be delivered without effort from the self and where 'success' is measured by external markers. Again this tends to make citizens robotic as they conform to 'external' measures of success rather than more internal criteria.

Fromm's arguments refer back to a more authentic version of humanity discovered via Enlightenment thought (Berman 1970). This was a vision where citizens lived more authentically by governing themselves, speaking truthfully and living imaginatively. Further, for Buber, Freire and Fromm the act of teaching and learning contained some level of authenticity where we cannot retreat into mere cleverness, producing a range of arguments that will simply be knocked down. Critical educators are invited to live relatively consistently with our beliefs and to encourage ourselves and others to engage in relatively honest forms of reflection. Again such a position tends to value the relatively unfashionable virtues of truthfulness, responsibility and connectedness above the endless play of irony so beloved by certain versions of postmodernism. There is, then, no genuinely challenging education that does not have to deal with fear. This might be the fear of rejection, changing our minds or simply finding our way to our own positions that may not be the ones upheld by our friends or the people closest to us. Education, when it is working well, is endlessly disruptive and unsettling, always asking us to think again or at least open our minds to possibilities that might at first seem threatening or beyond the pale. This is what makes it a permanent thorn in the side of more technocratic agendas.

Global education and histories

If the call for more genuinely authentic forms of education can be traced back to the Enlightenment today we find ourselves in a new kind of society. Citizens now, largely through the media of mass communication, are continually aware of a sense their global interconnectiveness. This has led many to argue not unreasonably that education should be reconstructed to articulate the principles of a global democratic citizenship based upon respect for different traditions and civilisations while being underpinned by human rights. This would also articulate a world of overlapping citizenships where we can be local, national, regional and global citizens all at once. Such a cosmopolitan view of education and citizenship is appealing in the extent to which it recognises a world of interlocking loyalties and bonds (Urry 2000; Tsolidis 2002; Rizvi 2003). However, despite the lure of such a universal view of global education it fails to appreciate a politics of cultural translation. If a cosmopolitan view is powerful because of how it identifies some of the key weaknesses of arguments that wish to return to a nationalist politics of secure states, it still has shortcomings of its own. There is an unacknowledged Eurocentrism to much cosmopolitan thinking and it fails to investigate how universal arguments are utilised and drawn upon in more local contexts. The handing down of arguments about human rights and the virtues of democratic participation is unlikely to take hold in contexts where these do not appear to be meaningful. Such views remain under appreciative of the extent to which political and cultural forms of struggle are shot through with antagonism and contradiction.

The idea of a genuinely cosmopolitan education owes a great deal to the intervention of Martha C. Nussbaum (1996). Nussbaum in her rightly celebrated essay is at great pains to warn the reader of the dangers of narrow celebrations of patriotism. She reasons that it is not enough to simply affirm the basic human rights of fellow global citizens, but that we should all be taught to think and act as citizens of the world. Such a position would need to reject narrow nationalism in favour of a more cosmopolitan identity. This would not be possible without the development of a genuinely cosmopolitan education. We citizens need to be taught to think from the point of view of the world rather than that of our host national society. For Nussbaum (1996: 7) we should start from the position that our national identity is 'an accident' and see that we share a prior identity as human beings through our ability to be able to reason and draw upon our capacity to act in the interests of the globe rather than the nation. It is not that we may continue to mostly define ourselves by our particular attachments, but that we need to learn to view ourselves through the lens of the other. Here the focus for civic education is not on the building of democratic capacities, but on the idea that all human beings are worthy of respect and concern.

Nussbaum concretises these suggestions through four proposals. To learn to view ourselves in our particularity we would need to engage in a number of debates concerning our differences and similarities with others. As a consequence what was thought of as 'normal' and 'universal' becomes more complex. If, say, the way 'we' organise our childcare becomes one option amongst others we are better able to examine the particularity of our own practices. In turn we would need to learn about the increasing interdependency of our global world. Notably, global warming does not recognise national boundaries and distinctions but is the product of the high-carbon lifestyles of the rich and prosperous parts of the globe that is likely to affect humanity everywhere. Next we would need to recognise the related point that we do indeed have moral obligations not only to the national 'we' but also to the global 'we'. Genuinely universalistic thinking needs to occupy the idea that human beings everywhere are deserving of love and respect. Finally, we need to make the effort to get children to think across national boundaries so that they are able to explore their 'humanness' in relationships that are informed by respectful forms of dialogue.

While Nussbaum mainly concentrates upon the ethical dimensions of cosmopolitan education there is little doubt that her themes are in tune with more global times. In my own teaching I have noticed how quickly students assent to the position being offered by Nussbaum. Despite her insistence (1996: 15) that 'becoming a citizen of the world is often a lonely business' many students seem intellectually excited at the prospect of a form of education that firmly rejects narrow nationalism in favour of a world of global responsibility and dialogue. Nussbaum's (1996: 17) intellectual challenge that 'puts right before country' seemingly connects to a shared desire to reject the intolerances and narrowness of the past and adopt a more imaginative and dialogic cosmopolitan identity. Listening to my students comment on the relatively closed and nationalist education system they have existed within, Nussbaum's essay seems to many like a breath of fresh air. For just a moment at least the flag-waving patriotism that produced the Iraq war, the daily reminders of Britain's role in the Second World War and the partially repressed memories of Europe's own empires are displaced. Yet in teaching this particular text I have become aware of more ambivalent feelings. Here my concern is that while Nussbaum's position offers a welcome break from the banal rituals of nationalism, her argument by its smoothness displaces a number of more critical questions.

Judith Butler (1996), in reply to Nussbaum, argues that she fails to consider that the meanings of cosmopolitan universalism are likely to be shot through with antagonism and cultural variation. In other words, what is missing in Nussbaum is any sense of how ideas of the 'universal' might be translated into particular histories and cultural locations. It is not surprising that so many of my students can identify with Nussbaum as what we are being asked to affirm is a political position where very little seems to be at stake. The point of contestation works through a binary logic that pits 'bad' nationalism against 'good' cosmopolitan universalism. Indeed, what of universal forms of thinking that are racist, ethnocentric or indeed Eurocentric? It is clear that Nussbaum's position is intended to be critical of these positions, but they are swept away rather than engaged with. While it is obvious that her essay is meant to contrast American nationalism with a more responsible form of cosmopolitanism what she fails to address is how such a dichotomy may be resolved through a strengthening of the languages and practices of empire. It is entirely possible that we could follow Nussbaum's arguments and end up rejecting American isolationism in favour of a renewed American imperialism that is meant to benefit global humanity.

The argument that a cosmopolitan education is best served through the ability to reason from the point of view of the community in the hope that these norms may lead to a more just world is questionable. Such a view not only misreads the current global crisis, it also neglects to connect cosmopolitanism with more complex understandings of culture and history. Nussbaum's ethical concern with paving the way for cross-cultural encounters is to be welcomed. However, the worry remains that she has underestimated both the resilience of history and the sheer difficulty of questioning deeply entrenched cultural hierarchies. My argument is that not only is cosmopolitanism more rooted in time, place and culture than Nussbaum allows, but that the cultivation of cosmopolitan horizons also requires more than empathy and tolerance. To try and think oneself into the position of the Other is important, and yet this cannot substitute for the practice of actually listening to the voice of the Other within a given social context.

The liberalism of much cosmopolitanism acts as a powerful antidote against a politics of nationalist regression, but does not do enough to locate itself within particular social and cultural struggles. Paulo Freire (2007) caught the distinction I am trying to describe when he contrasted the idea of a 'human right' to an education and what he called a 'liberating' education. The idea of human rights can give itself to a diversity of understandings and there is little to dissuade teachers who believe all should be educated from continuing to believe in the cultural inferiority of certain groups. Simply to insist upon the standards of democracy and human rights does little to press for an education that builds upon our shared capacity as learning and creative beings. As Paulo Freire well understood, missing from the liberal model of cosmopolitanism is a concern about the legacies of Western forms of colonialism and oppression. In the European setting the histories and cultures of colonialism live on today in the continuation of racialised discourses and presumptions about the inferiority of the Other (Bhabha 1994; Young 2001). Paul Gilroy (2000: 245) in this setting argued that imperial history in modern society often acts as a mostly obscured 'big rock beneath the surface of the sea'. David Theo Goldberg (2006) draws attention to the continuation of European amnesia in respect of the histories forming Europe's own colonial history. This often focuses upon the Holocaust as *the event* with the histories and continued cultural legacies of colonialism being assumed to have happened elsewhere. These assumptions not only fail to interconnect the histories of colonial dominance with histories of racial superiority they also sever the connection between colonialism and the Nazi era. As Franz Fanon (2001) suggests there remains a deep connection between the histories of colonialism and that of fascism. Perhaps the point is less to root our education in exclusive narratives of domination and in this case racial hygiene and to point to ways in which they remain interconnected. As Paul Gilroy (2000) has carefully stated to think only from the point of view of 'our' nation is an an attempt to deny any global sense of an interconnection with others, while also displacing the possibility of new narratives and forms of identification. The institution of European rule helps to promote ideologies and practices that were built upon the assumed inferiority of non-Europeans. According to Albert Memmi (2003) the European colonialists were initially lured by stories of privilege and adventure that allowed the most 'mediocre' citizens to indulge in fantasies of superiority and inferiority that were unavailable back home. The distinction between the 'primitive' and the 'civilised' was a key feature of the European culture that continues to have resonance today.

Notably the idea of 'the civilised' and 'the barbaric' has been revived by both the 'war on terror' and neoliberal forms of domination that have led to increasing forms of inequality in modern democratic societies. The war on terror has given a certain ideological legitimacy to ideas related to the clash of civilisations that reinforces an idea of Muslims who are, on the one hand, pre-modern but are also, on the other hand, anti-modern. This language, as Mahmood Mamdani (2004: 19) argues, not only reifies complex religious and civic identities, it also has a marked similarity with earlier colonial assumptions that Africans were savage and incapable of civilisation. Indeed wider languages of 'good versus evil' coupled with notions of democracy have at times sounded like an attempt to revive a civilising mission aimed at a barbaric Other. Missing in this rhetoric of course is a recognition of the United States' (and of course Britain's) own ability to undermine their own values through violence, human rights abuse, war and torture against those who are seen to be 'evil' and beyond redemption. Further, in the British context, if Muslims have been converted into a barbaric Other then so have poor citizens. Imogen Tyler (2008) reports that popular forms of abuse aimed at poor white working-class people are indicative of a growing sense of crisis and anxiety. These repeated and popular expressions of disgust widely circulated in popular media cultures not only redraw class boundaries, they also work to silence mostly young members of the working class. Neoliberal domination produces cynicism as well as the excluded Other. The expansion of aggressive forms of capitalism in the British context has not only led to war and the commodification of everyday life, it has also undermined the values of multiculturalism and intensified the normalised lifestyles of affluent middle-class people.

As Antonia Dardar and Luis F. Miron (2006) have commented, it is in the context of the extension of neoliberalism and the erosion of civil liberties that educators need to make sense of the world. This will only be effective if it enables students to make sense of their own lives in the context of wider cultures, histories and struggles. In order to do this, however, critical thinking in the context of education needs to be able to introduce new narratives and identities that will challenge much of the dichotomous discourses and forms of thinking that are currently popular.

Education needs to respond to the new agendas suggested by cosmopolitanism while recognising that the lives of most citizens most of the time remain connected to national forms of citizenship. Here it is only by recovering the ways in which citizens are located within more local debates and frameworks that we might begin to understand the global. For this we need to return to the seminal contribution of Henry Giroux (2006c) and add that students along with their tutors need to become critical border crossers. Thus the aim is to enable learners to negotiate complex languages of difference by appreciating some of the complexities involved in interpreting the different narratives and experiences that permanently displace ideas of the centre and the margin. For example, Raymond Williams' (1962) novel *Border Country* opens up a complex language involving the crossing of cultural as well as temporal and spatial borders. Centrally the novel maps a number of borders concerned with the country and the city, class background,' public and private, as well as past and present. Williams' own life was centrally concerned with borders and an appreciation of their political and personal significance. Here my argument is that a democratic and culturally inclusive education will inevitably be involved in complex processes that invite students to reinterpret and rethink complex borders in terms of their own reading and experiences. These features arguably become even more pressing in our shared global worlds. I would also argue there is a need to be able to locate a specifically national story within a global context. This is not a retreat into a form of narrow nationalism rightly feared by cosmopolitanism. Instead the narratives of citizenship would need to offer complex readings of a shifting national story that took account of features that were both internal and external to the nation-state. In Britain's case this would inevitably invoke stories of empire, relations with Europe and of course its increasingly multicultural make-up. Such a move would dispense with the argument that we can simply oppose cosmopolitanism with nationalism. Questions of cultural citizenship in relation to education are, then, concerned with issues of democracy, respect, responsibility, and of course cultural, historical and geographical borders.

Questions of cultural citizenship

After Paulo Freire's long exile he was appointed to the Municipal Bureau of Education for São Paulo in his native Brazil. Freire's account of this period covers how he was confronted by crumbling buildings and authoritarian teachers who thought very little of students. Consequently he spent much of his time seeking to rebuild schools and engage these teachers in extended forms of dialogue in order to persuade them to reconsider their teaching practice. In this context, Freire (1993: 81) affirmed that the central struggle in education was for the development of critical thinking and the liberty of human thought against 'elitism and authoritarianism'. The struggle against the authoritarianism in our own times is of course captured by the public erosion of democratic ideals. Here, however, I have also argued that the questions occupying 'our' time are somewhat different. Along with the struggle for a dialogic education we need to consider issues of respect, responsibility and, increasingly in a global age, borders. If education is indeed about complex processes of translation and learning then these features must be at the heart of our concerns. Further, the central threat to the development of a learning culture today is not authoritarian teachers but an increasingly market-driven and consumer-orientated society. In a market society individuals are now being asked to constitute themselves not as learning subjects, but as commodified selves who are competing with one another in a market. This ethos has arguably helped undermine the idea of learning and critical forms of engagement with the adoption of more pragmatic attitudes. Education becomes less and less about learning to debate, argue and listen as it becomes converted into a sellable commodity that ultimately offers a passport to success in the labour market. As Zygmunt Bauman (2007a: 57) has commented, it is the project of converting yourself into a sellable commodity that is the ultimate calling of the consumer society. As the logic of the market and consumerism increasingly determines the character of educational institutions, they have not only become more authoritarian, they have also excluded a more normative agenda that historically had become attached to a 'humanist' language of curiosity, development and emancipation. Here simply referring to a language of individual liberty or indeed a defence of republic duties can quite easily co-exist with the increasingly dominant consumerist orientation. Indeed, within such a language ideas of public (rather than simply private) responsibility are unlikely to make much headway embedded in a context where the good life has simply become the consuming life. As Henry Giroux and Susan Searls Giroux (2006) recognise these are deeply cynical times in respect of attempts to speak a language that questions the dominance of market metaphors and the degradation of ideals of learning and public service.

Throughout this text I have sought to revive the critical languages of education and make them relevant to our own times. I have mainly done this by linking education to questions of democracy, respect and responsibility. I have also argued that cultural citizenship as I have conceived it has tried to bring together an understanding of education that draws from those issues related to liberal socialism, human rights and global citizenship, feminism, multiculturalism and ecological thought. I have pursued the idea of cultural citizenship rather than democracy as I am keen to capture the extent to which critical possibilities within education are inevitably bound up with how we understood the cultural domain. Crucially what is at stake here is not only questions of autonomy and democracy, but also our ability to be able imagine human subjects as cultural and interpretative beings who are capable of acting both morally and ethically. In other words, in a globalised and ecologically sensitive society that is increasingly being run as though it was a business, education needs to reawaken its students to what Erich Fromm (1995) once called the art of living. This envisages joining together the possibility of institutional change and democratisation with the realisation that citizens have the agency to determine their own ways of living. We have, it seems, lost our ability to wonder and to think about how we might live. Alberto Melucci (1996) offers a wonderful image of the need to recover a language of the mysterious, the unexpected and the surprising within an increasingly instrumental and, as I have argued at length, fearful and consumer-driven culture. In doing this, however, I have also pointed out that we need to find our way back to the 'lost' languages of education that are mainly located in liberal or liberal socialist traditions. The main argument of the book has been for an imaginative recovery of these traditions in the context of the present in order to convert the idea of democracy into a reality in the context of most people's lives. This of course may not prove to be possible. However, the fact that education, despite attempts to impose from without a language of control through markets, calculable tests and other features, remains entangled within the uncertain languages of communication offered by teachers and learners itself is a cause for hope. Despite the considerable forces that have turned education into a commodity it retains within it elements which are never fully controllable and that still allow for human expression and creativity. This means that those of us who continue to dream of other possibilities can never finally give up on this. If these ideas remain some distance away from the ways in which education is currently constituted, the different traditions I have sought to bring together here remain messages in bottles that could yet open up the horizons of citizens of the future. In this respect, education has to operate within the realm of possibility rather than, as the pessimists suggest, structural determination and closure. However, if we are to build upon this sense of possibility, it must recover the moral narrative offered to it by the liberal socialist tradition in these new times.

Bibliography

Adams, W.W. (2007) 'The Primacy of Interrelating: Practicing Ecological Psychology with Buber, Levinas, and Merleau-Ponty', *Journal of Phenomenological Psychology* 38: 24–61.

Adorno, T. (1998) 'Education after Auschwitz', in *Critical Models: Interventions and Catchwords*, New York, Columbia University Press.

Alibhai-Brown, Y. (2001) 'After multiculturalism', *The Political Quarterly*: 47–56.

Anderson, P. (1992a) *English Questions*, London, Verso.

Anderson, P. (1992b) *A Zone of Engagement*, London, Verso.

Antonio, R.J. and Kellner, D. (1992) 'Communication, modernity and democracy in Habermas and Dewey', *Symbolic Interaction* 15(3): 277–297.

Appiah, K.A. (1998) 'Cosmopolitan patriots', in P. Cheah and B. Robbins (eds) *Cosmopolitics: Thinking and Feeling beyond the Nation*, Minneapolis and London, Minnesota Press. pp. 265–289.

Appiah, K.A. (2005) *The Ethics of Identity*, Princeton, Princeton University Press.

Apple, M. (2001) 'Comparing neo-liberal projects and inequality in education', *Comparative Education* 37(4): 409–423.

Arendt, H. (1958) *The Human Condition*, Chicago, University of Chicago Press.

Arendt, H. (1977) *Eichmann in Jerusalem: A Report on the Banality of Evil*, London, Penguin.

Arendt, H. (1990) *On Revolution*, London, Penguin.

Arendt, H. (1993) *Between Past and Present: Eight Exercises in Political Thought*, London, Penguin.

Arendt, H. (2000) 'Organized Guilt and Universal Responsibility', in P. Baehr (ed.) *The Portable Arendt*, London, Penguin. pp. 146–156.

Arendt, H. (2003) *Responsibility and Judgement*, New York, Schocken Books.

Aristotle (2004) *The Niomachean Ethics*, London, Penguin.

Arnold, M. (1861/1970) 'The Popular Education of France', in *Selected Prose*, London, Penguin. pp. 99–125.

Arnold, M. (1869/1970) 'Culture and Anarchy', in *Selected Prose*, London, Penguin. pp. 202–300.

Ball, S.J. (2004) 'Performativities and fabrications in the educational economy: towards the performative society', in S.J. Ball (ed.) *The Routledge*

Falmer Reader in the Sociology of Education, London, Routledge Falmer. pp. 145–155.

Barber, B. (1989) 'Public talk and civic action: education for participation in a strong democracy', *Social Education*, October: pp. 355–370.

Bauman, Z. (1992) *Intimations of Postmodernity*, London, Routledge.

Bauman, Z. (1993) *Postmodern Ethics*, Oxford, Blackwell.

Bauman, Z. (1997) 'Universities: Old, New and Different', in A. Smith and F. Webster (eds) *The Postmodern University?*, Buckingham, Open University Press. pp. 17–26.

Bauman, Z. (1998) *Work, Consumerism and the New Poor*, Buckingham, Open University Press.

Bauman, Z. (1999) *In Search of Politics*, Cambridge, Polity Press.

Bauman, Z. (2000) *Liquid Modernity*, Cambridge, Polity Press.

Bauman, Z. (2005) 'Education in liquid modernity', *The Review of Education, Pedagogy and Cultural Studies* 27: 303–317.

Bauman, Z. (2006) *Liquid Fear*, Cambridge, Polity Press.

Bauman, Z. (2007a) *Consuming Life*, Cambridge, Polity Press.

Bauman, Z. (2007b) *Liquid Times: Living in an Age of Uncertainty*, Cambridge, Polity Press.

Beane, J.A. and Apple, M. (2000) 'The case for democratic schools', in M. Apple and J.A. Beane (eds) *Democratic Schools*, Buckingham, Open University Press.

Beck, U. (1992) *Risk Society*, London, Sage.

Beck, U. (1999) *Democracy Without Enemies*, Cambridge, Polity Press.

Beck, U. (2006) *Cosmopolitan Vision*, Cambridge, Polity Press.

Beckett, F. (2007) *The Great City Academy Fraud*, London, Continuum Books.

Benjamin, J. (1990) *The Bonds of Love: Psychoanalysis, Feminism and the Problem of Domination*, London, Virago.

Benn, M. and Millar, F. (2006) 'A Comprehensive Future: Quality and Education for all our Children', London, Compass Pamphlet.

Berman, M. (1970) *The Politics of Authenticity*, London, Verso.

Bernstein, R.J. (1966) *John Dewey*, New York, Washington Square Press.

Bernstein, R.J. (1992) *The New Constellation: The Ethical-political Horizons of Modernity/Postmodernity*, Cambridge, MIT Press.

Bernstein, R.J. (2005) *The Abuse of Evil*, Cambridge, Polity Press.

Best, S. and Kellner, D. (2001) 'Richard Rorty and Postmodern Theory', in M. Peters and P.Jnr Ghiraldelli (eds) *Education, Philosophy and Politics*, Oxford, Rowman and Littlefield Publishers. pp. 101–110.

Bhabha, H. (1994) *The Location of Culture*, London, Routledge.

Biesta, G.J.J. and Burbules, N.C. (2003) *Pragmaticism and Educational Research*, Oxford, Rowman and Littlefield.

Blair, T. (1994) 'The Third Way: New Politics for the New Century', Fabian Society Pamphlet.

Bobbio, N. (1996) *The Age of Rights*, Cambridge, Polity Press.

Boltanski, L. and Chiapello, E. (2005) *The Spirit of Capitalism*, London, Verso.

Bourdieu, P. (1984) *Distinction*, London, Routledge.

Bourdieu, P. (1996) *The Rules of Art*. Cambridge, Polity Press.

Bourdieu, P. (1998) *Practical Reason: On the Theory of Action*, Cambridge, Polity Press.

Bourdieu, P. (2003) *Firing Back: Against the Tyranny of the Market*, London, Verso.

Bourdieu, P. (2004) 'The forms of capital', in S.J. Ball (ed.) *The Routledge Falmer Reader in Sociology of Education*, London, Routledge. pp. 15–29.

Bourdieu, P. and Darbel (1991) *The Love of Art*, Cambridge, Polity Press.

Bourdieu, P. and Passeron, J.C. (1977) *Reproduction in Education*, London, Sage.

Bourdieu, P. et al. (1999) *The Weight of the World*, Cambridge, Polity Press.

Bowers, C.A. (1993) *Critical Essays on Education, Modernity, and the Recovery of the Ecological Imperative*, Columbia University, Teachers College.

Bowers, C.A. (2003) 'Assessing Richard Rorty's ironist individual within the context of the ecological crisis', *The Trumpeter* 19(2): 6–22.

Bowers, C.A. (2006) 'Silences and double binds: why the theories of John Dewey and Paulo Friere cannot contribute to the revializing of the commons', *Capitalism Nature Socialism* 17(3): 71–87.

Brady, J. (1994) 'Critical literacy, feminism and a politics of representation', in P. McLaren and C. Lankshear (eds) *Politics of Liberation: Paths from Freire*, London, Routledge. pp. 142–153.

Buber, M. (1947) *Between Man and Man*, London, Routledge.

Buber, M. (1970) *I and Thou*, New York, Touchstone Books.

Buck-Morss, S. (2003) *Thinking Past Terror: Islamism and Critical Theory on the Left*, London, Verso.

Butler, J. (1996) 'Universality in Culture', in J. Cohen (ed.) *For Love of Country*, Boston, Beacon Press.

Callinicos, A. (2001) *Against the Third Way*, Cambridge, Polity Press.

Canovan, M. (1992) *Hannah Arendt: A Reinterpretation of Her Political Thought*, Cambridge, Cambridge University Press.

Carlson, D. and Dimitriadis, G. (2003) 'Introduction', in G. Dimitriadis and D. Carlson (eds) *Promises to Keep: Cultural Studies, Democratic Education, and Public Life*, New York and London, Routledge Falmer. pp. 1–38.

Carr, W. and Harnett, A. (1996) *Education and the Struggle for Democracy*, Buckingham, Open University Press.

Castells, M.(1996) *The Rise of the Network Society; The Information Age: Economy, Society and Culture, Volume 1*, Oxford, Blackwell.

Castells, M. (1997) *The Power of Identity: The Information Age: Economy, Society and Culture, Volume II*, Oxford, Blackwell.

Castells, M. (1998) *End of Millennium; The Information Age: Economy, Society and Culture (Vol. 3)*, Oxford, Blackwell.

Castoriadis, C. (1991) *Philosophy, Politics, Autonomy: Essays in Political Philosophy*, Oxford, Oxford University Press.

Castoriadis, C. (1997a) 'The Greek polis and the creation of democracy', in *The Castoriadis Reader*, ed. D.A. Curtis, Oxford, Blackwell. pp. 267–289.

Castoriadis, C. (1997b) *World in Fragments: Writings on Politics, Society, Psychoanalysis, and the Imagination*, California, Stanford University Press.

Chaney, D. (2002) *Cultural Change and Everyday Life*, Basingstoke, Palgrave.

Coben, D. (1998) *Radical Hereos: Gramsci, Freire and the Politics of Adult Education*, London, Taylor & Francis.

Collini, S. (1998) *Arnold*, Oxford, Oxford University Press.

Collini, S. (2006) *Absent Minds: Intellectuals in Britain*, Oxford, Oxford University Press.

Compass (2007) *The Commercialisation of Childhood* (Special Report), www.compass.org

Couldry, N. (2004) 'In the place of a common culture, what?', *Review of Education, Pedagogy, and Cultural Studies* 26(3): 3–21.

Crick, B. (2000) *Essays on Citizenship*, London, Continuum.

Crossland, A. (1956) *The Future of Socialism*, London, Jonathan Cape.

Crouch, C. (2004) *Post-Democracy*, Cambridge, Polity Press.

Darder, A. (2002) *Reinventing Paulo Freire: A Pedagogy of Love*, Oxford, Westview Press.

Darder, A. and Miron, L.F. (2006) 'Critical pedagogy in a time of uncertainty: a call to action', *Cultural Studies/Critical Methodologies*, 6(1): 5–20.

De Lissovoy, N. (2008) *Power, Crisis, and Education*, London, Palgrave Macmillan.

Debord, G. (1994) *The Society of the Spectacle*, New York, Zone Books.

Delanty, G. (2000) *Citizenship in the Global Age*, Buckingham, Open University Press.

Delanty, G. (2002) 'The university and modernity: a history of the present', in F. Webster and K. Robins (eds) *The Virtual University*, Oxford, Oxford University. pp. 3–19.

Dewey, J. (1916) *Democracy and Education: An Introduction to the Philosophy of Education*, New York, The MacMillan Company.

Dewey, J. (1933) *How We Think: A Restatement of the Relation of Reflective Thinking to the Educative Process*, Boston, D.C. Heath and Company.

Dewey, J. (1939) *Experience and Education*, New York, The MacMillan Company.

Dewey, J. (1977) 'Search for the great community', in D. Sidorsky (ed.) *John Dewey: The Essential Writings*, New York, Harper and Row. pp. 209–216.

Donald, J. (1992) *Sentimental Education: Schooling, Popular Culture and the Regulation of Liberty*, London, Verso.

Duggan, L. (2003) *The Twilight of Equality?* Boston, Beacon Press.

Durkheim, E. (1956) *Education and Sociology*, New York, Free Press.

Eagleton, T. (1990) *The Ideology of the Aesthetic*, Oxford, Blackwell.

Eagleton, T. (1996) *The Illusions of Postmodernism*, Oxford, Blackwell.

Eagleton, T. (2003) *After Theory*, London, Penguin.

Eagleton, T. (2007) *The Meaning of Life*, Oxford, Oxford University Press.

Edmundson, M. (2004) *Why Read?*, New York, Bloomsbury.

Eley, G. (2002) *Forging Democracy: The History of the Left in Europe 1850–2000*, Oxford, Oxford University Press.

Elias, N. (1998) 'The Society of Individuals-1', in J. Goudsblom and S. Mennell (eds) *The Nobert Elias Reader*, Oxford, Blackwell. pp. 68–74.

Elliott, A. and Lemert, C. (2006) *The New Individualism: The Emotional Costs of Globalization*, London, Routledge.

End Child Poverty (2008) www.endchildpoverty.org.uk (accessed 20.08.08).

English, R. and Kenny, M. (2001) 'Public intellectuals and the question of British decline', *British Journal of Politics and International Relations* 3(3): 259–283.

Etzioni, A. (1997) *The New Golden Rule: Community and Morality in a Democratic Society*, London, Profile Books.

Etzioni, A. (2000) *Next: The Road to the Good Society*, New York, Basic Books.

Fanon, F. (2001) *The Wretched of the Earth*, London, Penguin.

Faulks, K. (2000) *Citizenship*, London, Routledge.

Fielding, M. (2006) 'Leadership, personalization and high performance schooling: naming the new totalitarianism', *School Leadership and Management*, 26(4): 347–369.

Fine, R. (2000) 'Crimes against Humanity: Hannah Arendt and the Nuremberg Debates', *European Journal of Social Theory* 3(3): 293–311.

Fiske, J. (1989) *Understanding Popular Culture*, London, Unwin and Hyman.

Foucault, M. (1977) *Discipline and Punish*, London, Penguin.

Foucault, M. (1984a) *The Care of the Self: The History of Sexuality, Volume 3*, London, Penguin Press.

Foucault, M. (1984b) 'What is Enlightenment?', in P. Rabinow (ed.) *The Foucault Reader*, London, Penguin.

Foucault, M. (1989) 'Intellectuals and power', in S. Lotringer (ed.) *Foucault Live: Collected Interviews, 1961–1984*, Columbia University, Semiotexte(e). pp. 74–82.

Frankena, W.H. (1965) *Three Historical Philosophies of Education: Aristotle, Kant, Dewey*, Glenview, Scott Foresman.

Frankl, V. (1964) *Man's Search for Meaning: An Introduction to Logotherapy*, London, Hodder & Sroughton.

Fraser, N. (1993) 'Rethinking the public sphere: a contribution to the critique of actually existing democracy', in S. During (ed.) *The Cultural Studies Reader*, London, Routledge. pp. 518–536.

Fraser, N. (1994) 'Michel Foucault: a "young conservative"?', in M. Kelly (ed.) *Critique and Power: Recasting the Foucault/Habermas Debate*, Cambridge, Massachusetts, MIT Press.

Freire, P. (1970) *Pedagogy of the Oppressed*, London, Penguin Books.

Freire, P. (1974) *Education for Critical Consciousness*, London, Continuum.

Freire, P. (1993) *Pedagogy of the City*, New York, Continuum.

Freire, P. (1994) *Pedagogy of Hope: Reliving Pedagogy of the Oppressed*, New York, Continuum.

Freire, P. (1996) *Letters to Cristina: Reflections on My Life and Work*, London, Routledge.

Freire, P. (1998) *Teachers as Cultural Workers: Letters to Those Who Dare to Teach*, Boulder, Westview Press.

Freire, P. (2001) *Pedagogy of Freedom: Ethics, Democracy and Civic Courage*, Lanham, Rowman & Littlefield.

Freire, P. (2004) *Pedagogy of Indignation*, Boulder, Paradigm Publishers.

Freire, P. (2007) *Daring to Dream: Toward a Pedagogy of the Unfinished*, Boulder, Paradigm Publishers.

Friedman, M. (1982) *Martin Buber's Life and Work: The Early Years 1878–1923*, London, Search Press.

Fromm, E. (1941) *Escape from Freedom*, New York, Avon Books.

Fromm, E. (1978) *To Have or to Be?*, London, Jonathan Cape.

Fromm, E. (1995) 'On the art of living', *The Essential Fromm*, London, Constable. pp. 15–19.

Furedi, F. (2004) *Where Have All the Intellectuals Gone?*, London, Continuum.

Gadamer, H.G. (2001) 'Education is self-education', *Journal of Philosophy of Education* 35(4): 529–538.

Gamble, A. (2005) 'Public intellectuals and the public domain', *New Formations*, 53: 41–53.

Garnham, N. (1993) 'Bourdieu, the cultural arbitrary, and television', in C. Calhoun et al. (eds) *Bourdieu: Critical Perspectives*, Cambridge, Polity Press. pp. 178–192.

Garnham, N. and Williams, R. (1986) 'Pierre Bourdieu and the sociology of culture: an introduction', in R. Collins et al. (eds) *Media, Culture and Society: A Critical Reader*, London, Sage.

Geertz, C. (1973) *The Interpretation of Cultures: Selected Essays by Clifford Geertz*, New York, Basic Books.

Gerhardt, S. (2004) *Why Love Matters: How Affection Shapes a Baby's Brain*, London, Routledge.

Geuss, R. (1982) *The Idea of Critical Theory*, Cambridge, Cambridge University press.

Giddens, A. (1992) *Modernity and Self-Identity*, Cambridge, Polity Press.

Giddens, A. (1994) *Beyond Left and Right*, Cambridge, Polity Press.

Giddens, A. (1998) *The Third Way: The Renewal of Social Democracy*, Cambridge, Polity Press.

Giddens, A. (2003) 'Neoprogressivism: a new agenda for social democracy', in A. Giddens (ed.) *The Progressive Manifesto*, Cambridge, Polity Press. pp. 1–34.

Giddens, A. (2008) *Over to You, Mr Brown: How Labour Can Win Again*, Cambridge, Polity Press.

Gilroy, P. (1993) *The Black Atlantic: Modernity and Double Consciousness*, London, Verso.

Gilroy, P. (2000) *Between Camps*, London, Penguin.

Ginsborg, P. (2008) *Democracy: Crisis and Renewal*, London, Profile Books.

Giroux, H. (1983) *Theory and Resistance in Education: A Pedagogy for the Opposition*, Westport, Greenwood Publishing Group.

Giroux, H. (1988) *Schooling and the Struggle for Public Life: Critical Pedagogy in the Modern Age*, Minneapolis, University of Minnesota Press.

Giroux, H. (1989) *Schooling for Democracy: Critical Pedagogy in the Modern Age*, London, Routledge.

Giroux, H. (1992) *Border Crossings: Cultural Workers and the Politics of Education*, London, Routledge.

Giroux, H. (1993a) 'Literacy and the politics of difference', in C. Lankshear and P. McLaren (eds) *Critical Literacy: Politics, Praxis and the Postmodern*, Albany, State of New York Press. pp. 367–378.

Giroux, H. (1993b) 'Paulo Freire and the politics of postcolonialism', in P. McLaren and P. Leonard (eds) *Paulo Freire: A Critical Encounter*, London, Routledge. pp. 177–188.

Giroux, H. (1999) *The Mouse that Roared: Disney and the End of Innocence*, Lanham, Rowman & Littlefield.

Giroux, H. (2000a) 'Radical education and culture in the work of Antonio Gramsci', in *Stealing Innocence: Youth, Corporate Power and the Politics Culture*, New York, St. Martin's Press. pp. 109–136.

Giroux, H. (2000b) 'Paulo Freire, prophetic thought, and the politics of hope', in *Stealing Innocence: Youth, Corporate Power and the Politics of Culture*, New York, St. Martin's Press. pp. 137–156.

Giroux, H. (2003) *The Abandoned Generation: Democracy Beyond the Culture of Fear*, London, Palgrave Macmillan.

Giroux, H. (2004a) *The Terror of Neoliberalism: Authoritarianism and the Eclipse of Democracy*, Boulder, Paradigm Publishers.

Giroux, H. (2004b) 'War talk, the death of the social, and disappearing children: remembering the other war', *Cultural Studies/Critical Methodologies* 4(2): 206–211.

Giroux, H. (2004c) 'Education after Abu Ghraib: revisiting Adorno's politics of education', *Cultural Studies* 18(6): 779–815.

Giroux, H. (2006a) *Beyond the Spectacle of Terrorism*, London, Paradigm Publishers.

Giroux, H. (2006b) 'Border Pedagogy in the Age of Postmodernism', in C.G. Robbins (ed.) *The Giroux Reader*, London, Paradigm Publishers.

Giroux, H. (2006c) 'Border pedagogy in the age of postmodernism', in C.G. Robins (ed.) *The Giroux Reader*, London, Paradigm Publishers. pp. 47–66.

Giroux, H. (2006d) 'Cultural studies, critical pedagogy, and the responsibility of intellectuals', in C.G. Robins (ed.) *The Giroux Reader*, London, Paradigm Publishers. pp. 195–218.

Giroux, H. (2007) *The University in Chains: Confronting the Military-Industrial Academic Complex*, Boulder, Paradigm Publishers.

Giroux, H. (2008) *Against the Terror of Neoliberalism: Politics Beyond the Age of Greed*, Boulder, Paradigm Publishers.

Giroux, H. and Giroux, S.S. (2006) 'Democracy and the Crisis of Public Education', in H. Giroux *America on the Edge*, New York, Palgrave Macmillan.

Goldberg, D.T. (2006) 'Racial Europeanization', *Ethnic and Racial Studies*, 29(2): 331–364.

Gore, J.M. (1993) *The Struggle for Pedagogies: Critical and Feminist Discourses as Regimes of Truth*, London, Sage.

Gorz, A. (1994) *Capitalism, Socialism, Ecology*, London, Verso.

Gramsci, A. (1971) *Selections from the Prison Notebooks*, London, Lawrence & Wishart.

Gramsci, A. (1988) 'Language, languages, common sense', in D. Forgacs (ed.) *A Gramsci Reader*, London, Lawerence & Wishart. pp. 347–349.

Gunesch, K. (2004) 'Education for cosmopolitanism? Cosmopolitanism as a personal cultural identity model for an international education', *Journal of Research in International Education* 3(3): 251–275.

Gutman, A. (1987) *Democratic Education*, Princeton, Princeton University.

Habermas, J. (1976) *Legitimation Crisis*, London, Heinmann.

Habermas, J. (1981) *The Theory of Communicative Action (Vol. One)*, Cambridge, Polity Press.

Habermas, J. (1983) 'Modernity – an incomplete project', in H. Foster (ed.) *Postmodern Culture*, London, Pluto Press. pp. 3–15.

Habermas, J. (1985) 'Neoconservative culture criticism in the United States and West Germany: an intellectual movement in two political cultures', in R.J. Bernstein (eds) *Habermas and Modernity*, Cambridge, Polity Press. pp. 78–94.

Habermas, J. (1987) 'The idea of the university-learning processess', *New German Critique 41* (Spring–Summer): 3–22.

Habermas, J. (1989) *The Structural Transformation of the Public Sphere*, Cambridge, Polity Press.

Habermas, J. (1991) 'What does socialism mean today? The revolutions of recuperation and the need for new thinking', in R. Blackburn (ed.) *After the Fall*, London, Verso.

Habermas, J. (1996) *Between Facts and Norms: Contributions to a Discourse Theory of Law and Democracy*, Cambridge, Polity Press.

Habermas, J. (1999) 'The European nation-state and the pressures of globalization', *New Left Review* 235 (May/June): 1–12.

Habermas, J. (2001) *The Postnational Constellation: Political Essays* (translated, edited, and with introduction by Max Pensky), Cambridge, Polity Press.

Hall, S. (2000a) 'Conclusion: the multi-cultural question', in B. Hesse (ed.) *Un/settled Multiculturalisms: Diasporas, Entanglements, Transruptions*, London, Zed Books. pp. 209–241.

Hall, S. (2000b) 'Multicultural citizens, monocultural citizenship', in N. Peace and J. Halgarten (eds) *Tomorrow's Citizens: Critical Debates in Citizenship and Education*, London, IPPR.

Hall, S. (2003) 'New Labour's double-shuffle', *Soundings* (24): 10–24.

Hamilton, C. (2003) *Growth Fetish*, London, Pluto Press.

Hardt, M. and Negri, A. (2000) *Empire*, Cambridge, MA, Harvard University Press.

Harvey, D. (2003) *The New Imperialism*, Oxford, Oxford University Press.

Harvey, D. (2005) *A Brief History of Neoliberalism*, Oxford, Oxford University Press.

Harvey, D. (2006) *Spaces of Global Capitalism: Towards a Theory of Uneven Geographical Development*, London, Verso.

Havel, V. (1998) *The Art of the Impossible: Politics as Morality in Practice*, New York, Fromm International.

Hebdige, D. (1979) *Subculture: The Meaning of Style*, London, Methuen.

Held, D. (2004) *Global Covenant*, Cambridge, Polity Press.

Held, V. (2005) *The Ethics of Care*, Oxford, Oxford University Press.

Hickman, L.A. (1995) 'Science education for a life curriculum', in J. Garrison (ed.) *The New Scholarship on Dewey*, Netherlands, Kluner Academic Publishers. pp. 211–224.

Hoggart, R. (1957) *The Uses of Literacy: Aspects of Working-class Life with Special Reference to Publications and Entertainments*, London, Chatto & Windus.

Hoggart, R. (1970a) *Speaking to Each Other (Vol. 2): About Literature*, London, Chatto & Windus.

Hoggart, R. (1970b) *Speaking to Each Other (Vol. 1): About Society*, London, Chatto & Windus.

Hoggart, R. (1982) *An English Temper: Essays on Education, Culture and Communications*, London, Chatto & Windus.

Hoggart, R. (1995) *The Way We Live Now*, London, Pimlico.

Hoggart, R. (2001a) *Between Two Worlds*, London, Aurum Press.

Hoggart, R. (2001b) 'Adult Education: the legacy and the future', www.gla.ac.uk/adulteducation/lastestnews/RichardHoggart.html (accessed 1.10.2008).

Hoggart, R. (2004) *Mass Media in a Mass Society*, London, Continuum.

Holub, R.C. (1991) *Jürgen Habermas: Critic in the Public Sphere*, London, Routledge.

Honneth, A. (1995) *The Struggle for Recognition*, Cambridge, Polity Press.

hooks, b. (1994) *Teaching to Transgress: Education as the Practice of Freedom*, London, Routledge.

hooks, b. (2000a) *Where We Stand: Class Matters*, London, Routledge.

hooks, b. (2000b) *Teaching for Community*, London, Routledge.

How, A. (2003) *Critical Theory*, Basingstoke, Palgrave Macmillian.

James, O. (2007) *Affluenza*, London, Vermilion.

Jones, P. (1994) 'The myth of "Raymond Hoggart": on "founding fathers" and cultural policy', *Cultural Studies* 8(3): 394–416.

Kahn, R. and Kellner, D. (2004) 'New media and internet activism: from the "Battle of Seattle" to blogging', *New Media and Society* 6(1): 87–95.

Kalantzis, M. and Cope, B. (1999) 'Multicultural education: transforming the mainstream', in S. May (ed.) *Critical Multiculturalism: Rethinking Multicultural and Anti-racist Education*, London, Falmer Press.

Kaldor, M. (2003) *Global Civil Society: An Answer to War*, Cambridge, Polity Press.

Kapur, J. (1999) 'Out of control: television and the transformation of childhood in late capitalism', in M. Kinder (eds) *Kids' Media Culture*, Durham and London, Duke University Press. pp. 122–138.

Keane, J. (2003) *Global Civil Society*, Cambridge, Cambridge University Press.

Kellner, D. (2000) 'New technologies/new literacies: reconstructing education for the new millennium', 11(3): 245–265.

Kellner, D. (2003) 'Toward a critical theory of education', *Democracy and Nature*, 9(1): 51–64.

Kellner, D. (2003) *Media Spectacle*, London, Routledge.

Kellner, D. (2005) 'Globalization, September 11, and the restructuring of education', in G.G. Fishman et al. (eds) *Critical Theories, Radical Pedagogies and Global Conflicts*, Lanham, Rowman & Littlefield. pp. 87–114.

Kenny, M. (2004) *The Politics of Identity*, Cambridge, Polity Press.

Klein, N, (2008) *The Shock Doctrine: The Rise of Disaster Capitalism*, London, Routledge.

Kohli, W. (1993) 'Raymond Williams, affective ideology and counter-hegemonic practice', in D.L. Dworkin and G. Roman (eds) *Views Beyond the Border Country: Raymond Williams and Cultural Politics*, London, Routledge. pp. 115–132.

Law, S. (2006) *The War for Children's Minds*, London, Routledge.

Layard, R. (2005) *Happiness: Lessons from a New Society*, London, Allen Lane.

Lister, R. (2007) 'Inclusive citizenship: realizing the potential', *Citizenship Studies* 11(1): 49–61.

Lister, R. (2008) 'The irresponsibility of the rich', *Red Pepper* 161 (Aug./ Sept.).

Lyotard, J.F. (1979) *The Postmodern Condition: A Report on Knowledge*, Manchester, Manchester University Press.

Lyotard, J.F. (1988) *The Different: Phrases in Dispute*, Minneapolis, University of Minesota Press.

MacIntyre, A. (1981) *After Virtue: A Study in Moral Theory*, London, Duckworth.

MacIntyre, A. (1988) *Whose Justice? Which Rationality?*, London, Duckworth.

MacIntyre, A. (1998) *A Short History of Ethics: A History of Moral Philosophy from the Homeric Age to the Twentieth Century* (Second Edition), London, Routledge.

MacIntyre, A. (1999) *Dependent Rational Animals: Why Human Beings Need Virtues*, Chicago, Open Court.

Mamdani, M. (2004) *Good Muslim, Bad Muslim: America, the Cold War, and the Roots of Terror*, New York, Three Leaves Press.

Mann, M. (2003) *Incoherent Empire*, London, Verso.

Marcuse, H. (1964) *One Dimensional Man*, London, Routledge.

Marshall, J.D. (1996) *Michel Foucault: Personal Autonomy and Education*, Boston, Kluwer Academic Publishers.

McNay, L. (1994) *Foucault: A Critical Introduction*, Cambridge, Polity Press.

Mead, G.H. (1934) *Mind, Self and Society*, Chicago University Press.

Melucci, A. (1996) *The Playing Self: Person and Meaning in the Planetary Society*, Cambridge, Cambridge University Press.

Memmi, A. (2003) *The Coloniser and the Colonised*, London, Earthscan Press.

Midgeley, M. (1989) *Wisdom, Information and Wonder: What is Knowledge For?*,London, Routledge.

Midgley, M. (2001) *Science and Poetry*, London, Routledge.

Mill, J.S. (1859/1974) *On Liberty*, London, Penguin.

Mill, J.S. (1873/1924) *Autobiography*, London, Oxford University Press.

Mills, C.W. (1954) 'Mass society and liberal education', pamphlet, Centre for the Study of Liberal Education for Adults.

Modood, T. and May, S. (2001) 'Multiculturalism and education in Britain: an internally contested debate', *International Journal of Educational Resource* 35: 305–317.

Morrow, R.A. and Torres, C.A. (2002) *Reading Freire and Habermas: Critical Pedagogy and Transformative Social Change*, New York and London, Teachers College Press.

Moschonas, G. (2002) *In the Name of Social Democracy: The Great Transformation: 1945 to the Present*, London, Verso.

Mouffe, C. (2000) *The Democratic Paradox*, London, Verso.

Mouffe, C. (2005) *On the Political*, London, Routledge.

Moutsios, S. (2008) 'The decline of democratic politics in "knowledge societies" and the initiatives for citizenship education', in M. Peters, A. Britton and H. Blee (eds) *Global Citizenship Education*, Rotterdam, Sense Publishers.

Mulgan, G. (1994) *Politics in an Antipolitical Age*, Cambridge, Polity Press.

Neil, A.S. (1962) *Summerhill: A Radical Approach to Education*, London, Victor.

Noddings, N. (2002) *Educating Moral People: A Caring Alternative to Character Education*, New York, Teachers College Press.

Noddings, N. (2003) *Happiness and Education*, Cambridge, Cambridge University Press.

Nussbaum, M. (1996) 'Patriotism and cosmopolitanism', in J. Cohen (ed.) *For Love of Country: Debating the Limits of Patriotism*, Boston, Beacon Press. pp. 2–17.

Nussbaum, M. (1997) *Cultivating Humanity: A Classical Defense of Reform in Liberal Education*, Cambridge, Harvard University Press.

Nussbaum, M. (2010) *Not For Profit: Why Democracy Needs the Humanities*, Princeton, Princeton University Press.

Nuyen, A.T. (1995) 'Lyotard and Rorty on the role of the professor', in M. Peters (ed.) *Education and the Postmodern Condition*, Westport, Bergin and Garvey.

O'Hear, A. (1991) *Father of Child-Centredness: John Dewey and the Ideology of Modern Education*, London, Centre for Policy Studies.

Orr, D. (1992) 'Environmental literacy: education as if the earth mattered', Twelfth Annual E.F. Schumacher Lecture (pamphlet available from the Schumacher Society).

Orr, D. (1994) 'What is education for?', in S.J. Goodlad (ed.) *The Lost Best Hope*, Jossey-Bass. pp. 231–242.

Orr, D. (2004) *The Last Refuge: Patriotism, Politics, and the Environment in an Age of Terror*, Washington, Island Press.

Orwell, G. (1999) *Nineteen Eighty-Four*, London, Secker & Warberg.

Orwell, G. (2001) 'The intellectual revolt: four articles', *Orwell and Politics*, London, Penguin. pp. 415–438.

Parekh, B. (2000a) *Rethinking Multiculturalism*, London, Macmillan.

Parekh, B. (2000b) *The Future of Multi-Ethnic Britain*, London, Profile Books.

Peters, M.A. (1995) 'Introduction: Lyotard, education, and the postmodern condition', in M.A. Peters (eds) *Education and the Postmodern Condition*, Westport, Bergin & Garvey.

Peters, M.A. (2006) 'Lyotard, nihilism and education', *Studies in the Philosophy of Education* 25: 303–314.

Power, S. and Whitty, G. (1999) 'New Labour's educational policy: first, second or third way?', *Journal of Educational Policy* 14(5): 535–546.

Pring, R. (2005) *Philosophy of Education: Aims, Theory, Common Sense and Research*, London, Continuum.

Pring, R. (2007) 'The common school', *Journal of Philosophy of Education*, 41(4): 503–521.

Putnam, R. (2000) *Bowling Alone: The Collapse and Revival of American Community*, New York, Simon & Schuster.

Rawls, J. (1972) *A Theory of Justice*, Oxford, Clarendon Press.

Rawls, J. (1996) *Political Liberalism*, Cambridge, MA, Harvard University Press.

Readings, B. (1996) *The University in Ruins*, Cambridge, MA, Harvard University Press.

Reay, D, and Ball, S. (1997) 'Spoilt for choice': the working class and educational markets', *Oxford Review of Education* 23(1): 89–101.

Reay, D. (2004) 'Finding or losing yourself? Working-class relations to education', in S.J. Ball (ed.) *The Routledge Falmer Reader in the Sociology of Education*, London, Routledge Falmer. pp. 30–45.

Reay, D. (2005) 'Beyond consciousness?: the psychic landscape of social class', *Sociology* 39(5): 911–928.

Ricoeur, P. (1991) 'Life: a story in search of a narrator', in M.J. Valdes (ed.) *A Ricoeur Reader: Reflection and Imagination*, London, Harvester.

Rizvi, F. (2003) 'Democracy and Education after September 11', *Globalisation, Societies and Education*, 1(1): 25–39.

Robin, C. (2007) 'Dragon-slayers', *London Review of Books*, 29(1): 18–20.

Rogers, M. (1999) *Barbie Culture*, London, Sage.

Rogers, P. (2008) *Why We're Losing the War on Terror*, Cambridge, Polity Press.

Rorty, R. (1985) 'Habermas and Lyotard on Postmodernity', in R.J. Bernstein (ed.) *Habermas and Modernity*, Cambridge, Polity Press.

Rorty, R. (1989) *Contingency, Irony and Solidarity*, Cambridge, Cambridge University Press.

Rorty, R. (1991a) *Objectivity, Relativism and Truth: Philosophical Papers Volume 1*, Cambridge, Cambridge University Press.

Rorty, R. (1991b) *Essays on Heidegger and Others: Philosophical Papers Volume 2*, Cambridge, Cambridge University Press.

Rorty, R. (1996) 'Response to Simon Critchley', in S. Critchley et al. (eds) *Deconstruction and Pragmaticism*, London, Routledge. pp. 41–46.

Rorty, R. (1997) *Truth and Progress: Philosophical Papers Volume 3*, Cambridge, Cambridge University Press.

Rorty, R. (1998a) 'Human rights, rationality and sentimentality', *Philosophical Papers*, Vol. 3, Cambridge, Cambridge University Press. pp. 167–185.

Rorty, R. (1998b) *Achieving Our Country*, Cambridge, MA, Harvard University Press.

Rorty, R. (1999) *Philosophy and Social Hope*, London, Penguin Books.

Rosaldo, R. (1994) 'Cultural citizenship and educational democracy', *Cultural Anthropology* 9(3): 402–411.

Rosaldo, R. (1999) 'Cultural citizenship, inequality and multiculturalism', in R.D. Torres et al. (eds) *Race, Identity and Citizenship*, Oxford, Blackwell.

Rose, J. (2001) *The Intellectual Life of the British Working Classes*, New Haven and London, Yale University Press.

Rose, N. (2000) 'Governing cities, governing citizens', in E.F. Isin (ed.) *Democracy, Citizenship and the Global City*, London, Routledge. pp. 95–110.

Ross, H. (2003) 'Rethinking human vulnerability, security and connection through relational theorising', in W. Wallis (ed.) *Comparative Education, Terrorism and Human Security*, New York, Palgrave Macmillan.

Ruddick, S. (1989) *Maternal Thinking: Towards a Politics of Peace*, Boston, Beacon Press.

Russell, B. (1926) *On Education: Especially in Early Childhood*, London, George Allen & Unwin Ltd.

Rustin, M. (2007a) 'The Long Revolution revisited', *Soundings: A Journal of Politics and Culture*, 35: 16–31.

Rustin, M. (2007b) 'What's wrong with happiness?', *Soundings: A Journal of Politics and Culture*, 36: 67–84.

Rutherford, J. (2005) 'Cultural studies in the corporate university', *Cultural Studies* 19(3): 297–317.

Ryan, A. (1970) *The Philosophy of John Stuart Mill*, London, Macmillan.

Ryan, A. (1995) *John Dewey and the High Tide of American Liberalism*, New York, W.W. Norton & Company.

Ryan, A. (1998) *Liberal Anxieties and Liberal Education*, New York, Hill & Wang.

Ryle, M. and Soper, K. (2002) *To Relish the Sublime? Culture and Self-Realisation in Postmodern Times*, London, Verso.

Sadovnik, A.R. and Semel, S.F. (1999) 'Durkheim, Dewey and progressive education', in G. Walford and W.S.F. Pickering (eds) *Durkheim and Modern Education*, London, Routledge. pp. 142–163.

Said, E. (1988) 'Michel Foucault, 1926–1984', in J. Arac (ed.) *After Foucault*, London, Rutgers University Press.

Said, E. (1994) *Representations of the Intellectual*, London, Vintage.

Salzberger-Wittenberg, I. (1999) 'Beginings', in I. Salzberger-Wittenberger, G. Williams and E. Osborne (eds) *The Emotional Experience of Learning and Teaching*, London, Karnac Books.

Schumacher, E.F. (1979) *Good Work*, London, Jonathan Cape.

Schumacher, E.F. (1993) *Small is Beautiful: A Study of Economics as if People Mattered*, London, Vintage.

Seiter, E. (1999) *Television and New Media Audiences*, Oxford, Clarenden Press.

Sennett, R. (1970) *The Uses of Disorder: Personal Identity and City Life*, London, Penguin.

Sennett, R. (1998) *The Corrosion of Character*, New York, W.W. Norton.

Shor, I. and Freire, P. (1987) *A Pedagogy for Liberation: Dialogues on Transforming Education*, South Hadley, Bergin & Garvey.

Sidorkin, A.M. (1999) *Education, the Self and Dialogue: Beyond Discourse*, New York, State University of New York Press.

Silverstone, R. (2007) *Media and Morality: On the Rise of the Mediapolis*, Cambridge, Polity Press.

Skeggs, B. (1997) *Formations of Class and Gender*, London, Sage.

Skeggs, B. (2004) *Class, Self and Culture*, London, Routledge.

Spivak, G. (2002) 'Righting wrongs', in N. Owen (ed.) *Human Rights, Human Wrongs*, Oxford, Oxford University Press. pp. 164–227.

Stallabras, J. (2006) 'Spectacle and terror', *New Left Review* 37(Jan./Feb.): 87–106.

Steedman, C. (1986) *Landscape for a Good Woman: A Story of Two Lives*, London, Virago.

Stephen, A. (2007) 'Iraq: the hidden cost of the war', *New Statesman*, 12 March.

Stevenson, N. (1995) *Culture, Ideology and Socialism*, Aldershot, Avebury.

Stevenson, N. (1999) *The Transformation of the Media*, Longman.

Stevenson, N. (2001) *Understanding Media Cultures*, London, Sage.

Stevenson, N. (2003) *Cultural Citizenship: Cosmopolitan Questions*, Buckingham Open University Press.

Stevenson, N. (2006) *David Bowie: Fame, Sound and Vision*, Cambridge, Polity Press.

Stevenson, N. (2007) 'Cosmopolitan Europe, post-colonialism and the politics of imperialism', in C. Rumford (ed.) *Cosmopolitanism and Europe*, Liverpool, Liverpool University Press.pp. 51–71.

Tawney, R.H. (1961) *The Acquisitive Society*, London, Collins.

Tawney, R.H. (1964) *The Radical Tradition*, London, Penguin.

Taylor, C. (1979) 'What's wrong with negative liberty', in A. Ryan (ed.) *The Idea of Freedom: Essays in Honour of Isaiah Berlin*, Oxford, Oxford University Press.

Taylor, C. (1989a) *Sources of the Self: The Making of the Modern Identity*, Cambridge, Cambridge University Press.

Taylor, C. (1989b) 'Marxism and socialist humanism', in R. Archer (ed.) *Out of Apathy*, London, Verso.

Taylor, C. (1995) 'Liberal politics and the public sphere', *Philosophical Arguments*, Cambridge, Harvard University Press. pp. 257–288.

Thompson, E.P. (1970) 'Highly confidential: a personal comment by the editor', in E.P. Thompson (ed.) *Warwick University Ltd*, London, Penguin Special. pp. 146–166.

Thompson, E.P. (1978a) 'The peculiarities of the English', in *The Poverty of Theory and Other Essays*, London, Merlin Press. pp. 35–91.

Thompson, E.P. (1978b) 'An open letter to Leszek Kolakowski', in *The Poverty of Theory and Other Essays*, London, Merlin Press. pp. 92–192.

Thompson, E.P. (1980) *Writing by Candelight*, London, Merlin Press.

Todd, S. (2003) *Levinas, Psychoanalysis, and the Ethical Possibility of Education*, New York, State University New York Press.

Todorov, T. (2005) *The New World Disorder*, Cambridge, Polity Press.

Todorov, T. (2009) *In Defence of the Enlightenment*, London, Atlantic Books.

Tomlinson, J. (1999) *Globalization and Culture*, Cambridge, Polity Press.

Tomlinson, S. (2003) 'Comprehensive success and bog standard government', Third Caroline Benn Memorial Lecture, Socialist Educational Association, www.socialisteducation.org.uk/CB3.htm.

Tomlinson, S. (2006) *Education in a Post-welfare Society*, Maidenhead, Open University Press.

Touraine, A. (2000) *Can We Live Together?*, Cambridge, Polity Press.

Toynbee, P. and Walker, D. (2008) *Unjust Rewards: Exposing Greed and Inequality in Britain Today*, London, Granta Publications.

Tsolidis, G. (2002) 'How do we teach and learn in times when the notion of "global citizenship" sounds like a cliché?', *Journal of Research in International Education*, 1(2): 213–226.

Turner, B.S. (2006a) 'British sociology and public intellectuals: consumer society and imperial decline', *British Journal of Sociology* 57(2): 169–188.

Turner, B.S. (2006b) *Vulnerability and Human Rights*, Philadelphia, Pennsylvannia University Press.

Tyler, I. (2008) 'Chav mum chav scum', *Feminist Media Studies* 8(1): 17–34.

UNICEF (2007) *Child Poverty in Perspective*, Report Card 7, www.unicef.org.

Urmson, J.O. (1988) *Aristotle's Ethics*, Oxford, Blackwell.

Urry, J. (2000) *Sociology Beyond Societies*, London, Routledge.

Usher, R. and Edwards, R. (1994) *Postmodernism and Education*, London, Routledge.

Vincent, C. and Ball, S. (2007) '"Making up" the middle-class child: families, activities and class dispositions', *Sociology* 41(6): 1061–1077.

Wall, J. (2005) *Moral Creativity: Paul Ricoeur and the Poetics of Possibility*, Oxford, Oxford University Press.

Webster, F. and Robins, K. (2002) 'The virtual university', in F. Webster and K. Robins (eds) *The Virtual University*, Oxford, Oxford University. pp. 3–19.

Weiler, K. (1994) 'Freire and feminism', in P. McLaren and C. Lankshear (eds) *Politics of Liberation: Paths from Freire*, London, Routledge. pp. 12–40.

Westbrook, R.B. (1991) *John Dewey and American Democracy*, Ithaca and London, Cornell University Press.

Wilby, P. (2008) 'The toxicity of poverty', *New Statesman*, 3 March, p. 15.

Wilkinson, R. (2006) 'The impact of inequality', *Social Research* 73(2): 711–732.

Wilkinson, R. and Pickett, K. (2009) *Why More Equal Societies Almost Always Do Better*, London, Allen Lane.

Williams, R. (1958) *Culture and Society 1780–1950*, London, Pelican.

Williams, R. (1960) *Border Country*, London, Chatto & Windus.

Williams, R. (1962) *Communications*, London, Penguin.

Williams, R. (1964) *Second Generation*, London, Chatto & Windus.

Williams, R. (1965) *The Long Revolution*, London, Pelican.

Williams, R. (1968) 'Culture and revolution: a comment', in T. Eagleton and B. Wicker (eds) *From Culture to Revolution*, London, Steed & Ward. pp. 22–34.

Williams, R. (1980) *Problems in Materialism and Culture*, London, Verso.

Williams, R. (1985) *Towards 2000*, London, Pelican.

Williams, R. (1989) *Resources of Hope*, London, Verso.

Wirth, A.G. (1966) *John Dewey as Educator: His Design for Work in Education (1894–1904)*, New York, John Wiley & Sons.

Wolff, J. (1990) *Feminine Sentences: Essays on Women and Culture*, Cambridge, Polity Press.

Young, I.M. (2000) *Inclusion and Democracy*, Oxford, Oxford University Press.

Young, R.C. (2001) *Postcolonialism: An Historical Introduction*, Oxford, Blackwell.

Young, R.E. (1989) *A Critical Theory of Education: Habermas and Our Children's Future*, London, Harvester Wheatshef.

Yuval-Davis, N. (2006) 'Belonging and the politics of belonging', *Patterns of Prejudice*, 40(3): 197–214.

Index